HE SAID WHAT?

WOMEN WRITE ABOUT MOMENTS WHEN EVERYTHING CHANGED

Edited by **VICTORIA ZACKHEIM**

SEAL PRESS

OTHER TITLES BY VICTORIA ZACKHEIM

FICTION
The Bone Weaver

ANTHOLOGIES
*The Other Woman: Twenty-one Wives, Lovers, and Others Talk
Openly About Sex, Deception, Love, and Betrayal*

*For Keeps: Women Tell the Truth about Their Bodies,
Growing Older, and Acceptance*

*The Face in the Mirror: Writers Reflect on Their Dreams of
Youth and the Reality of Age*

He Said What?
Women Write about Moments when Everything Changed

"At Home in the World," by Joyce Maynard, copyright © 1999 by the author, is reprinted by permission of Picador, an imprint of St. Martin's Press, LLC.

Published by
Seal Press
A Member of the Perseus Books Group
1700 Fourth Street
Berkeley, California

Library of Congress Cataloging-in-Publication Data

He said what? : women write about moments when everything changed / edited by Victoria Zackheim.
     p. cm.
  ISBN 978-1-58005-336-5
  1. Man-woman relationships. 2. Sexual fantasies. I. Zackheim, Victoria.
  HQ801.H42 2011
  306.7092'2--dc22

                              2010033373

9 8 7 6 5 4 3 2 1

Cover design by Kimberly Glyder
Interior design by Tabitha Lahr
Printed in the United States of America by
Distributed by Publishers Group West

For Aviva and Leon, with love.

CONTENTS

INTRODUCTION

I *love you. I want a divorce. The meeting ran late. Please don't tell the folks, but I'm gay.* One little phrase, one casual lie, one devastating announcement, and our lives are turned upside down forever. We all know that the children's rhyme boasting "sticks and stones can break my bones, but words will never hurt me" is a crock. Words can hurt—deeply—and they frequently do. But they can also soothe, cajole, enliven, educate, entertain, and remind us that loving, cheating, losing, and gaining are all part of that human condition we call life. This book is a collection of gifted writers, women sharing their most intimate, true-life experiences of how one phrase, a few little words, changed their lives. Some of these stories are poignant, a few might be considered frightening, and others are laugh-out-loud funny.

When journalist Dianne Rinehart was sent to cover the United Nations Conference on Women's Rights in Beijing, how could she have known that while the Chinese were doing their best to undermine the conference (let's face it, the sisterhood wasn't exactly brimming over with international support!), her husband was at home, doing his best to undermine their marriage? As for best-selling author and screenwriter Beverly Donofrio (*Riding in Cars with Boys*), she's had so many "yeah, he really said that" experiences that she wondered if she should write about the veterinarian who announced, "I'm into animal as protein" or the New York City commissioner who ignored her because of his fixation on writing the Great Novel, a *Watership Down* story in which, instead of rabbits, he featured miniature pigs.

Kathi Kamen Goldmark, the founder and lead singer of the (in)famous Rock Bottom Remainders, shares her rock 'n' roll story about love, deception, and revenge. Novelist Carrie Kabak, whose humor rings out loudly on every page, tells us, "By the time I entered college, I wasn't sure I wanted to meet a man's willy. But encounter one I did, and I hold Rowland Jones responsible for making it such a traumatic experience." Internationally known novelist (*To Die For*) and memoirist Joyce Maynard reveals how she felt when, at age nineteen, after having given up Yale and an already nationally recognized writing career to live with middle-aged international phenom J. D. Salinger, he told her to pack her bags and get out.

Abby Frucht opens her essay with "It began with a pestilence of flies . . . " and ends it with a devastation foisted on her family by Ponzi schemer Bernie Madoff. And Sherry Glaser-Love—playwright, actress, and writer-performer of the longest-running off-Broadway one-woman show in history—kissed her husband goodbye one lovely morning and watched him drive off to meet his buddies for a round of golf, never imagining that he would play half the course . . . and then disappear forever. And noted novelist Caroline Leavitt reveals how experiencing emotional abuse from a college boyfriend forced her to discover her inner strength and self-respect.

Whether the life-altering comment is made by a psychotic boyfriend, a dying father, someone's husband, teacher, or doctor, a Russian journalist, a boss, or a frightened brother facing the threat of AIDS, the talented authors in this book offer everything from drama to delight, from havoc to the outright hilarious, from the philosophical to the whimsical, and they will remind you of that moment in your life—or, for some of you, the many moments!—when you thought to yourself, *He said what?* and it changed the way you looked at your life for that precise moment . . . or forever.

FULL CONDOM

Dianne Rinehart

I'm so dead-dog tired and emotionally drained that nothing can faze me. So when my colleague Jonathan Manthorpe, attractive in a teddy-bearish, mountain-man manner, bellows, "Full condom!" at me, I don't get all hormonal.

Instead I nod, retrieve my bags from security guards, who've been searching them for weapons, dig out a plastic packet, and pull out a huge, thick, military-green rubber poncho that is so heavy, it's like donning Chernobyl's sarcophagus—or a condom, as Jonathan endearingly calls it.

I wrestle it on and see myself reflected in the glass doors protecting us from the monsoon outside. I look like Woody Allen in *Everything You Ever Wanted to Know About Sex But Were Afraid to Ask:* a large green version of his Sperm character, about to be launched into the unknown.

And this is definitely that.

I'm on tour as a reporter of the daily and unspeakable cruelties "manifested" on women around the world, at a United Nations Conference on Women's Rights in Beijing, circa 1995.

And besides: my eight-year marriage is on the rocks.

Small stuff in this sea of misery, I realize. But hey, the personal is the political, and this environment is definitely one in which women celebrate that special bond: that men, no matter how hard we fight—and some do so to the death—still, apparently, hold all the power. Indeed, at this moment, the Chinese authorities are using theirs—formidably—to prevent women who have come from around the world, supported by bake sales and their own thin pocketbooks, from demanding their rights at a UN conference *established* for that singular purpose!

Authorities are seemingly so out of touch with their raison d'être for walking around secure UN sites with guns—so cocksure of their ability to control women, and so clearly contemptuous of either our gender or our cause—that they've actually hung an enormous banner that boasts Shopping Is Enjoyment at the site where the human rights activists will meet to discuss rape, abduction, forced prostitution, wife burning, and other quaint cultural practices.

How do I capture that singular act of ignorance and viciousness for my readers—a demeaning provocation of women attending the conference who are not allowed to marry without their father's permission, divorce without their husband's, travel without their brother's, drive without the government's, or work without the authorities', or, yes, shop without someone's okay?

But now the security guards are shooing me along, so I heft my computer bag and briefcase over separate shoulders, slipping them under the poncho to protect the thousands of briefing documents on women's rights I'm collecting that describe the indescribable acts done to half the planet's population on a daily basis.

Where is the doomsday clock measuring *that?*

But I'm at least prepared for the devastation of it, because of a preview at the 1992 UN conference on human rights in Vienna, where women told their stories at a "tribunal" that will be repeated in Beijing: young girls' genitals mutilated (an act so abhorrent that I cannot even imagine it until one day, fourteen years later, when I turn a page in Ayaan Hirsi Ali's book *Infidel* and scream as she describes, without fanfare or warning, having hers snipped off, at her grandmother's instigation, while she is held down screaming); South Asian wives' faces burned with cooking oil over disagreements with their husbands; a Brazilian beauty queen whose boyfriend disfigures her face with acid after she breaks up with him; an American who, as a toddler, was diagnosed with gonorrhea (or was it syphilis, or both?) sores lacing her mouth, but no doctor thought it unusual enough to report, so her father continued to coax her to his bedside and insert his penis into her mouth; an incredibly composed Korean "comfort woman" who tells of being raped by multitudes of Japanese soldiers during the Second World War and left barren from her internal injuries.

Covered in my condom, I push through the glass doors and out into the monsoon with my coworkers, a group of tired self-styled "freedom" fighters marching out to a war we will fight with words, dressed in impenetrable rain gear that seems symbolic of the mass media's inability to penetrate either the heart of the human rights abuses women face or the front pages of our papers.

As horrible as this conference is turning out to be, it is not a *disaster,* and that's what it would take—some massacre, some rampage, some tsunami—to make it lead the TV news and scream from the front pages of the world's top papers.

And the news hook we do have for this story—it's a historic world conference focused on women's rights!—is being thwarted by a Chinese government notorious for shutting down human rights activities, even, incredibly, one it put in a bid to host.

Not that there wasn't warning: In the lead-up, journalists and organizers wrote stories protesting how Chinese authorities denied visas to countless human rights organizations around the world, ones whose attendance the UN had actually pre-approved—the ones most likely to create some news, perhaps, such as the Tibetans.

But the UN and the leaders of the world's most powerful governments do not act, which is why Chinese authorities can later drop the bigger bomb with impunity.

Only months before the long-anticipated congress, China announces it is moving the location of the parallel conference of human rights organizations from the UN conference facilities in Beijing, where the non-governmental organizations (NGOs) were expecting to participate in negotiations with officials on the declarations—the norm at UN conferences, and part of the bid plan—and will instead exile them to an outpost called Huairou, forty-five miles outside of Beijing, though first the Chinese have to build it.

How hospitable.

They strategically announce this change of plan late in the game, anticipating (and not being disappointed) that Western nations won't demand that the UN change the site of the long-planned conference to—I'm just saying—a country that actually gives a damn about human rights.

And it's impossible to know whether the Chinese authorities cannot conjure up a finished site in time for the NGOs because they left the announcement until so late, or because they actually don't care that women attending the conference are listening to speakers in unfinished buildings, some (you will think I'm making this up) actually roofless—in monsoon season.

It's a wonder the speakers at mics don't get electrocuted.

Who else but the UN, the same body that in 2003 put Libya in charge of the UN Human Rights Commission, could have handed over the keys of a historic human rights vehicle to the Chinese? Suspiciously strategic, I wonder. Another way to make women "shut the fuck up," as a Canadian senator says so memorably on the issue of abortion fifteen years later.

So, poorly funded, unheralded women's organizations find their voices snuffed out (at their own conference!) by militaristic men, so frightened by the notion of females actually speaking to each other, and perhaps infecting Chinese women with their thought crimes, that they not only have banished them to Huairou, then failed to deliver on transportation they've promised to get the women there each day from their Beijing hotels, but also have actually created mini–"prisons for protests."

NGOs arrive at the site to find a very small square, maybe the size of a tennis court, created with white lines painted on black asphalt. They will be permitted to hold demonstrations to voice their protests, but only if they book this little site.

They're kidding, right?

Women marching in circles, inside the painted lines of a tiny square of asphalt, in a secured, isolated site, chanting their messages to the converted? They have come from around the world—from villages where women pooled their money to send one representative—for this right?

So we journalists ferry back and forth, desperately trying to capture the news at the NGO conference each morning and catch up on the UN conference in the afternoon. As if that weren't challenging enough, Chinese authorities refuse to let local cab drivers near many of our hotels—they don't want them fraternizing with us—so I set out each morning at six, laptop and briefcase on my shoulders, and walk a mile or so to secure a cab, get to Huairou, cover the event, file a story, taxi back to Beijing, track down a story at the UN conference, file another report, attend an evening event, write another story, and drop into bed for four hours before my alarm goes off.

Needless to say, I'm not sleeping.

I'm lying there thinking about the day's horror stories, deadlines, and—pathetically—my missing-in-action husband.

Exhausted, the mostly female reporters are about as effective at covering women's rights stories here as at home, where they watch male colleagues climb to the top of the career ladder by writing on more "important" issues.

We are impotent. Which reminds me of my husband.

As I'm drowning in despair at the horrendous human rights abuses against women in this world, and at my own inability to effect change, he is, I believe, anything but ineffective or impotent, and likely carrying on an affair with the woman he told me, before I left for Beijing, he'd broken up with . . . to be with me!

Since he was "with" me before he had the affair, I'm not sure what the commitment he's making here is, nor how it is he "broke up" with her while he was married to me. But never mind. I am, he suggests, apparently not sufficiently grateful for his sacrifice.

Why, he wondered, was I not just accepting my good fortune that he chose me, in the end, and shutting up about it? And perhaps that—my determination that we can't rebuild our relationship without actually talking about it!—is what has driven him back into her arms.

What else can it be?

She's about ten years younger than I, tall, blond, beautiful, successful, and rich. Okay, she may be every woman's nightmare, but I still cannot fathom what he sees in her, because she's got the brainpan of an armadillo and a sense of humor as sophisticated as a five-year-old's.

Apparently, though, the big attraction is not those qualities, but this one: she thinks he's perfect. I point out to him that this may be how she is in the throes of competing for him, but that eventually she, too, will notice that he doesn't pick up his dirty socks—or anything else.

And who could want that acquiescence anyway? Where is the fight, the dance, the tease, the passion of their relationship? Is love so worthless that we give it up to be told what we want to hear?

And if they've broken up, why can't I reach him? Why is he never home when I call? Why is he not *returning* my calls?

I admit it: In the face of horrors so unimaginable, I weep when I hear women testify to their ordeals at the conference, while I also worry about such a trifling thing as *Does my husband still love me, or does he love her?*

This concern is met with total disdain by one of my colleagues, an older "dame" of a reporter from the UK, who tells me on our trek to Huairou one morning that I need to stop worrying about him and start thinking about what I want. Her relationship, she says saltily, is the opposite of mine: She is the one who has affairs. Her husband, who is wealthy, accepts them, and she lives a rich life of sexual adventure while he maintains their stable home life.

I'm feeling so lackluster.

During another shared cab ride, a tall, blond, blue-eyed, drop-dead-gorgeous, Pulitzer Prize–winning journalist takes my hand and, without pretense, hits on me. I pry his hand from mine to reveal my wedding band. "So?" he challenges. So, I don't have affairs, I insist. What I don't confess, however, is that this last year of living dangerously, during my husband's indiscretion, has worn down that resolve. Still, his grin reveals he can smell my vulnerability—or the pheromones of a discarded woman exploding—because there are four of us squished into the back seat and his leg (I think it's his leg) is pressed firmly against mine.

And so the fifteen days go. There is no time for dinners or time off, except for one day, a holiday to celebrate a month with two full moons. The city and the conference close, and I head out on an outing with my blond-haired Wonder Boy and a group of lesbian feminists, who are the only ones making headway at the conference. They've managed to score world headlines by getting arrested, after unfurling a banner at the UN site with a message that must be anathema to authorities who thought women were there to shop: LESBIAN RIGHTS ARE HUMAN RIGHTS!

Apparently, genital mutilation and honor killing do not sell papers, but, thankfully, arrests do.

So we, like any tourists, hit the Great Wall and then a famous Peking-duck restaurant. We are packed on the second floor, and suddenly flashbulbs are popping and people are gasping. I look over the railing: It's former president George Bush. He's not in town to draw attention to the women's conference with his high profile or heft, though. That's left to Hillary Clinton, a simple *wife-of* at that time. (If more people had watched her take on the Chinese authorities, they would have voted for her to be president.) She is the sole official representative who speaks out on Chinese human rights abuses against women in their own country, and she skewers them like shish kebabs, then puts their feet to the fire on their treatment of activists at the conference. Better yet, she does it in a pink suit. It's perfect: Pink Power. And it smells sweet, more like victory than napalm ever could.

Truth is, I have been shamed by Canada's ass-kissing speech given by Sheila Finestone, an ineffectual politician who never cracked the cabinet but who is as high up the food chain as the Canadian government thinks a historic UN conference on women's rights is worth. And I have watched as each delegation sacrifices women's rights—at a women's rights conference—at the altar of political expediency, literally kowtowing to the Chinese regime that, among other human rights abuses too numerous to outline here, abducts pregnant women in the middle of the night, forces them into trucks, and takes them to abortionists where the sin of even conceiving a second child is cut out of them. Then Hillary stands up, all pink and pretty and deadly determined, and the world takes notice—for that day.

After Peking duck, my blond-haired buddy insists we are close enough to his hotel to walk there, and that I can get a cab back to mine after a drink. We walk for two hours and I have no assurance, except his, that he actually knows where he is going. This is adventuresome, but not romantic. Walking through the major arteries of communist Beijing is the equivalent of walking alongside a freeway in California. And our conversation is anything but titillating or tender. Like all journalists, we are arguing—screaming at each other, actually—about whether or not General Romeo Dallaire, heading up UN peacekeeping troops during the Rwandan massacre, was a hero or a coward. (I am arguing the hero side—and I am right.)

Then it's there, in front of us, unbidden and forbidden: Tiananmen Square, a worldwide symbol of the fight for human rights, by and for *both* genders. On June 4, 1989, as I was reporting on the blooming of democracy in Poland during the Solidarity election, it was simultaneously being trampled in China beneath tanks rolling into Tiananmen Square to "fight" the democracy protesters.

They're nothing if not consistent on human rights issues—I give the Chinese authorities that.

So at 2:00 AM, exhausted and now finally silent out of respect for the dead freedom fighters, we walk into the starkly empty, moonlit square, listening only to the tinkling of halyards on the flagpoles, when there is a cacophony of commotion: doors slamming, boots pounding toward us on pavement blocks, and we see far off, then so quickly not so far off, a group of screaming soldiers racing at us. Neither of us understands Chinese, but we know with certainty that we are being told to get the fuck out of Dodge, and we flee.

After that encounter, we quicken our pace, and finally we are at the door to his hotel. We have a drink and it's almost time for me to get up for the next day's work, so I exit.

And each day I file reports to newspapers across the country that are looking for a story bigger than the female NGOs can deliver from behind Huairou's iron curtain.

Would they have done this to men? the activists ask.

And speaking of men, where is mine?

By this time, the physical exertion of being soaked to the bone in monsoons, hiking for cabs, lugging 1995-weight laptops for twenty hours each day, mostly without sleep and with little time to eat, coupled with the stress of the stories I'm covering and the conflicting direction dictated from various editors—and did I mention my husband is missing in action?—have caused me to drop fifteen pounds. I'm now holding my clothes up with safety pins.

And each day, as I make my call home, my lovely colleague Jonathan, a man who talks sweetly about how much he's missing his wife and family, watches from the hotel bar, then, without a censoring word about the futility of my attempts, offers his support: Do I need him to carry my heavy computer? Let's go get something to eat! How about a drink?!

When I finally get hold of said husband, only days before the end of the conference, he, a man who could file a story from communist Siberia—and did—has the most ludicrous of excuses for not calling: "I didn't have my cell phone with me. I was down in the U.S., and I didn't have change for a telephone booth."

I know he is lying. I know he didn't want to talk. I know he is guilty. I know, now, he is leaving. But most of all, I know he thinks I'm an idiot!

The flight home is a hellish twenty-four hours, during which I'm too exhausted to sleep, so I exchange war stories with the NGOs at the back of the plane, though we are all feeling defeated.

And then, finally, I am home.

My last pleading request to my husband, before I left for

Beijing, was to water the plants, a chore he has never once taken on during our marriage.

And as the cab drives up, I know it's the end—and no condom, full or otherwise, can protect me: The bushes, trees, flowers, and hanging planters surrounding our lovely home are all desiccated, as is, I then know, our marriage.

I walk in, and I can see it in his drowsy eyes as he rouses himself from the sofa where he's been waiting. He can't fake excitement or even warmth at seeing me. Waiting up has been a chore.

And as much as it's not *my* idea, at this moment I am certain the end is a good idea. I am so completely exhausted, not from the lengthy travel, or the three weeks of impossible deadlines and obstacles, or the horrors I've reported, but from trying to be *this* for the past six months or year or however long he has been unfaithful—trying ridiculously, self-demeaningly, and desperately to be the woman he loves.

But it's impossible to compete with those mythical other women. They aren't themselves when they're competing; they're who their target wants them to be. They're a dream of perfection, devotion, and love. And, in my worst nightmares, hot sex.

Does he know, at this moment, in this emotional wasteland, how relieved I am? I am sure not. But he will notice—likely with relief—as the months roll by after he has left that I am not begging him to come back.

The truth is, if I'd wanted to submit to his terms—accept the affair, never discuss or understand it, just move on—I could have. But he is denying me the basic building blocks to reestablish trust, and as incomparable as it is to human rights abuses, it is part of that bigger picture.

To submit is to do what all Western nations allowed China to do: snuff out any sense of female self-respect and partnership in this world. I know with my husband it will never be about us; it will always be about him.

So I won't submit to his thought control, his absolute authority to dictate the makeup of our marriage. Submission's never gotten women anywhere. We can never debase ourselves enough.

And I draw inspiration on my own small battlefield from a phrase passed at the conference. It is a statement so obvious, so simple, that one can't believe the UN delegates argued about it for three weeks—and for years in the lead-up to the conference: Women's rights are human rights.

They are inalienable. Culture and tradition—or a man's discomfort—cannot excuse withholding them.

That's what it says on paper, anyway.

It's not just about educating girls or stopping genital mutilation, rape, and murder. It's about living with Kant's conviction that our human rights and dignity are innate.

They cannot be taken from us without our acquiescence.

And so I will not let him take mine. He doesn't hold all the power, after all. No man does.

It is the least I can learn from those women in Beijing.

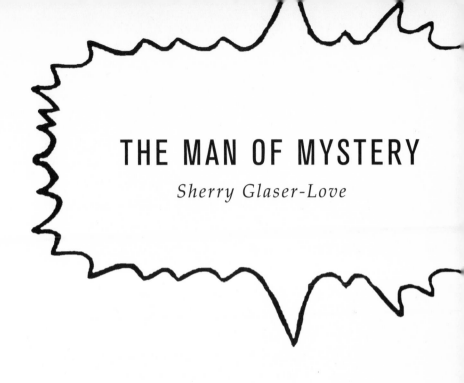

THE MAN OF MYSTERY

Sherry Glaser-Love

I was cleaning out the little cream Honda civic, when I reached into the leather pouch behind the passenger seat, scavenging for candy wrappers and rotting cheese or fruit, which somehow always managed, with the complicity of my children, to take refuge in secret hideouts in my vehicles. My hand touched something cold, metal. At first, I thought it was a toy, the little silver .22-caliber gun was so tiny, but there was a weight to it, a heaviness that indicated that, yes, in fact, this could kill someone.

A gun? In my car? In my car, in the back seat, where children could find it, play with it, kill with it? Whose was it? What was it for? Would somebody die because of it? Would it be me? My family? My cocker spaniel?

I ran in a circle, crying, holding the tip of the gun between my index finger and thumb like a stinky diaper. Not even knowing how to check if it was loaded. No experience here, uh-uh—this was new to me. I went below the house and found a nice place under the deck and dug a hole like a dog, with both my paws. The gun lay next to its grave in the dirt. I threw it into the hole and buried it. I took a long shower and cried for a long time. My husband was out on a hike with the baby. I needed time to get my shit together, figure out a plan.

Things had been really difficult for us for the past two years or so, ever since our show had closed in New York. *Family Secrets* turned out to be the longest-running one-woman show in off-Broadway history. It was based on my life story.

My husband, Greg, and I wrote it, and he directed it. This should have been a pivotal point in his life, one that turned it into an unquestionable success, but he was sinking ever deeper into depression. When the show took off for its national tour, he wasn't invited to redirect in the new theaters. Not only that, but he had a mad ambition to prove himself "on his own merits," and he had convinced himself that *Family Secrets* was my solo success. Many of us tried our damnedest to recognize and honor him for his vital contributions, but those efforts only bounced off him like bullets off Superman's chest.

When the tour was over and we returned to our little town in Northern California, I wanted so much to have another baby. I'd been waiting eight years for my career to stabilize, and with the success of this show, I could take a break and have one—a baby, that is. I could write something new. Other actresses would audition for *Family Secrets*, and Greg would direct them at regional theaters.

He wasn't that into it. He was busy writing his own screenplays and stage plays; every day, he was tippity-tapping away at the keyboard. Yes, he was determined to prove that he was talented unto himself and could provide for the family. But the opportunity to do this—something he had been asking for, becoming head of household—was obviously overwhelming. He was drinking a lot, smoking pot even more. And saddest of all, there was no affection or physical relationship between us, and it was unbearable to me. His distress seemed to hinge on his level of masculinity, and he had been in the "female" role of raising our daughter and keeping house while I went to work. Later on, his mother would accuse me of emasculating him, though a stay-at-home husband was, to me, a very sexy dynamic.

Greg wouldn't touch me. I am dependent on touch; I need it to survive. I am addicted to flesh and sex and sensuality. There was none. He had taken to sleeping downstairs, he wouldn't even look at me, and when I would look at him, he would tell me to stop staring. The loneliness was cutting me into pieces, and I would struggle every day to find a connection, to leave a door open for intimacy, sex, anything. But I was left alone with my journal, bitterly scribbling my utter confusion about where my husband had gone. We would fight, I would beg for attention, he would run to town and get drunk. He would promise to touch me the next day, would offer a massage or to have sex with me, but he would forget and I'd be the last person to bring it up.

On our ninth wedding anniversary, we did manage to get pregnant, but it took a bottle of champagne and an afternoon fuck on the roof of our cabin. That was probably the only time we had had sex in two years.

N ow, with this gun buried under my porch, what should I do? Soaking my head under the shower, I was strategizing about what the hell I was going to say. How would I put this to him without provoking a strange, and potentially violent, reaction? Would he kill me with his bare hands? A few minutes later, I heard him coming up the wooden stairs to the deck, where I was toweling off. "How was your walk?" I asked.

"Great."

"Good. So . . . I was wondering if you wanted salmon or steak for dinner."

"Whatever you think, honey."

"Okay, um . . . why do you have a gun?"

"Where is it, you cunt?"

Holy shit, now what? "I'm not going to tell you."

"Fuck you, bitch. Where's my gun?"

"You think I'm going to tell you when you're scaring the shit out of me? And why do you have a gun? Are you going to kill us?"

"I have a gun because I'm an American, and I have a right provided to me under the Second Amendment of the Constitution."

Oh my God, is he crazy? "The Second Amendment?"

"Yes, and I have the right to protect my family from mountain lions. Now give me my gun."

"No."

He looked so pissed, and went on an obscene verbal tirade that I won't subject you to. I said, "I'll give you back your gun, under certain conditions."

He got a cigarette from his breast pocket. He had just started smoking, and it still looked silly to me.

I said, "I will give you back your gun if you consent to go to therapy, because obviously we need help."

He said, "No," blowing smoke through his nostrils like a dragon.

I pleaded, cried, begged, for the sake of our kids, for our marriage.

"Okay," he said, "but I'm not going to one of your feminist therapists who just wants to slice my balls into carpaccio."

I said, "You pick the therapist."

And he did, and I gave him back his gun.

He just happened to know a therapist who would even be willing to drive eighteen miles to Comptche and three miles up our dirt road and counsel us at home. Wasn't that convenient? I thought (and, yes, a little too convenient). I wanted so desperately to believe my husband. To believe that he cared deeply enough about our relationship that he had actually put that much effort into finding just the right therapist, one even willing to come all the way to our remote outpost to mend our hearts.

When Jonathan showed up, he looked a bit grizzly, but confident. Easy. We sent our elder daughter over to her friend's house. The baby napped upstairs and we got down to business.

Jonathan suggested we organize our therapy, prioritize things so we could deal with them methodically. I liked that. "Number one," I said, "the gun. That's why we called you here."

"Right, the gun. What would you like to have happen, Sherry?"

"Well, I'd like the gun to disappear forever. But that notwithstanding, I'd like Greg to disclose to the other families who live on this land that he has a gun, so they can make decisions about

whether or not they feel safe with their children coming over here."
I could see Greg rolling his eyes and shaking his head.

"Okay," said Jonathan. "That seems reasonable."

Wow, could this really be happening, or was it a dream? A
therapist of Greg's choosing was agreeing with me. Far out. I told
Jonathan how disconcerting it was to have found the gun. I also
told him that I'd had suspicions when I found the hardware bill for
a whopping $245, and that Greg had offered the lame explanation
that it was for a generator. And yet there was no generator to be
found. "It's scary to deal with Greg's lies. I don't understand why
he won't just tell me the truth."

"What about it, Greg? Is it hard for you to tell Sherry the
truth?"

"Well, no, not really," he said. "Even if I don't tell her, she
always finds out. It's like she has sonar, and whatever I'm up to she
just . . . knows."

"Do you think you could open the doors to more honest
communication?"

"I don't know," Greg said.

"That's honest." His doctor was giving him a gold star; I sat
there ashamed and embarrassed that my husband of ten years was
afraid to tell me the truth. That was my gold standard.

"Greg," said the therapist, "would you agree to disclose to the
people here that you have a gun?"

"Yes."

The therapist turned to me. "What else?"

I said, "Well, that he'll keep the ammunition separate and
locked away at all times, out of reach of the kids."

"Greg?"

"Yes."

"And that he'll sign an agreement that says so."

Greg said, "Oh, that's bullshit."

"Well, Greg, actually," said the therapist, "that's a good idea. That way, all parties can see what they are agreeing to, and you can go back and reference it, unlike a verbal agreement."

"Okay, fine."

"Well, that's done," Jonathan said, and then turned to me. "What else, Sherry?"

"Wow, that was easy," I told him. "Let's hope this is just as agreeable: It's about Greg's drinking."

"Oh, here we go."

Jonathan said, "No, wait, Greg, remember that's why we're here today: to make good agreements. Now, Sherry, what is it you need around Greg's drinking?"

"Well," I said, "for him to at least admit that he's an alcoholic, and that his behavior is directly affecting our family, making us both miserable, and scaring our kids."

Greg argued with me—defending, resisting, rationalizing— but after a little while and a really good show, he said, "Yes, I am an alcoholic. But I'm a functional alcoholic."

Jonathan suggested that we find ways to reduce the harm to the family; maybe Greg could drink under certain circumstances, certain occasions. *Yes*, I thought, *we could work that out*. I felt this enormous relief, a huge sigh, a welcome dose of truth, reality, and solution.

This guy was good. Our first hour was up, and since Jonathan had come all this way, I offered not only to pay him $70, but also to make him a nice fish dinner. We closed our session, agreeing that the following week we would deal with the reality of the gun. I went into the kitchen and started preparing the salmon.

Greg opened the fridge and said, "Hey, J, want a beer?"

"Sure, thanks," said the therapist.

Huh? What did he say? I squeezed my eyes closed, giving my best effort to control myself. As I heard the ever-familiar pop-top spritz, and as the hops vapors scented the room, I tried to stay calm. Foxtrotting around my tiny kitchen, creating my usual masterpiece of marinated fish, rice pilaf, salad full of our garden greens, cucumbers, I maintained a decorum, an air. No matter what was happening in reality, I would keep myself tucked into a delightful fantasy that, yes, even though they were both drinking and we had just talked all about alcoholism, it was simply an unorthodox form of therapy. And hell, I might as well have a beer, too. Join the party. Whereas I had been so present for our counseling, I mentally left this scene after the first loud burp.

I made a lovely dinner and it tasted great, but it made me sick to my stomach. I just stuffed my mouth and swallowed it. I couldn't lie to my soul, but I also couldn't bring myself to question these two men. I knew deep down that this whole exercise wasn't true, but I was still relishing the feeling of being heard, of hearing myself out loud, and of saying things in front of Greg with a witness, whoever he was.

It's a debilitating kind of pain to have spent ten years with someone, have children with him, create an award-winning play for the stage with him, and suddenly not know who he is. In effect, doubt becomes a constant companion, not just around his true identity, but around mine as well. Perhaps it was I that was the problem: needy, nagging.

I didn't think my demands about the gun were too oppressive. I mean, he still had it, after all. Sure, there was a little dirt in the barrel, but I was certain it could still put a hole in my head. I began to think that every disagreement from that point on would be reason for him to murder me. I was still trying to convince myself that it wasn't going to be a murder-suicide situation, or at least the end of our dog, Daisy, whom he threatened to kill on a weekly basis because she tore into the compost and urinated wherever it was most convenient.

Still, he'd been acting so strange. Take the television episode—see, I had bought a twenty-six-inch television set on sale at Target, and it had turned out to be a piece of crap because it had no sound. Greg had wanted to throw it away, but I had insisted that I would return and exchange it. But life and its busyness had gotten in my way, and now it irked him every time he tried to watch a movie and had to rely on subtitles.

One night, when I returned from the city after a weekend of performances, the television lay smashed in the front yard. I didn't know if it had fallen or been pushed. I had a feeling he had chucked it off the deck. I found out later that he had shot the television in front of the kids. I had never examined it closely; if I had, I would have seen the bullet wounds. Later, I found out that not only had he shot the television, but he went out to practice shooting in the evenings. One night he targeted an old car that had broken down on the back forty acres. Somehow the bullet ricocheted off the car and back toward him, and got him in the groin. Ha. That must have been hilarious. Wish I coulda seen it.

After our brief therapeutic intervention, Greg said that he was feeling better and would try to be a better husband. But then he said that if things got to a certain point, "I'll just disappear."

It was a rare moment of intimacy. I felt this love, compassion. I think it was more motherly than wifely, but it was good.

He also said, "I feel like I'm the obstacle between you and your success."

I said, "Without you, I wouldn't have the success I do now. You were the one who discovered me in the comedy crowd and said, 'Do your own show.'"

It was ten years prior to that when he came to me with a joke for one of my characters, Bernard Gluck, a retired dentist, borscht-belt style. He gave me the joke: "What's a dentist's favorite song?"

"I don't know," I said. "What?"

"Fillings, nothing more than fillings."

Greg was in law school when I met him, looking to follow in his father's footsteps. He was recently divorced from a woman who had his same birthday and looked just like his mother. He moved into a ramshackle place next to my little bungalow in the Golden Hills district of San Diego. We began as friends and racquetball buddies, but after a few months, I realized how much I really liked him, and we became lovers. One of the most precious elements of our early love affair was that at night, after we made love and before we fell asleep, he would tell me a bedtime story, made up right on the spot. I told him as I was falling asleep in his arms each night, "You're not a lawyer, you're a writer."

As it was, our first child was due during his final exams.

He missed his finals and dropped out of school, and we became collaborators on *Family Secrets*, which made theatrical history.

I missed my friend, my collaborator. He was a complicated and frightening mystery to me now.

Greg had had so many setbacks in the last year, and the death of my father from liver cancer had nearly destroyed him. They weren't close when my dad was healthy, but Greg spent a lot of nights with him in the hospital, dressed up, tie and all, reading to him from *The Great Big Book of Baseball*. Losing my dad just drove him deeper into despair.

"**H**ey," I told him, "you mean the world to me and the kids." I reminded him how talented he was, how brilliant his latest play, *Lazarus*, was. I thought the story of the unlikely allegiance of Lazarus and Jesus, who joined forces to get Jesus elected as governor of Judea after Jesus brought Laz back from the dead, was the funniest play I'd ever read. I said, "Your time is coming. Don't give up." There was a tenderness between us, a gentleness. I got to lay my head on his chest, my favorite place, all soft and warm and a little fuzzy. I thought, *We'll be all right. We have our beautiful lives, our daughters, our careers—everything will turn out for the best.*

It was mid-April when he woke up one morning and declared, "I'm going to Harbin Hot Springs so I can detox, stop drinking and smoking pot, and be a good husband. Honey, I'm just killing myself."

We had booked a six-week run of our new work, *Oh My Goddess!* at the Carl Cherry theater in Carmel. I had a one-year-old toddler and a nine-year-old daughter we were homeschooling, and my father had died six months prior, and *he* needed a break? But if he was willing to admit he had a problem, and even willing to address it, so be it.

He shared with me a lifelong dream to open a health institute, which he called the Living Institute, or "boot camp for the stomach." He wrote in his journal:

> *We are going right inside you and change completely the way your stomach and colon work. This in turn will change the way the rest of the body functions. It will prove a catalyst for a realization of human potential. Let's attack our food addictions. Let's live! An addict cannot gauge how precious and delectable life can be. Let's free ourselves from our addictions and fly.*

Oh, this sounded like just the ticket for us. *Family Secrets* was so successful in New York that our next show would certainly be the same huge success, if not even beyond. We could take the profits from the theater and open the Living Institute. Yes, that was the plan. Meanwhile, he had to get himself with the program.

I said, "Okay, honey, you go save your life and I'll keep nursing ours along. No problem—I can handle it all by myself. You just go to Harbin and get well."

Harbin Hot Springs is a gorgeous retreat center in Northern California, nestled in the central hills, surrounded by lakes and mighty rivers. It offers all kinds of healing modalities, from yoga to Watsu (which involves being held by a therapist, like a baby floating in a hot-water pool, and gives you the sensation of being back in the womb). Ten days.

I didn't mind the time alone; I had had plenty of it in the course of our marriage. Greg would be home with our daughter for weeks while I was on the road. During our previous hiatuses, I had worked on my book. I figured that when he was gone, I could sleep, dance, exercise, even watch movies. I liked the solitude.

But once he was at Harbin, I didn't have time for any of that. Our baby was just a year old and wobbly-walking at best. We lived in a rickety old cabin that had once been a chicken coop. The steps to the deck were treacherous, and the baby liked to climb things better than she liked walking. I was busy on her trail, and rehearsing whenever I could. Plus, I was keeping an eye on our nine-year-old and cooking, cleaning, shopping. Despite the constant activity, I was really loving life and even missing my husband. Hope, yes—I had it like a fever. It burned through the past year or so of struggle, conflict, and curses.

Those were the days before cell phones, mind you, so Greg would have no service in the Clear Lake area, where the high desert cradles hot springs and sprouts fig trees. But he did call on the seventh day.

"How's it going, hon?"

"Great," I said. "We miss you, but we're great. The baby's talking up a storm, and she runs more than she walks. What about you—how's the withdrawal going?"

"Oh, yeah," he said. "I'm doing great. Having some detox headaches, but otherwise I'm okay. I'm drinking a lot of carrot juice. I'm turning orange."

"Ha," I laughed. He always made me laugh.

"Okay," he said, "gotta go. Time for yoga."

"Yoga? I'm so proud of you."

"Okay, I love you."

"I love you, too."

Three days later, he rolled down our dusty road in the little cream Honda. He looked pretty good: big smile, happy to see the kids. He handed them a box of fudge and they ran off. In his other hand, he had a shopping bag with the brand name LA MIRAGE printed on its side.

Hmm. Fudge—from Harbin?

"Yes," he said.

"And what's this?" He handed me the bag. There was a box inside containing a lady's Rolex.

"They sell Rolex watches at Harbin Hot Springs?"

"No, it was a roadside stand."

La Mirage. Rolex watch. He had been to Vegas. Las Vegas!

I wondered where the gun was, and if I could get to the ammunition. Visions of homicide danced through my head as he slunk by me. I felt my engines roar. I was about to mow him down, when something just clicked. I felt an eerie calm come over me. I found language. I said, "You made enough money in Vegas to buy me a Rolex? Why didn't you just bring the money home so we could pay the rent?"

He said, "Because time is the greatest gift."

I had to laugh. I said, "What am I going to do with you? I'm so tired of being mad at you."

He said, "Just love me, Sherry, just love me."

So I ruffled his hair and kissed him and loved him and let it go.

A s we were about to depart for our six-week engagement in Carmel, heading out the door, Greg said, "Oh, by the way, honey, my will and insurance policy are under the desk, in a manila envelope."

"Hmm, okay," I said, "good to know."

It wasn't the strangest thing he'd ever said to me. I thought the timing was a bit odd, but we needed to get on the road, so I didn't give it much thought; I was distracted with the upcoming show and a one-year-old shouting for me from the back seat of the little cream Honda.

It wasn't until he disappeared off the thirteenth hole at Rancho Canada Golf Course three weeks later that I thought, *Wait, what did he say?* To this very day, I relive the moments, the clues, the foreshadowing that may one day help me to discover where on earth that man went.

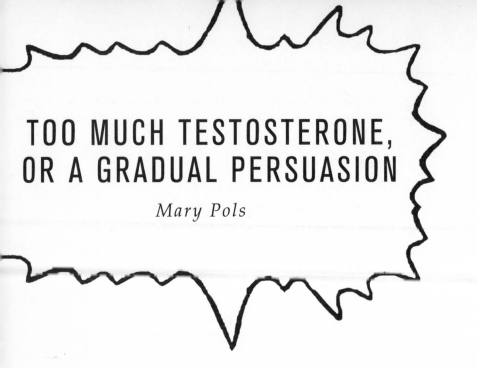

TOO MUCH TESTOSTERONE, OR A GRADUAL PERSUASION

Mary Pols

Spring 1992. Inside a rental car. Driving on a surface street in Los Angeles, somewhere in South Central. My male classmate Josh and I are on our way to an assignment for our political reporting class. As we drive through these streets, I marveling at how tidy this legendarily troubled neighborhood looks, at the green lawns and cute houses, we are discussing my twisted romance with another classmate, Josh's friend, who has been leading me on a merry dance for a year, phoning, flirting, telling me how much he'd like to be with me, if it weren't for his long-term relationship with his live-in girlfriend, whom he has been with for many years. Seven years, this guy will say to me sometimes, shaking his head as if I were asking him to break up a marriage. Then he'll make some gesture, like leaving an envelope of autumn leaves in my mailbox at school, with a note saying how much he thought about me while gazing at the fall foliage on a recent trip to the East Coast.

I'm confused by all of this. I want what I want. I never fake it. I don't get the idea of pulling someone to you and then pushing her away. It seems wasteful and dishonest, against my Yankee upbringing.

(In retrospect, I have such a hard time picturing this particular man scrabbling around on the ground, collecting leaves for me. So close to the dirt! And he liked white pants. It seems more likely that he had some girl in New York, whom he also had in some flirtation harness, and sent her out to pick him some leaves, to remember her by, and then he neatly passed them on to me, as any multitasking philanderer would.)

At any rate, I say to his friend Josh, in the car on that day in Los Angeles, with a tone of no-doubt-righteous indignation, "It's not like I started this! I never asked him to break up with her! But if he likes me so much, why doesn't he just tell her the truth, end it, and we'll give things a try? Why must we waffle? Why can't we just take action?" For emphasis, I hit the steering wheel with the heel of my hand when I say "action."

Josh sighs. He's like those smart guys who probably don't do well with women because they have the furtive look of a library mole, but in truth, he would likely treat women much better than, say, his flirtatious friend if he got more chances with them. But I am not smart enough to know this yet. "I think you've got too much testosterone," he says. He sniggers a bit when he says it.

Years later, we reconnect on Facebook and I discover that Josh is one of those guys who combines their name with their wife's. It usually creates some hideous amalgamation that bears no resemblance to an actual name. I'm influencing the story by telling you this now, because it suggests that within the classic framework of "manhood," Josh is perhaps himself not in possession of enough testosterone. And although I do believe he was attempting to devalue my own "womanhood" with that comment, it doesn't seem nice to devalue his 'hood in retaliation, especially twenty years later. But here we are, in the age of Facebook, when I have the capacity to frame his statement that way I feel a little guilty bringing it up, but if you're going to dissect tossed-off remarks made twenty years ago, you might as well bring all pertinent information to the table.

At the time, I did little more than stare at him. What had I said to produce such criticism? My young self considered: Was it my vehemence? I probably self-consciously ran a finger up my shin, to see if my legs seemed particularly hairy. (Unlikely. At twenty-seven, you never know when you might get laid, so I maintained a general state of preparedness.) Was Josh responding to my insistence that it wasn't right for his friend to be jerking me around? Which, in truth, must not have been particularly insistent, because here I was, a good six months into this romantic torture chamber, deluding myself that a) this douche was going to leave his girlfriend for me and b) he wasn't a douche.

I do remember feeling a little hurt because, by this juncture in my road-tripping weekend with Josh, I had come to the conclusion that he was a good guy. I wonder now whether it was because I insisted on driving. Wait, did I insist on driving? Was I even driving, or does my memory put me, hopped up on inappropriate testosterone, in the driver's seat?

B eing invited to participate in an anthology of essays with a title like this one's—*He Said What?*—is, in a sense, an invitation to indignation. I said yes to it without knowing what I'd write about, but thinking, Oh, Christ, so much material. A heterosexual woman in her midforties who's never been married? Naturally, she has some indignation in her past, some bitter things she could dwell on.

I told myself I'd have no problem coming up with something. I did consider, briefly, trying to do something counterintuitive, like writing about the time a man said, "You are beautiful and fabulous and perfect for me, and let's never leave each other's side." I'm sure there would be material there, too—like about the pitfalls of perfection, and about being put on a pedestal, and about claustrophobia within relationships—but the fact is, no one has ever said that or anything like that to me, so instead I did my due diligence on weird or outrageous statements made to me over the years.

(Once the guy from graduate school, the leaf collector and friend of Josh, suggested to me that we, together, in our postgraduate school lives, could be just like Neil and Susan Sheehan—respectively, the author of *A Bright Shining Lie* and a former *New Yorker* contributor, who happened to be visiting our graduate school for a week—if we wanted. I now believe that was his way of saying, "You are beautiful and fabulous and smart, etc.," but at the time, I thought, *That is one big ego you've got there, my friend.*)

Here are a few of the prospective *"He said what?"* lines I considered and dropped, along with the reasons for dropping them.

COMMENT: "Your thighs have gotten much bigger since you started college."

Speaker: father.

Situation: me walking by him while wearing bikini (for perhaps last time ever; certainly last time without shorts covering my bottom half).

Emotional reaction: humiliation mixed with feminist revolt, the germ of a desire—an unformed desire, or I would have done it—to turn on him and say, "You, the man who gave me confidence in the first place, do you want me to turn into a nutso vomiter/self-starver like most of the poor sad scared insecure girls at college? That's how they get that way, you know; that's how they end up wearing the enamel off their teeth. I mean, I'm, like, a size 6. Shut the fuck up."

Reason for rejection as topic: As a parent now, who marvels— out loud, nearly every day—at how her son has grown in this or that way, I recognize the sort of ownership associated with being a parent, for right or wrong, and how these beings we create are notable in every way. Also, technically, my thighs did get bigger at some point. Let's blame college. Let's blame Domino's pizza.

COMMENT: "She's just a friend. She's not even attractive. If you could see her, you would know there was no way I could be sleeping with her."

Speaker: first serious boyfriend.

Situation: I, suspicious.

Emotional reaction: grossed out by the demeaning of said "friend" while simultaneously pleased by reassurance, even though I didn't believe it. As I shouldn't have.

Reason for rejection as topic: On the rare occasion when I think about this guy, I do a little mental jig that I did not marry him and end up living in New Jersey, having his babies.

COMMENT: "I'm thinking about clay pots."

Speaker: not-serious boyfriend—a determination confirmed in 2010 by the fact that I had trouble recalling his last name for this mental exercise.

Situation: It is approximately 1993. I have just mentioned, in what I thought was a fairly sexy way, that I was thinking about giving him a blow job.

Emotional reaction: chagrin. Hurt. Desire to flee. A lingering insecurity about my blow job abilities.

Reason for rejection as topic: It was odd, and maybe for a while there I pictured that it would make a good line in a scathingly clever short story in which I would shamelessly imitate Lorrie Moore. It was a great indication that we were out of sync. But really, it's more of a curiosity than a leaping-off point. Also, being forty-six and single means you really don't have to worry about blow jobs anymore.

COMMENT: "If we live together, you can't cook meat in my house." Followed shortly by: "We can get a dog, but only if the children want one."

Speaker: serious, beloved boyfriend.

Situation: It's 1997, and we are in the last months of relationship talks before he gives me the heave-ho. I am totally in his thrall.

Emotional reaction: *Not even my mother's spaghetti sauce with ground beef?* Coupled with a deep desire to excuse myself and go call a girlfriend to ask whether or not that sounded dictatorial to her, too. Also, deep in my brain, a tiny longing that in the future we could all have handheld devices, like those jumbo ones they give us at the newspaper before they send us off to cover a shootout or an earthquake or something, so that I would be able to slip into the bathroom and get confirmation of relationship dictatorship. (Note: I have no spark of entrepreneurial spirit; otherwise, I'd have gone on to invent the iPhone, or at least work at Apple in some capacity.)

Reason for rejection as topic: Ultimately, I really like to eat meat, so I think it all worked out nicely.

COMMENT: "Maybe you can get your head out of the movies."

Speaker: father.

Situation: I've just told him I may get a journalism fellowship that would allow me to spend a year at Stanford. If it comes through, I plan to use the year to take film courses. I have, at that point, been a movie critic for five years, fulfilling a roughly thirty-year dream. But I'd like to get better at it, and classes will help.

Emotional reaction: hurt and annoyance. Did I ever tell him to get his head out of Aristotle's arse when he was devoting sixty-some-odd years to being a philosopher?

Reason for rejection as topic: He wasn't right to say it, but five years later I could see the wisdom in getting my head out of the movies, at least somewhat. They are a huge time-suck. Eight times out of ten, they're terrible. Movie criticism is a treadmill. Also, I did in fact run down the whole philosophy-as-profession thing every time I suggested to him that he should use his great love of the mystery genre to write a book that "people might actually want to read." Also, all he ever wanted was the best for me, even if his idea of the best didn't always match up with mine. I miss that man every day of my life.

COMMENT: "Oh, so you want to see how many inches it is?" [Wink, wink.]

Speaker: an editor at a large metropolitan daily in Southern California, who eked out every bit of double entendre he could from that statement.

Situation: I have turned in my first really big story for the paper, about a crazy, ambitious, dreamy tribute to shared beachfront, an enterprise called Coastwalk, which hosted an annual event where people walked the entire California coast from Oregon to Mexico. The story is a long one. I am sitting side by side with this editor, cutting it, trying to get it into more manageable shape for the paper. I am absolutely high on life—I've been walking and camping with these people and doing a daily journal of our trip through Ventura County. It's about nine o'clock at night. There are very few people left in the newsroom at that hour. I am young and cute. And vulnerable. We've just made a cut that I think might get it down to the required length, so I say, with jubilance, "Let's measure it!"

Emotional reaction: brought down to earth with a giant, disgusted thud.

Reason for rejection of topic: Sexism in the workplace unfortunately continues apace, but this twerp deserves no more than a paragraph anywhere.

COMMENT: "Bitch."

Speaker: close male friend, married to one of my best friends.

Situation: We've been discussing a recent tabloid magazine cover featuring a pair of women on a dating show, the last two candidates vying for the affections of a man who may or may not present one of them with a ring. Each woman has been identified with a one-word phrase, which, blessedly, I can't remember. This word is intended to sum up her entire being. The three of us have been discussing the horror of being reduced to one-word descriptors. We ask him what one-word descriptor he'd give his wife if she were to appear on the cover of *People* magazine. I believe he said, "Beautiful." We asked him how he would describe me. The answer: "Bitch."

Emotion: initially, a sort of sputter of humor, appreciation for his audacity, some hurt, some sense of *Really? Is that all?*

Reason for rejection as topic: At that point in my life, I *could* be kind of a bitch. I still can, but I'm less attached to that part of myself. She's less useful to me than she used to be. But I still admire her wherewithal. She got things done.

What do we have here? These remembered words floating back to me, from "too much testosterone" to "bitch," what do they mean? They reflect only moments when my own inadequacies intersected with the casual cruelty of men, the sexism inherent in our society, or an indication of either men's lack of regard for me or discomfort with my choices. And, of course, their own fears. I clearly made Josh uncomfortable with my proclamation that his friend and I should just give it a try.

Today, thinking back to my pointless interest in Josh's friend, which was obviously an emotional dead-end, I make myself uncomfortable. If I were a Labrador retriever, I'd be the one who is hugely affectionate and loyal but who never learns to drop the ball. I'd be in the corner of the park, holding that stupid ball in my mouth, missing so many opportunities to go play with other dogs.

My ability to recall these lines is evidence that I have dwelled far too much and too long on *What He Said.* What matters is not so much what he said, but what I heard. I am not alone in putting too much emphasis on what a man says—virtually every woman I know does or has done this. Nor do I feel particularly guilty about it. The problem was clearly linked to my childbearing years, the era in which I longed for and needed, or thought I needed, a male partner for any number of reasons (love, validation/completion, companionship, sex, security guard, sperm source, carpentry, sounding board for recipes, more sex, and so forth). None of which I actually need, I realize, as I reach the end of the childbearing years, although the love and sex would obviously be nice.

On one level, it was biological: I couldn't help myself. On another level, it was cultural, societal, inescapable. In that day and age, few of us could help ourselves, especially women like me who gobble up romance novels in their early adolescence, and this may be just as true today, in the era in which young girls read Stephenie Meyer, the Georgette Heyer of the twenty-first century. I had no idea that I didn't need a man, none at all. I had an appreciation for the independent life, but no role models representing what that kind of life might look like. I ended up becoming a single mother, a life I was dragged into by fate, a life I've found to be harder logistically than the other life, the waiting-to-be-completed life, but much easier and richer emotionally.

My father, the philosopher who thought I should get my head out of the movies, once wrote a book called *The Recognition of Reason* (not a mystery novel, and possibly requiring a PhD in philosophy to understand). I like to think of these past few years I've lived with my son as being the recognition of my reason.

The truth is, the mental exercise entailed in picking over these past events served to solidify something that had been bouncing around in my head for a while: I no longer give a shit what "He" said. Which has made it extraordinarily hard to write this essay.

There are good men, there are great men, there are men I love and some out there I will perhaps be loved by. I have friends who long for this last thing for me: a man and a mate. What I long for is good health for my son and my family, for the strength and ability to work and to provide a good home for my child. I would like a dog to keep me company (a retriever, I'm guessing). For this second half of life, I will hear what "He" says through different ears—ears less tender, less reactive—without such need. What I fix (bitchiness) or don't fix (thighs, red-meat cravings) about myself is my business. It was always my business. To feel that finally is to know women's liberation. To have known it but not felt it all those years is to understand why the need for women's liberation existed in the first place. As a girl, I knew we had already come such a long way, baby. But I never realized until now how important it would be to travel that road myself in order to see it.

WE CAN'T TELL ANYBODY THAT

Benita (Bonnie) Garvin

I stepped out of the first-class cabin of a United Airlines jet from New York and into a fantasy shared by millions before, during, and certainly after me: Hollywood. I left New York on a cold winter's morning in a torrent of rain and wind that conjured up images of *The Wizard of Oz*, and arrived in Los Angeles to glaring sun, powder-blue skies, and the scent of jasmine. Randy Newman's "I Love L.A." played softly on my internal jukebox. And if that weren't heady enough, a stocky man wearing dark glasses stood at the baggage claim, holding a cardboard sign with BONNIE GARVIN in bold, black letters. It wasn't a marquee, but it was the next-best thing.

I had arrived. Not just in a physical sense, but in a superego sense. In the Hollywood that existed in my mind, status could be measured most easily in perks. Lunch at the Ivy signaled being wooed by one of the major talent agencies, like ICM or William Morris, or a possible script or development deal with a studio. Lunch at a chain restaurant like Hamburger Hamlet or, worse yet, in a mini-mall along Ventura Boulevard meant you were on your way out of the business, or barely had a toe in it.

I struggled for years to break into the film and television industry. It was a complicated and difficult process under any circumstances, let alone mine. I arrived at the party when most of the others were sated and sanguine and secure. I was, if you calculated my age in Hollywood years, beyond a late bloomer. In fact, I was dried and ready to be potpourri. It's true that I had enjoyed a successful career as a publicist in Detroit. However, by the time I typed my first *Fade in*, Hollywood considered me as having one foot in the grave. It is a business in which the prime age for a writer is thirty and the ideal gender, male.

Age and gender weren't the only things that worked against me; subject matter was also a drawback. I was drawn to characters who challenged the status quo. And although it made for compelling drama (a good thing), it also made for *issues* (a bad thing). Issues meant controversy, which could, in turn, translate to low ratings. And most issues that drew high ratings weren't really issues; they were exploitation posing as issues. Take, for example, Amy Fisher, the Long Island Lolita, as she was branded in the media. She inspired not one, but three, television movies. Unfortunately for me, my issues lacked the titillation of Amy, much less lust or murder. Instead, I chose to shine a light on corners of our society where problems or issues had yet to be illuminated.

Over the previous several years, I had made numerous trips to Los Angeles to pitch film and television projects. From the outset, I had been well received. A dozen or so projects had been optioned, and I had been given numerous shots at the brass ring: selling a film. But none of the many possible yeses had resulted in anything other than nos (or "passes," as they say in the film business). This time, not only was I being flown out to pitch an idea for an original television movie to one of the three major networks, but the network was paying for my trip. It wasn't just rare that an unproduced writer would receive such treatment; it was virtually unheard of. The economic risk to the production company was far too great.

In the entertainment boom times of the late 1980s and early 1990s, it was once estimated that more than 1,200 television movie projects were pitched weekly. Since only a fraction of those ideas were ever bought, let alone made into films, executives who wanted to keep their jobs didn't spend their budgets shuttling unknown East Coast writers to pitch meetings. It was undeniable that this trip was a supreme vote of confidence in my project and me. It also signaled that my years of anonymity were about to end.

I found the inspiration for the story that would transform my career where I found most of my stories: in little-known but widely practiced social injustices. Years earlier, in a high school history class, I had learned about the Triangle Shirtwaist Factory fire, considered one of the greatest industrial accidents in U.S. history. The 1911 blaze etched itself into my imagination and never disappeared. The images of young, innocent immigrant girls eking out an existence in sweatshops, toiling under impossibly inhumane working conditions, and perishing as a result of their employers' greed were ones I couldn't forget. I often think these memories might have been the seeds that later germinated into my social consciousness and political activism.

Cut to two decades later. I read an article in my hometown newspaper, *The New York Times*, that said the same abhorrent conditions that led to the Triangle fire were flourishing only a mile or so from my apartment in the West Village. I batted away delusions of winning a Humanitas Prize, as my creative juices bubbled up. Like millions of other baby boomers obsessed with Watergate, I, too, had youthful pretensions of being the next Woodward or Bernstein. I had spent a few years in radio news and knew the value of proper research. If I was going to develop a great story, I had to investigate my subject first.

The New York City garment business was a burgeoning industry at the turn of the twentieth century. By the late 1960s, what had once been considered a basic essential, an article of clothing, or a *schmata*, had evolved into a social force. Clothing had morphed from the rag business to the highly profitable fashion industry. What you wore made a statement, signaling your status or individuality, or a lack of interest in either. Clothing designers were household names. It was a safe bet that the average American could identify Calvin Klein over any member of the Supreme Court. Having risen to the level of artists, clothing designers were as influential as writers, poets, or painters, but had bank accounts that rivaled those of royalty. Unlike other artists who create with their own hands, a fashion designer relies on nameless and faceless others. It was those *others* who were going to be the heart of my story.

I contacted the inspector from the Labor Violations Board mentioned in the *New York Times* article, told him I wanted to write a movie about modern-day sweatshops, and asked if I might accompany him on some of his site visits. He agreed.

What struck me on my first visit was the juxtaposition of heaven and hell. Seventh Avenue was home to the garment industry, its designer showrooms filled with haute couture. Samples of the future season's collection, hanging in plastic bags, could be seen being transported on racks across the avenue, dodging cars. Inside the showrooms, pencil-thin models with permanently affixed pouts substituted for mannequins, while cutters and patternmakers draped their size 2 figures in swaths of luxurious fabrics.

But turn the corner off Seventh Avenue, onto Forty-third or Forty-fourth or Forty-fifth, walk into a nondescript building, and take the claustrophobic, creaky elevator up a few flights, and it was as if you had stepped backward in time. Rooms of illegal immigrants, primarily Hispanic, Asian, and Caribbean girls and women, sat hunched over sewing machines. Cotton and other fibers hung like moss from the dim fluorescent lighting and the machines. The fibers that didn't stick to the overhead lighting floated through the air and directly into their lungs. It was a steamy summer's day, and the bank of windows that lined the room was closed. Nailed shut. Small children with no place to go scooted in and out as if on a playground, while their mothers slogged away slavishly for below-minimum wages. Garbage overflowed from the trash cans, and the cloud of stale cigarette smoke felt potent enough to cause secondhand lung damage.

Until that day, I had succeeded in living in New York without ever having gazed upon a rat. I knew that on any given day I could see one or two of the ugly vermin traveling on the tracks of the subways, so I studiously averted my eyes. But now, not having been forewarned, I cried out when a rat the size of a beaver ran over my feet.

There was nothing around me to suggest we were in the post-industrial age, except the incessant hum of the sewing machines. These images replicated those I'd seen in documentaries on the Triangle factory as it had existed nearly a century earlier. It was shockingly apparent that another man-made catastrophe was looming. And it wasn't a matter of *if*, but of *when*.

Our sudden and unannounced appearance in the sweatshop seemed to spark a wave of fear. The female workers didn't speak a word of English, and their supervisor—the only adult male in the room—was a small, stern Asian who pretended that he didn't, either. What they didn't know was that the labor investigator had about as much power over them as I did, because although there were an estimated five thousand–plus sweatshops in the five boroughs of Manhattan, there were a mere five inspectors.

The fashion world clearly had all the elements for a provocative drama. I decided to take the two parallel universes—glamour and beauty, exploitation and suffering—and show how they were inextricably linked. After all, it was still Hollywood and it was still television, meaning that advertisers had to be lured and commercials sold. Although my story would be a work of fiction, I would ground it in the reality of the garment industry, offering viewers a peek into a universe that existed just outside their peripheral vision. I felt confident that I had brilliantly camouflaged the social issue at the core of the story, balancing that aspect with commercial realism.

I pitched the idea to my agent. He thought it could be sexy. Whereas I saw sweatshops, he envisioned supermodels. He put in a call to a producer named Vanessa*. I'm sure he never stopped to consider whether the subject of the film would appeal to her sensibilities, only that she had a successful track record as a television-movie producer.

Vanessa was a tall, frosty blond who would more likely be taken for the headmistress at an elite private girls' school than for a producer bargaining with the Teamsters to work an hour of overtime and do it off the books. Later, when I met her, judging this book by its cover, I wouldn't have thought that she would respond to my story with such enthusiasm.

Vanessa and I were opposites in every way but gender. She was soft-spoken, I was loud. She was reserved, I was outgoing. She was self-possessed, I was insecure. She felt a sense of entitlement, whereas I had only wonder. She was thin and knew it. I was thin but thought I was fat.

A fter I arrived in L.A., I checked into my hotel, the Hollywood Roosevelt. In 1929, before television and mind-numbing production numbers with forgettable music from unmemorable films, the first Academy Awards took place here, under the roof of this historic Spanish colonial revival hotel whose decor evoked the glamour that was once Hollywood: Spanish tiles; painted ceilings, arches, and fountains; and the pièce de resistance, a pool painted by David Hockney. It was easy to imagine Clark Gable and Carole

Lombard having a cocktail in the bar, or Errol Flynn hitting on an underage waitress.

Vanessa's travel department had originally booked me at the Sportsmen's Lodge in Studio City, thinking it would be convenient for me to get to the network for my pitch. It was a reasonable, practical decision based on logistics. However, they were unaware that, for me, logistics didn't enter the equation. This was about living the dream. So when the travel office delivered my itinerary, I had a "not on your life" moment.

It wasn't that I had any misconception about my place in the Hollywood hierarchy—I knew I had yet to reach the heights of the Beverly Hills or the Hotel Bel-Air—but what respectable writer wanted to arrive in a black chauffeur-driven sedan, only to be greeted by the moose head that hung over the entrance of the Sportsmen's Lodge? I placed a call to the Hollywood Roosevelt, found that its rates were comparable, alerted the travel office, and had my booking switched.

The first thing I did after dropping off my luggage was to go shopping. A Santa Ana wind had blown in, bringing the average sixty-five-degree winter's day temperature to a toasty one hundred degrees and a stifling 110 in the Valley, where I was going to pitch the film. Everybody was running around half-naked, dressed in white linen, shorts, and T-shirts. Usually, I preferred looking like a New Yorker when I was in Los Angeles, but my all-black wardrobe, with my leather jacket, suede skirt, and boots, reminded me of the Orthodox Jewish men I'd see in the subway, each one wearing a hundred pounds of black clothing and a big fur hat. Only they could sustain perfect composure under the most extreme heat. Just looking at myself in the mirror of my air-conditioned room made me break into a sweat.

As I stood at the register in an overpriced Melrose boutique, credit card in hand, waiting to purchase a beautiful, gauzy print skirt and handkerchief-thin, tomato-colored cotton shirt, I couldn't help but wonder about their origins. How could I be sure they hadn't been sewn by some poor, indentured ten-year-old Haitian child in a sweatshop on Forty-third Street? Wasn't I poised to put a substantial sum of money on my credit card in the hope that I could pay for it when the bill came in, because I had sold a movie about how female immigrants are exploited so that women like me can be comfortable and look fashionable?

For a moment, I considered putting the clothes back on the rack. But then I imagined walking into my pitch in my black NYC wear, looking like something akin to Vampira. I had to ask the tough question: What was best for the movie? If I wanted to shine a public light on the plight of the inhumane working conditions of thousands of garment-industry workers, there was only one thing I could do: I handed the clerk my MasterCard.

I showed up for my network meeting the following day feeling confident about my appearance. It was meant to assure the network executives that they wouldn't be buying a polemic from a left-leaning New York Jew who would pollute the airways with communist propaganda. Rather, I was one of them. My new apparel spoke for me. It said I realized that wearing featherweight, light-colored fabrics and tooling around L.A. in a convertible in February were superior to bundling up in itchy wool and trundling around New York City, underground, in a moving urinal. I "got it," the "it" being Hollywood. It was safe to buy a project from me.

I knew I had pulled it off when I walked into the waiting room and saw the relief on Vanessa's face. She even used the "p-word," telling me what a pretty outfit I was wearing. For the first time since we'd met, she began to warm to me. Her modulated voice barely rose above a whisper as she expressed her love of the story and the clever way I had brought two disparate worlds together. My characters' milieu was original and fresh. She told me that *we*, meaning the audience in the *fly-over states*, hadn't seen it before, yet it touched all of our lives. Even people in L.A., second only to NYC in its number of industrial sweatshops, hadn't yet seen this story. My story was *important*, which separated it from the ordinary ones she was pitched day in and day out. She had fought to spend the money to bring me out here, and the company had agreed because she had good instincts. She knew a winner when she found one.

A novice might have had her head swell under this mountain of praise, but I was no novice. I knew compliments passing from producers to writers were handed out like wafers at Communion, part of the ritual of winning over the flock. Of course, I believed in my project. And, of course, she believed in my project. Otherwise, neither of us could sell it convincingly.

What made me believe in the inevitability of our success was the moment I learned the most astonishing fact about the executive to whom we were about to pitch: Prior to overseeing such highbrow television fare as *A Bunny's Tale*, he had been a priest! Even with the imagination of a writer, I couldn't map the trajectory from the priesthood to television-movie executive. Under the usual circumstances, I would've found his credentials disconcerting to the point of distraction. An atheist at birth, I naturally recoiled in the presence of clerics or true believers of any kind; they made me do something I cannot do in front of anybody else: clam up. Not something that would serve me well in a pitch.

Yet, to my utter amazement, I found comfort and reassurance in this man's bizarre and inexplicable midlife career change. Surely, my story of good and evil would resonate with a man of the cloth. (Maybe the genesis of "man of the cloth" had sprung from their interest in fashion?)

Vanessa and I were led into Patrick's office, where she introduced me to the ex-priest. He was a gentle man with kind, sad eyes. I couldn't help but wonder whether so-called sinners could see his eyes when they took (or is it gave?) confession. Vanessa, speaking in her barely audible voice, took the seat closer to Patrick, which made it difficult to hear much of what she was saying. But I knew that she was giving me a generous introduction, based on the way Patrick kept glancing at me and smiling. When she stopped talking and turned to me, I moved seamlessly into my story pitch.

I've pitched dozens of stories before and dozens of stories since. I've been blessed with a natural ability to pitch well, which isn't always the case with writers, I've been told. But there was something about looking into Patrick's eyes that elevated me to new heights. I felt an invisible connection between the two of us; it was metaphysical. It didn't matter that I don't believe in divine intervention, it was happening anyway. I couldn't deny what I was experiencing. Patrick sat there as if enraptured by my tale of a talented young immigrant who struggles to work her way out of poverty by putting in fourteen-hour days in a sweatshop. She is like every girl who has a dream to raise herself above her circumstances.

Halfway into my pitch, the unthinkable occurred: A tear

rolled down Patrick's cheek. He quickly wiped it away, but it was too late—Vanessa had seen it, too. Patrick had violated the cardinal rule of the network pitch: no display of emotion by an executive. Although Patrick, like any other television-movie executive, had no power to actually buy my pitch, he had the power to reject it, thereby guaranteeing that it wouldn't be heard by or sold to his boss, who would make the decision after hearing his pitch of my pitch. Moving an executive to tears was an admission of how deeply he or she had been touched. It signaled that the executive would fight for the project. It was a commitment.

I finally came to the ending, which struck just the right balance: hopeful but not overly sentimental. Then the room fell silent as the three of us digested the story I had just told.

Patrick spoke first, and Vanessa and I tried to hide our excitement. "I can't believe that things like that still go on today," he told us. Vanessa animatedly chimed in about how the horrors were straight out of a Dickens novel, yet all true and based on my meticulous research. It dawned on me that I probably should've bought the shoes I had passed up the day before. Patrick looked first to me and then to Vanessa, and then he stated, "That is one of the most terrible things I've ever heard."

Vanessa and I nodded our enthusiastic agreement in perfect sync. As far as I was concerned, the movie was as good as made.

"However . . ." he added.

My heart stopped. However! However . . . what?

"We can't tell anybody that," he announced.

Now, a writer must always be ready to respond to some off-the-wall comment with an attitude that conveys both her appreciation for getting the profoundly stupid input and her willingness to fix the fatal flaw in the story. But in the face of Patrick's response, words failed me. Thoughts failed me.

Vanessa leapt from her chair, porcelain skin blood-red, blue eyes purple with rage. If she had been carrying a weapon, I'm convinced she would've used it. She berated him mercilessly, telling him that was the most idiotic comment she had ever heard and how he, of all people, should relate to this story, given his background. The last thing I remember was her calling him a hypocrite. Patrick listened politely, unmoved and unfazed. I suddenly understood how religion had prepared him for a life in network television.

As we walked toward our cars, I thanked Vanessa for defending the story. I told her that I had never seen such an unbridled display of passion, that she had said everything I had wanted to say. Of course, I assumed we would try the remaining networks, as was often the case when one turned you down. But, as if her internal thermostat had turned back to full freeze, she said, "I have to reevaluate the project." And then she checked her watch and said it was best to forgo our scheduled lunch so she could get back to the office and work. The project had already cost enough money.

I recently read in my hometown newspaper, the *Los Angeles Times*, that sweatshops are still flourishing. But we can't tell anybody that.

* Pseudonyms have been used to camouflage characters' identities.

THIRTEEN SECRET LOVERS

Starhawk

He said, "I don't think this is going to work out."

Ten minutes into our blind date, and it wasn't going well.

Since we had barely said hello, I wondered how he'd known so quickly that our future together was doomed. I admit I'd had my own doubts from the beginning, when we'd had to juggle all of our household's cars to make room for his fancy sports car in our garage. He was afraid to leave it on the street in the Mission district, our lively Latino neighborhood in San Francisco, where cars do get vandalized, but only occasionally. Experience has taught me this Rule of Life: *Do not expect much from a relationship with anyone who is afraid to park on your street.*

I can't remember what make of car it was, which shows my own deficiency of interest in the subject. Nonetheless, his fancy car was one of the selling points when my friend Diane set up this blind date. She knew that I'd been "between relationships" for eight or nine years at that point, ever since I'd divorced my highly charming but bipolar husband Eddie, the yogi plumber. Eddie and I remained friends, and he always gave us a discount on the plumbing. Still, I'd come away with another Rule of Life: *It's cheaper to hire a plumber than to marry one.* Even now, when they make more per hour than lawyers, I still stand by that rule.

Diane herself was a lawyer who worked in child welfare, and my date—we'll call him Michael—was a social worker she had met through a court case. Diane thought that I, an adult child of two social workers, might bond with someone in the family business. Besides, she said, he was extremely good looking—café-au-lait skin and warm dark eyes, kind of like the young Harry Belafonte, but shorter.

I was appreciative of her efforts on my behalf. In the eight or nine years since Eddie had taken his crescent wrench and his van with the FORCE, IT WORKS! sticker on the back and ridden off into the Sunset district with some broad he'd picked up at a party, I'd had buddy sex, friendly fucks, sexual adventures, flings, and heartbreaks aplenty. Now I was nearing forty, and I wanted to have a baby. I was ready to bond but finding singularly few bondable guys—or gals, for that matter—in my vicinity.

My lifestyle may have had something to do with the problem. I was an author who had at that point published three fairly successful books on the Goddess and the intersections of feminism, spirituality, and politics. I spent much of my time traveling, teaching, leading workshops and rituals—for mostly female audiences. While I was certainly not averse to women and considered myself bisexual, I hadn't yet found a woman to share my life with. Or rather, I already did share my life with a woman—my best friend and housemate, Rose. We'd lived together in collective houses since the aforementioned split-up with Eddie, and still lived together. Rose was (still is) my best friend, confidante, buddy, surrogate sister, but never lover—the juice just wasn't there. And in the most secret depths of my heart, if I were brutally honest, I'd have had to admit I was looking for a guy. I've often pondered this underlying heterosexuality, when a nice lesbian relationship would have made my life so much easier, but there it was. A therapist might attribute it to the early loss of my father, who died when I was five. Perhaps I was unconsciously trying to replace him, still longing for that energetic connection I never got enough of as a child. But whatever, there it was.

By rights, men ought to be attracted in droves to a spiritual tradition that says sex is a Good Thing, and in which women outnumber them by about five to one. But alas, for most of them, it's a bit too scary, or weird, or uncomfortable. Especially for men of my generation, who'd spent their formative years in the 1950s and early '60s. Men were scarce on the ground in my world, and many of those who were around were either too feminist or just downright scared to blatantly put the moves on a powerful woman. I needed help, human or supernatural, maybe both.

On the night of the Fateful Date, I had just come back from a long summer tour doing talks and workshops and trainings in Europe. I had put the time to good use, magically speaking. On the windswept moors of Dartmoor, at an ancient standing stone, with wild ponies racing over the heather and rain clouds scudding on the wind, we'd done a ritual. "Ask for something," I suggested to the women. "I ask for world peace," one said. "I ask for an end to hunger," said another.

I was the spiritual leader, and felt some responsibility to set a good example, to Think of Others and display my selfless commitment to the greater good. However, I put that all aside and decided to ask for what I really wanted. "I want a lover," I said. A number of the women immediately revised their wishes and announced, "Ooh, me, too!" Possibly, that explains the continuance of war and hunger to this very day.

But just in case that ritual wasn't powerful enough, I followed it up with a visit to Avebury, an ancient ring of giant megaliths on the plains of Wiltshire. My English friend Ann, who drove us there, suggested we go sit on the Wishing Stone—a particular huge block of rock with a natural seat in it. You sit in the seat and make a wish, she said. Then, to seal the wish and make it come true, someone must take your picture. Done.

On the summer solstice, I found myself in northern Spain, spending the night alone in a friend's stone farmhouse. I was driving back from a hike in my rented car, and I began humming an impromptu chant, a little song to the Goddess, with the basic theme of *With all I do for you, Goddess, the very least you, as Goddess of the sacred erotic, could do for me is send me a lover. A long-term-relationship kind of lover.* I proceeded to enumerate all the qualities I thought were important.

So, coming back home with these three powerful rituals behind me, I was ready. When Diane suggested this date, I was prepared for an answer to prayer, although not quite convinced Michael would be it. Deep in my heart, I wanted a hero, someone brave and romantic, not a social worker, albeit one with a James Bond car.

But when Michael arrived, I was in a strange and vulnerable state. That afternoon, I'd gotten a letter from my Aunt Ruthie in Minneapolis. Ruthie was married to Hi, my father's younger brother, and along with my dad they were the communist wing of the family. Back in the '30s, they'd been members of the party, and, while they lived otherwise utterly conventional suburban lives, they still liked to sing the old songs and reminisce about the old days. Uncle Hi, before he retired, had been a recreational therapist, Ruthie a secretary, and they had both worked for the Veterans Administration, which Ruthie always said was the closest thing to socialized medicine we had in this country.

Ruthie had been cleaning up old papers and found a letter from my father, which she sent on to me. He had written the letter to Hi at the end of World War II, when they were both in the service. My father was in the army, which he hated, and Hi was in the navy. "I joined the navy because I heard it was a clean life," Uncle Hi used to say, "but I never knew who cleaned it until I got in." He would say that over and over, and then tell me how many sit-ups he'd done that day and how far he'd run. Aunt Ruthie would sing satirical ditties about political scandals of 1947 and cook horrible food I didn't want to eat. My aunt and uncle taught me at an early age that people can belong to radical, outlaw political organizations and still try to serve you Ritz cracker–and–peanut butter sandwiches dipped in chocolate and bore you with accounts of their exercise regimes.

Uncle Hi, we learned years later, had Alzheimer's, which was why his conversations tended to circle back around and around the same set of exercises. When his care finally got to be too much for Aunt Ruthie and he had to go to the Jewish old people's home, she fell into a deep depression. Before long, she, too, was in the old people's home—on a different floor. I thought it was tragic that they were so close, yet rarely saw each other, as Ruthie refused to go up and visit him. When I went to see her, I insisted and dragged her up to the seventh-floor ward.

There was Uncle Hi, davenning, praying from the Jewish prayer book. Communist that he was, this was out of character. He had no yarmulke, no skullcap, but instead wore a pair of Mickey Mouse ears. I don't know where they came from.

But when I walked in with Ruthie and he saw her, his face became transfigured with a look of pure, absolute love that beatified the mouse ears and everything around him. He was glowing, radiant. My Aunt Ruthie was no beauty—she had no chin and protruding teeth. But Hi looked at her as if she were the goddess of love incarnate, beaming and smiling with such pure joy that the room glowed.

He took her in his arms and kissed her passionately. Suddenly, I could see what a handsome young man he must have been, and how sexy, filled with masculine strength and tenderness. I stood in the presence of a great love, and it made my simple Uncle Hi into a hero, my plain aunt into a muse.

In Jewish mythology, there are supposed to be thirteen secret righteous men upon whom the universe depends. Simple, modest, unremarked-on, and unrenowned, they hold the worlds together with their honesty and steadfastness, but nobody will ever know who they are.

I wondered if perhaps Uncle Hi was one of thirteen secret

lovers. Perhaps they lurk in the world somewhere—plain, utterly ordinary, even a bit dull, yet with a hidden radiant love that kindles the world into being.

"Take me home," he said. "Come on, Ruthie, let's go home." Over and over he said it, while Ruthie shook her head and said, "I can't stand it. Let's go."

"He won't remember after you're gone," the nurse said.

We fled.

At the time I got the letter from Aunt Ruth, however, she and my uncle were still sharing domestic bliss in their tract home near the airport. I appreciated her impulse to send me this memento of my father.

The letter contained his scathing assessment of the war office and his advice to Hi to apply early on for benefits. It wasn't exactly an intimate, poetic outpouring of his inner soul, but it conveyed his authentic voice—a voice I had no conscious memories of, since he'd died when I was so young. Reading that letter, I felt that for one brief moment he'd come back to life. Out of my hazy memories emerged a full-fleshed human being—a person I might have known and loved, talked politics with, argued and fought with. I was overwhelmed with a sense of loss. I wanted to just sit down and have a good cry. But at that moment, the doorbell rang. Michael had arrived, so the juggling of cars began and I stuffed down my grief and tried to look like a woman eager for dinner and accustomed to fancy cars.

W alking into our collective house, Michael already looked nervous. Immediately he began to complain about his stomach, and went to the bathroom. When he emerged, he looked deathly pale. "I'm not interested in a casual affair; I really only want a long-term, committed relationship," he said. "And this isn't it."

Was it something in the bathroom? I wondered. Perhaps the bowl of condoms on the back of the toilet seat? Rose made her living doing sociological studies of AIDS and drug users. As a sex educator, she felt it her civic duty to distribute condoms wherever they might be needed. She could also do a great trick: In response to those who said, "I can't use condoms; I'm just too big for them, *heh heh heh*," she would stretch one over her head, covering her nostrils, and proceed to blow it up like a giant balloon. That could well send a man fleeing out the door, I supposed, but she wasn't even in the house at the moment, let alone lurking behind the toilet to scare off suitors.

Was it the array of menstrual products we kept out on a shelf? Pads, tampons, stick-on light-day shields, all sizes and dimensions, just in case a visitor might prefer some unique configuration of products. Maybe that was just too graphic for him?

Maybe it wasn't the bathroom at all; maybe it was the clutter in the house, or the reality of collective living, or the parade of housemates coming in, out, and through. Our English housemate, Laura, and her Senegalese husband, Charlie, kept coming in with their baby daughter, Florence, asking for my car keys. I'd offered to lend them my car for the evening, thinking I was going out on a date in a fancy car, but now that plan seemed to be deteriorating, and so every time Laura would say, "Can I have the key?" I'd say,

"Wait a few minutes, okay?" If Michael was afraid to drive his fancy car, we might have to take my Toyota.

"It's just dinner," I said to Michael. "No strings, no commitments."

But he was hemming and hawing and fidgeting, looking more and more nervous. Was it me? I wondered. Was I too earthy, too fat, too strange? He fled back to the bathroom.

"Can I take the car now?" Laura asked.

"Wait a few minutes, okay?" I said.

Maybe it was the spirit-guardian masks that lined the hallway—perhaps he thought they were demons and that he'd strayed into the home of devil worshippers. Or the Venus of Willendorf figures that Charlie had stenciled all over the walls?

"I'm not feeling well," he said, emerging again from the toilet.

"Can I take the car now?" Laura asked, coming down the hall.

"Wait just a minute," I said.

"I'm sorry, I just don't want to waste your time or mine on something that I know isn't going to work out," he said.

"You don't want to chance dinner?" I said.

"I'm a busy person," he said.

"Can I take the car now?" Laura asked.

"I think I might need it," I said. "Wait, and I'll drive you."

"I'm sure you understand," he said.

"I'll let you out of the garage," I offered.

After another session of car shuffling, I came back upstairs and looked for Laura. Where had she gone? I was feeling low. Not that I'd had great hopes for the date, but to be so firmly rejected in the first ten minutes just didn't do much for my self-esteem or my faith in magic. I picked up my father's letter and settled down in a big chair to reread it and have that good cry.

At that moment, the door opened down below and David Miller walked in. Laura had been nanny to David's two younger daughters before she'd gone traveling to Mexico and met Charlie. David and his wife were newly divorced; he had his daughter for the weekend, and that was where Laura and Charlie and the baby were attempting to go in my car. But Laura had finally gotten tired of waiting and called David, and he'd come to pick them up.

"Hello, sweetie," he said.

I looked at him and heard the warmth in his voice, and something in me shifted. I had been avoiding David since his wife had run off with the sign language interpreter at our big Halloween ritual and they'd split for good. We'd had a long friendship, punctuated by a one-night stand we'd had years before, and a longer fling I'd had with his wife. They had had an open relationship—which worked for them, to a point, better than it worked for me. Another Rule of Life: *Open relationships are great for fun, but being the opening to someone else's couplehood is just not the same as having a long-term, committed relationship of one's own.*

With all that convoluted history, I had long ago decided that if he were the last man on Earth, I would steer clear of a relationship with him. When he and his wife had split up, I had been determined not to be his Source of Sympathy.

But now, when he walked in and said, "Hello, sweetie" and I heard the warmth in his voice, it was as if a door I'd slammed shut had just swung open a crack. *You know, he's a really nice man,* I thought. And since I had to eat dinner somewhere, I got out the Toyota and went over to his place—in my own car, so I could leave early if I wanted. I wasn't ready to commit to more than dinner.

David is nine years older than I. At that time, he was in his late forties, tall, with an athletic build, bald, with a gingery mustache and beard, and had eyes that shifted from steel-gray to hazel in different lights. He looked, I have to admit, a lot like my father in all the pictures I have of him, except that my father's face was narrow and his nose aquiline, while David's is broad and Celtic, his *goyishe* nose round on the end as a Ping-Pong ball. For that matter, he looks a bit like my uncle Hi and all the other men in my family: tall, pale, and bald.

We ate pizza together with Laura and Charlie and Florence and David's youngest daughter, Julie, who was ten years old. Laura and Charlie wanted to leave early, to put the baby to bed. David offered to take me back later if I wanted to stay. *Well*, I thought, *I have nothing better to do*, so I offered them my car keys.

We talked. I talked about my father's letter and he talked about wanting to write a book about his life. David had been the first person to burn his draft card after the government made it illegal to do so during the Vietnam War. He'd spent two years in federal prison—a genuine hero. Now he was a child-welfare lawyer, representing families in cases of neglect and abuse—a kind of anti–social worker. Most of his clients were in jail, and social workers were the opposition.

Finally, he put Julie to bed and drove me home. It was only a few blocks away, and he didn't intend to be gone long. He drove a battered red Honda of archaic vintage that no self-respecting thief would bother to hijack or vandalize.

He pulled into my driveway and leaned over to give me a brotherly peck on the cheek.

That's when it happened. Suddenly, we were clenched in a passionate kiss, as if our magnetized bodies had snapped together and refused to come apart.

Some power had caught us. I was stunned, immobilized, like a deer in the blinding headlights of some supernatural vehicle driven by one of thirteen secret lovers, holding me in their glow. I couldn't pull away. I shut my eyes and kissed and kissed. From time to time, I tried to open them, but the radiant glare was too strong. Finally, ever thinking of the environment, I managed to croak out a soft suggestion.

"Maybe you should turn the engine off," I said.

After another long while, I said, "Maybe you should come in."

We snuck quietly up the stairs, avoiding all my housemates. I didn't want to get sidetracked by conversation or have to answer awkward questions. We ducked into my bedroom and made wonderful, passionate love. Then he snuck back out to go home to his daughter.

In the morning, when I staggered into the kitchen for breakfast, Rose looked up from the paper. In her warm, sisterly, supportive manner, she said, "You slut! You didn't come home last night!"

"I did, too," I protested innocently. "I've been here all night long."

She frowned, clearly not convinced.

"Okay, I think I might be with someone," I said.

"Who?"

"You have to promise not to laugh."

"Who is it?"

"David Miller," I said.

She laughed.

R eader, I married him. That was nearly twenty years ago, and despite all the ups and downs, disappointments, and rough spots of any relationship, we are still married. And so, as it turned out, I was the one to end up in a long-term relationship that night—a gift, I'm convinced, of spirits, ancestors, and matchmaking relatives. Maybe that's how they work, those thirteen secret lovers, who care not for fancy cars or expectations but shed their radiance on the everyday. One last Rule of Life: *When your heart is cracked open with grief and sorrow, look for that soft light somewhere you don't expect to find it.* Trust it. Love makes heroes of us all.

NIGHT VISION

Clea Simon

"Every woman needs a biker in her past," my therapist was telling me. "It's what we do. It gives us character."

It was hopeless. I didn't want character; I wanted my biker back. Only, despite the charming metaphor, my missing love—the ultimate Mr. Wrong—was not a biker. Was, in fact, nowhere near that tough or picturesque. But he was just as bad for me, just as wrong. And he had finally broken my heart.

I had known from the start that he didn't play by the rules. That was why I'd chosen him. Five foot ten, with short, spiked hair and a body like a weightlifter, he was unlike any of the college kids I had dated. He looked tough, streetwise. Only his thick Coke-bottle glasses gave him away, but to me they looked vulnerable—a sign of sweetness.

"Who's he?" I remember asking my buddy. We were both in our twenties, smitten with the live-music scene and working our butts off trying to build our careers. That night, like so many others, we were out at a club, hanging by the bar, when I noticed him. "Is he in a band?"

"Nuh-uh," she answered, biting on the lime that took the edge off our tequila shots. "He's at that new radio station—you know, 'outlaw rock'?"

Okay, so it wasn't outlaw rock. Its tagline was something that would sound a lot more trite today. But back then, when "new music"—punk, new wave, experimental sounds—was challenging the rock'n'roll establishment, anything outside was good.

"Is he on-air?" I'd been a music critic for only a year or so, but I already knew to stay away from the mic hounds. They had egos as big as their voices, but usually their bodies weren't this nice.

My friend shook her head and took the beer chaser I handed her. "Music director." She took a swallow. "I'm servicing him." And I thought, *I'm in!*

You have to understand, this was the '80s. And we, in our small way, were part of a brave new world. Music had changed, radically, right as we listened—established bands were being overtaken by newcomers. People we knew were picking up and plugging in. Yes, both leg warmers and lingerie were acceptable nightclub fashion, but there was more to it than that. Things were happening, and our generation was making them happen. I'd graduated college only a year or two before, but that world—with its hushed libraries and late-night philosophizing—seemed so old-fashioned. It was a new era, and me and my new friends? We were cool.

The buddy I was with that night—I'll call her Dot—worked at the local branch of a record label. It was her job to make sure all the new "product" (never "records" and not yet "CDs") got to the right people to get airplay. It was a dreary job; she was more of a gofer than anything else. But it was in the industry. She had contacts, and in the lingo of our world, she was telling me that she knew him professionally.

"Come on." She grabbed the two longnecks that the bartender—another friend of the moment—had lined up, and jerked her head in Radio Guy's direction. "I'll introduce you."

"Cool station," I said, once my friend had done the basics. The band had started playing by the time we worked our way over, which kept conversation to a minimum.

He nodded in acknowledgment. "I've seen your stuff," he said.

"You know these guys?" This was the band's first gig at this club. We were always checking out new bands in those days.

Radio Guy nodded again. "Caught 'em in London," he said, the stage lights glinting off those glasses. I was hooked.

Crash—I'll call him Crash, since those were the days when everyone was reinventing him- or herself, days when guys named Ed routinely became Oedipus or Shred—and I hooked up that night. Before long, we were a media couple to be reckoned with. Crash wasn't on-air, but he liked being onstage, introducing the new bands that his station played when the others chickened out. And I liked having access to the advances—advance tapes, advance albums, even simply advance word—before the latest thing from Leicester broke in Boston, playing to our friends in some basement club on a Tuesday night. This was what I had longed for all those years with Ivy League sweethearts: no more talk, talk, talk. We were out there, living the life. This was real.

But it was hard being cutting-edge and also in love. And as time went on, we got to see more of each other's daytime selves, the less glamorous ones. For me, the big issue was self-sufficiency. My folks couldn't understand why I wasn't in some career track at a newspaper or a glossy magazine. I'd dropped off the radar, as far as most of my old college friends knew. When I wasn't out being a rock journo, discovering the acts that would matter, I was working as a secretary with a part-time morning gig that had me groggy and sleep deprived most days. The goal was to get enough writing assignments that I could give up the typing and filing. And Crash? Well, he lived with his mother. But it was temporary. While he got his shit together. Just for now.

Still, I probably should have wondered how a man with a full-time job and no rent managed to always be short on cash. "Hey, babe, I've got to take these guys out, just for a while. Can I borrow a twenty?"

After a while, I would start asking, "Can I come?"

"Babe," he'd say, those big blue eyes looking into mine. "You know I'd love that. But this is business." And so I'd hand over the money and make plans to meet him at the Rat, at Spit, or whatever club of the moment had managed to book the band of the moment. And if my guy didn't show till closing, I knew it was business—the life we'd chosen. Besides, we were nocturnal, weren't we? *We belong to the night . . . after dark, we come alive . . .* Ellen Foley, she got it.

But I was burning the candle at both ends. My editor, a slightly older, slightly worn-down gentleman, was sympathetic, even as he tried to guide me. "It's exciting," he told me when I sauntered in, draped in black leather, "when your generation starts to take over the scene. But you've got the range. You can write about more than just one kind of music. And really, do you think housewives in Quincy care about the Godfathers?

"Why don't you head out to Cohasset tonight?" he'd say, looking over a desk calendar on which various assignments were scrawled. "Anne Murray in the first of three sold-out concerts."

"But the Black-Eyed Arseholes are going to be at the Rat," I'd protest.

"So spread your tiny wings and fly away . . ." he'd sing, and Anne Murray it was.

I wanted to make the scene. I needed it, but I needed to eat, too. As I progressed in my chosen career, I ended up missing more and more gigs with Crash. I also started gaining weight, all that beer making my blue snakeskin mini a little too tight for comfort.

Crash did, too. We were all hitting that club-crawl wall, when our relative youth could no longer outmaneuver the blatant unhealthiness of our lifestyles. But on Crash, I thought it looked good. He'd been a high school football player, back in some distant suburban past, and he held it well. I found his paunch masculine and kind of sexy, and when he pinched my too-soft waist, I only held my breath. Androgyny was the rage for women rockers. I stopped eating.

As we neared our first anniversary, we'd fallen into a pattern: Two or three nights each week, I'd end up at some suburban theater, trying not to be sarcastic on deadline; three or four nights each week, we'd meet up at a club. The few nights that I wasn't out, I was home—alone, usually, because for Crash the music was a full-time commitment. But increasingly, I'd go over to my buddy Dot's and we'd play old country records, drink, and talk about our homes. She'd majored in Anglo-Saxon, she told me one night, and had spent a semester at Cambridge, the one in England, as an undergrad. We laughed about our student days, our nerdy pasts, discovering a shared love for the late-Victorian novel.

Sometimes I'd go home and sleep the sleep of the dead. I'd gone into therapy by then, the fatigue and the loneliness getting to me. It was hard building a life outside of established career lines. But I had my friends, women who were making it up, making a living as we went along. I had the music, which sustained us all. And I had Crash, the man who came with the music. My soul mate, my partner in the beat. I couldn't talk about books with him—not without getting that look, the one that said, *What the hell are you talking about?* The one that didn't expect an answer. It was okay, though—we had other interests: the music, the scene. Sex. Though, as time went on, I started to pick up on some discordant notes.

"Did you hear about the crackdown at the station?" One of my more connected friends sidled up to me one night. "That new guitarist? They found him passed out in the general manager's office. He'd used it to shoot up in, and now they're saying no more junk of any kind on the premises."

I laughed. It was all part of the scene. We had it under control.

Other rumors worried me more. "Who's the chick with the hat?" Another journo, a male friend, gestured to the bar. A cute girl, her curls popping out from under a derby, was smiling up at Crash.

"That's his new intern." I'd be introduced at some point.

"Nice gig," said my friend. He didn't mean the internship.

"Hey, Crash." When I finally caught up with him, I tried to sound casual. "What's this I hear about new rules at the station?"

"Don't get me started." He'd roll his eyes at any mention

of The Man. "It's crazy. I mean, we've got connections. We're just hanging with these guys. Speaking of which, I had to put a new muffler in my car and the label guys want to grab a drink. Can you?"

"Yeah, sure." I fished out my wallet. "Come by later?"

"Sure thing, if I'm not too wiped."

It was the stress; I was sure of it. Crash was still crashing at my place probably three or four nights a week, but our sex life had nearly vanished. I didn't want to think it was the coke. I didn't want to think it was me. He was tired. I was tired, too. But I knew better than to complain.

I'd already tried, as subtly as I could. "So I thought maybe, if you could come by a little earlier . . ."

"Please," he'd said, putting the pillow over his head and turning away. "You're beginning to sound like my mother."

Still, we had some good times: the night his station planned a live broadcast by the Godfathers, and on the air the band dissed the other rock station in town. The night the guys from the New Music Seminar told Crash he'd be getting that award. His birthday, when I scrapped the dinner I'd planned so we could drive to New Haven to catch the Poodle Boys.

Nights like that made up for a lot. Like when I'd just been talking one night, rambling about nothing, really, like I'd do with Dot. Until I caught him looking at me. "You're weird, you know that?" he said. Despite our shared punk aesthetic, he didn't mean it as a compliment.

The worst, however, was the night at the Paradise.

It wasn't like we'd be side by side, ever, in the clubs. I'd wander off to greet a friend, and we'd hang out in the relative quiet of the bathroom for a while. He'd duck backstage, intending to share a little something with the road manager, who might then wave him in to hang with the band. Often, we'd not see each other for an hour or more, ending up smiling at each other from opposite sides of the stage by the time the music kicked in. It didn't really matter; I'd catch up with him at the bar at some point, after the music had ended. He'd be drinking with the staff, all of them talking a mile a minute on the coke.

But this night, he never came back. No smile and nod from the bouncer, telling me I could head upstairs to what they called the dressing room. No word left at the bar, telling me to wait till he got back from the band's van. Nothing, and by the time the bouncer came downstairs to tell me that even the band had taken off, I didn't know what to do. In the stark house lights, the club looked ugly and sad. I knew I didn't look much better, and finally the bartender took pity on me.

"Go home, Clea," he said. "I'm sure he'll call. There was some kind of mistake. Maybe he's waiting for you."

He wasn't, and I called everyone I knew, certain he had been taken to the hospital—the coke, his heart—or been mugged. I was so frantic that by the time he did call—I'd bothered somebody enough—I could barely speak.

"You left." I was all cried out, gasping for air. "You *left* me there." It wasn't the club; the club was my second home. It was the act of leaving. Abandonment. Desertion. I couldn't fathom the concept.

"Babe, I'm so sorry. Please, babe, stop crying."

I did my best. He didn't like it when I got sloppy. And besides, I was tired. But this time, "sorry" wasn't going to cut it.

"What happened?" Something in my voice must have been different. Something signaled that I was serious.

"Why did I leave? I couldn't find *you*, that's why," he said finally. "I assumed you'd left *me*." He was drunk, I could tell, and he sounded so sad that I believed him. I asked if he wanted to come over. But when he said he didn't think he should drive, I accepted that. He was being responsible, and I knew his eyesight was bad. Besides, he made me promise never to leave a club without him. "I was so afraid I'd lost you," he said, though I couldn't imagine how he could have.

But then the next time—a week or maybe two later—I was a little less easygoing.

"You know, I said I'd wait for you." It was the next morning by the time I found him. I was at work, talking softly and angrily into the phone. "I waited until they turned the lights up, and Brian said he had to kick me out."

The groan that greeted me was supposed to gain my sympathy. "Babe, if you knew the night I had. Those label guys, they're murder. They're all twenty-three, and they drink like professional wrestlers."

"Label guys?" Crash had stopped introducing me by then, although that hadn't stopped him from hitting me up for cash. "Label *guys?*" I'd seen his intern the night before. She'd been laughing and chatting with the bar staff, and looked fully capable of handling any schmoozing duties.

"Babe, get off my case, will you?" He was the injured party now. "I didn't see you, all right? You know about my night vision."

"Night vision?" I didn't know whether to laugh or cry. Soon enough, I found out: He left me for his intern, the girl with the hat. The woman with fewer than my twenty-five years who, nevertheless, had more sense than to take him seriously. Almost as soon as I heard about them, I heard it was over.

And I began to find out why. "I never knew how to tell you," one friend finally confessed, "but he made a pass at me when you were covering something out at Worcester one night. I didn't know if it meant anything. I mean, he was pretty wasted."

"I wasn't sure how to tell you," began the next confession, only to shock me with the revelation "but I'm pretty sure he was freebasing in the studio. I mean, he had me on speakerphone, but the sound of a blowtorch is pretty distinctive."

I was inconsolable, briefly. Even my therapist seemed helpless. I didn't want to hear about how I'd ignored the signs. I certainly didn't want to hear about the ways in which Crash had been imperfect, dismissive of my talents and envious of my past. And so, finally, she resorted to the biker line and I calmed down.

Finally, the cold, clear day dawned when I could see: Crash was a loser, the kind of boyfriend you chalk up as a learning experience, and over time I became grateful that the tuition had been only $600. But at night, with my night vision, well, Dot and I still laugh about that.

THE IRISH FLU

Christine O'Hagan

The last time I saw my father alive was on a blazing August day, inside a freezing hospital room, where the "Irish flu" had put him yet again.

For the previous week, he'd been in and out of heart failure, in and out of respiratory failure, in and out of the ICU. He was still too weak to walk, his feet so filled with fluid that he could hardly stand. He'd had the last rites three times.

All of this, and yet, amazingly enough, his doctor said he was "responding well to treatment" and that maybe he'd even be home soon.

My mother thought this was good news. Despite thirty-five years to the contrary, she still believed she could save him. Where there's life, she liked to say, there's hope.

I didn't think sending my father home was a good idea at all. Joe Camel was waiting for him there, along with Johnnie Walker Red.

We're only a mile from the bay, yet some August nights on Long Island are suffocating because there are no ocean breezes anywhere. During the August when my father was in the hospital, our house was so hot that we hardly slept at all. We had no air-conditioning, only old metal fans rattling in the bedroom windows, and crickets chirping underneath them, a duet that, to me, in my sleep-deprived state, sounded like a ringing phone.

Dawn brought with it not only twisted, sweaty sheets, but a huge sense of relief: My father had made it through one more night.

Every morning after my husband left for work, I sat at the kitchen table with my nightgown stuck to my back, sipping iced coffee, preparing myself (white-knuckle driver that I am) for the hundred-mile-plus trip to the hospital. The boys were eleven and fourteen then, unwashed, smelly, senseless-fighting ages, rolling around so much in the back seat that the car often felt ready to tip over.

I dreaded the Long Island Expressway, the car traffic, the truck traffic, the car haulers, the eighteen-wheelers, the construction crews standing too close to the car, the car itself, and the asphalt it sometimes stalled in, thick and black as mud.

I was afraid to go and afraid to stay home, unwilling to waste even a bit of my father's hospital-enforced sobriety. Without a cigarette in one hand and a drink in the other, he was a stranger to me, a stranger I had spent thirty-four years desperate to know. I was sure that there was some huge and pressing secret about him that would make every terrible thing he did fall into place, and I wanted to be there to hear it. I was like an adoptee searching for her real father for most of her life.

One morning I was in the shower, thinking that the kids were in the yard playing baseball with other kids, but instead, somewhere in the wrecked house, they had found the camera and were walking around our property taking pictures, making an accidental documentary of a difficult time. In the photos, the house and the front porch need painting; the lawn is not only overgrown, but parched. The white curtains in the bay window are limp and seedy-looking, while crooked pots of straggly red and white impatiens hang on either side of the front door—where I'm standing, in my pink seersucker robe, my face pale and worried, hoping against hope (and every time I see that picture, I remember that sick feeling rising in my chest) that the Irish flu wouldn't get him just yet.

When I was a kid and the Irish flu was on my father, he said that I didn't eat to live, I lived to eat. He also said I had a "bulbous" nose, and called me W. C. Fields. When I started wearing glasses, he said I should get a seeing-eye dog and sell pencils on street corners.

When the Irish flu was on him, my father watched me sitting on the apartment steps with my nose in a book, while all the other kids were running around playing tag, and said that I was lazy—so lazy that I'd shit in bed and kick it out.

I was eight years old the night my father hurled a hot baked potato the length of my grandmother's dining room table and struck me square in the chest. My sobbing grandmother, who had buried three of her four children, dragged me into the bathroom, sat on the side of the tub, wedged me between her bony knees, and rubbed Vaseline into the burn.

"Ach, Christ," she cried, "yer da's a rummy."

My mother said that it wasn't my father at all, but "the drink" that threw the hot potatoes, "the drink" that sent me off to the senior prom with a huge bruise on my upper arm that I blamed on a vague inoculation, "the drink" that punched me in the other arm when I was not only married but eight months pregnant, something I never told my husband until long after my father was dead.

Whatever he said, whatever he did, my mother said that he didn't mean it, he was sorry, I should pay no attention, he wasn't in his right head, he didn't think I was a "whore" at all, at all—he just had the Irish flu.

Man takes a drink, my mother (distracted by my handicapped brother and hanging on to Irish respectability by her nonexistent fingernails) said, then the drink takes the man. It's the curse of our tribe.

Irish flu or not, my father's words and deeds half killed me, and the only way I knew how to cope was to fill page after page of an old composition book with all of his insults, like Rain Man, and with my rebuttals, all the "answering back" that I couldn't do, as I fell deeper and deeper into a well of anxiety, failure in school, depression that my child's mind had no words to express. I spent my after-lunch recess in church, shuddering from what I now recognize as St. John of the Cross's *Dark Night of the Soul*, praying to God to help me, a prayer that, eventually, felt answered.

It was either God who cured me, or time itself.

M y father's hospital room was at the end of a long hallway. When I walked into his room, he was sitting on the edge of his bed, swinging his enormous feet from side to side, the green oxygen mask on top of his head. His swollen liver made his hospital gown taut across his middle. (I wished I could have poked his belly with a finger, teased him about his taste for spaghetti and meatballs or chocolate cake.) Staring at that swollen belly made it easier for me to ignore the bundles of tubes and wires, his skeletal arms, blackened by too many needles, his sticklike legs, his emaciated frame, despite the years of my mother's roasts and stews, the Irish pride she took in "running a fine table" from which he increasingly refused to eat.

He preferred cheese crackers or saltines, what he called "tid-bits," to actual meals, although he hardly ate any of them, either.

Ice cream was the only thing he ever asked for, and when he did, my mother was grabbing her purse and flying out the door for a half gallon of the fudge ripple he'd eat a few tablespoons of before she stashed it in the freezer to grow frost.

I was alone with my father, this father who had caused me such heartache, and yet the fear and vulnerability I saw in his huge hazel eyes were almost unbearable to behold. He was so frail that I wanted to gather him up in my arms. He stared at me, steadily, continuously, openly, seemingly about to say something, then changing his mind. I told him about the heat, the traffic, the construction, the boys in the back seat. He said nothing. I was so uncomfortable, I could hardly wait for my mother to show up.

My mother, the narrator of the silent film that was my father's life. To help us understand him, and her theories of how he caught the Irish flu in the first place, she told us that there were only two things Dad really wanted, and he had been denied both. The first was a healthy son, not a son handicapped by muscular dystrophy, always my father's "get-out-of-jail-free card." (My mother had been denied a healthy son, too, but she never seemed to think about that while she was pulling my brother, eight times a day, back and forth to school on a little blue bike with training wheels, up and down three flights of stairs at school and four flights at home.)

The second thing he was denied was a military career. My grandfather Harold was a decorated World War I veteran of both the navy and the army, a "doughboy" who was gassed in the Argonne forest, a hero who saved the lives of five others. He died, eventually, of his injuries, and his wife, my grandmother Rachel, died of TB; they were both gone much too young. My great-grandmother, who raised both my father and his young sister after their parents died, said she wouldn't stand in his way. She said that Dad's sister, who was in high school, was fine living with her, as she'd been doing for most of her life. After all, Dad's grandmother told him, there's a war on, and you'll be drafted anyway.

When my father went to enlist in the marines, he was with his black friend Jimmy Mack, whom the recruiter turned away. Jimmy Mack went home, and my father went to the Army Air Corps, where he decided to make the service his life's work.

Yet before my father was sent overseas, Grandma found, not only that caring for a teenager was too much for her, but also that without my father's Woolworth's paycheck, they had hardly enough to eat. So the old lady wrote to the American Red Cross, explaining her plight, and after a short time in Texas, my father came home and the "action" (as he called it) he so desperately wanted to be part of came to him secondhand, in letters from his boyhood friends Marty and Pete.

When he came home, my father got a job selling storm doors at Sears. Instead of earning a Purple Heart, he earned a paycheck that he put on the table every week. That money fed his grandmother, his sister, and him, and he made sure that his sister graduated from high school, something my father, who left high school when his parents died, was denied.

He also bought himself a Harley and a black leather jacket and started a motorcycle club, and the minute he punched out of Sears's back door, he was off riding (banned forever from Duffy's Tavern when, on a bet, he rode the motorcycle from the front door all the way through the place and out the back), a rebel with nothing visible to rebel against.

After my parents were married, my father applied to the police department—something close, I imagine, to a military life. He wanted to be a motorcycle cop (a combination, I suppose, of vocation and avocation), and he aced the test, but my mother, who thought it too dangerous, deterred him, not yet realizing that all the real danger her husband faced was on the inside.

Therefore, instead of the police department, my father went to work for the telephone company in New York City, where he ignored his inner demons and created outer ones, tossing his toolbox from one rooftop to the next and then leaping across the wide chasm, instead of using the stairs, like a normal person.

The other installers in his crew refused to work in watery cellars, terrified of the rats, but my father had no problem, hypnotizing the large rodents with a flashlight while he worked.

It wasn't the Argonne forest, but he kept us going, grabbing all the overtime he could, working on weekends as an electrician's helper, driving a delivery truck, working, at times, three different jobs.

He kept a roof over our heads, food in our bellies, and clothes on our backs, sent us to private schools, did everything he was supposed to do—everything, that is, but make us feel safe, something both my sister and I were lucky to find in our very-early marriages.

Our sick brother and my father's thwarted career, according to my mother, were what gave him the Irish flu.

Those were reasons as good as any others.

And there we are, a lifetime later, staring at each other, I in the chair, closer to tears than I had expected to be, my father in his hospital bed, his collarbone piercing the neckline of his gown.

"I was a lousy father," he says finally.

"Never apologize, never explain" has always been his motto, and suddenly, with these five words, it's as if we've turned a corner, opened up our life together for discussion, and I feel as though a window has opened in a dark house, letting in a sliver of light. I start to stand and go to him, gratefully, eagerly, desperately, yearning so much to offer him understanding and forgiveness that I am practically drooling. But then, seemingly out of nowhere, my smiling mother, carrying a shopping bag, comes through the door.

"The doctor says you're holding your own," she says brightly, while my father just looks at her, as she takes from her bag a tin of butter cookies, a quart of orange juice, a pair of wool socks. When she opens the juice and pours it into a cup, my father and I watch intently, as if she were a priest consecrating wine.

The last memory I have of the two of them together is my mother kneeling at my father's feet, like Mary Magdalene before Jesus, pulling on his socks.

Then there are breathing treatments and technicians, and nurses and doctors in the room, and when they are gone, my mother and I leave him reading the *Daily News* and go out for a late lunch.

I'm sitting across from my mother in a steak house, of all places (thinking to myself that leaving a hospital and going to a steak house is guaranteed to make a person queasy), where I'm devising a plan. When I get back to the hospital, I think, I am going to remind him about the fishing pole he once bought me, and the hi-fi he bought me after that, and how all the little girls at my birthday party, with their crinolines flashing under their party dresses, lined up to dance with him. And I can't forget the time he came to get me at the movies when I was afraid to walk home after seeing *Frankenstein 1970*. (It doesn't matter what his huge and pressing secret is. It doesn't matter to me now.)

I am going to give credit where credit is due, and let him see that our father-daughter thing isn't a total loss, that I love him, that I forgive him. But I don't get the chance.

When my mother and I come back to his room, he's gone. He looks surprised, his dark eyebrows raised quizzically. His ice-cream spoon is halfway to his mouth, his head lolling against his shoulder.

My mother runs to him, stands with her hands on either side of his face, screaming, screaming, screaming his name.

CRAZY

Barbara Abercrombie

He's banging on the bedroom door that opens onto the deck. When I let him in, he says, "You locked the doors."

I say, "It's 4:30 AM."

He says, "I forgot my keys."

I say, "Where were you?"

"It was a late dinner."

"*It's 4:30 AM.*"

What he doesn't say is, *I don't want to be married anymore. I want to leave. I think I'm in love with someone else.* Instead he says, "You're crazy."

Oh, how I loved this man. I was obsessed with him from the moment I laid eyes on him at the beach in Puerto Rico. Then married him three weeks later in New York, had two children with him, and lived with him for twenty-six years. I left one career for him and never looked back. I followed him halfway around the world to a war. When he quit his job as a stockbroker at age forty-three and bought a sailboat, I abandoned our teenage daughters to sail with him to Greece. I even handed over my second career to him. "Of course you can write a book!" I told him.

He looked like Harrison Ford, and during the sailing years he got leaner and tanner and somehow younger. I, on the other hand, acquired sun damage and took up smoking again.

I didn't know him when I married him. Only three weeks! He was a naval officer, a lieutenant, just a few years out of Annapolis and on his way to Vietnam. I was an actress in New York, about to go into rehearsals for an Arthur Kopit play at the Actors Studio. We met at a small hotel called La Playa on the outskirts of San Juan, Puerto Rico. It was on the beach, the *playa*, and the air was tropic and the water was warm, and in New York that week it was snowing. My hotel reservation had been lost and I didn't have a real room, just a spare one for $5 a night—it might even have been a rather large closet.

Years later, we'd joke that I spent the rest of the week in his room because I wanted a bathroom upgrade. I was twenty-four and he was twenty-six, taking a week's vacation before going to Vietnam. It was 1964, and both of us were dumber than skunks. Truly and deeply dumb in the ways of the world and the heart. We both smelled of Bain de Soleil, and that first night on a blanket on the beach, he said he was usually more charming but the mosquitoes were driving him nuts.

The second night, he proposed. I'd had five years of dating men in New York, the kind of men who had to check in with their shrink before making any form of commitment, such as going out of town for a weekend, so I was truly enchanted by a man who was so impetuous, so decisive. I said no, of course. I told him I was really flattered and all, but I had a career and a life.

My mother called me from New York in the middle of the week and started to yell that she knew I was "at the bottom of this." I was "the instigator." I had no idea what she was talking about. She was known in our family for sudden emotional outbursts, but usually I knew what had set her off. "Don't pretend you don't know what I'm talking about!" she yelled from Westchester County. The hotel phone was in a little room off the courtyard of La Playa; it was hot and humid and I could smell flowers and I was confused by this phone call. How had she found me? And why? Finally, she clarified things: "Your brother has dropped out of college and has gone to join you in Puerto Rico."

It was true. She gave me the address in San Juan where he was staying, and the lieutenant and I got into a cab to go looking for him. "My family is not really like this," I said. But in retrospect, we were. We were exactly like this. We were the kind of people who drop out of college and fly to Puerto Rico at a moment's notice. Twenty years later, my mother would take off from East Hampton, New York, after a fight with my father and come to this same hotel, and then return home fewer than twenty-four hours later. (There was a certain sleaze element to the hotel by then, she would tell me.) The fact was, we were a family of lunatics putting up a pretty good front.

We found my brother and got him a job as a bartender at La Playa. So here he was, in the middle of my affair with the handsome lieutenant, serving us drinks every night.

At the end of the week, I returned to New York for rehearsals of Kopit's play *Mhil'daim.* I had the lead: Sally, a Peace Corps volunteer who eventually gets boiled and eaten by the people she's trying to help. The lieutenant said he'd come to New York; I didn't believe him. But a few days later, he appeared at my door in the middle of the night. The next morning, he got on the phone and called my mother, introduced himself, and said he wanted to marry her daughter before he had to leave for Vietnam. Oddly, this struck me not as new looniness for our family, but as sanity. I thought he was deeply and impressively sane. My mother, who by now knew he was a graduate of the United States Naval Academy, was all for it. A wedding in ten days? No problem.

It was my lunch hour during rehearsals. My mother was dressed in a hat, suit, stockings, coat, and heels. I wore boots and jeans and an old plaid jacket. We were in the bridal department at Lord & Taylor to buy my wedding dress, and I was embarrassing my mother, not only because of the way I was dressed, but also because of my attitude (something that had embarrassed her for the past twenty-four years). I wanted to whip through this whole business as quickly as possible. "I'm looking for a long, simple white dress," I told the wedding saleslady. And lo and behold, she pulled out the perfect dress: white satin, lots of sweet little buttons down the back, high neck, long sleeves, and simple. "This, of course, is for a winter wedding," she said.

"It is a winter wedding," I said.

"Oh, good, so we have plenty of time for alterations and . . ."

"It's *this* winter. It's next week," I said.

"The wedding? *Next week?*" The wedding lady looked at my mother, who nodded.

"Nine days," said my mother, looking both brave and relieved at the same time.

I then became known at Lord & Taylor as the girl who was having the "quickie wedding." And in 1964, that meant only one thing. Though, of course, if I had been pregnant, I wouldn't have found out yet, since I'd known him for only two weeks.

My closest friend, who would be my maid of honor, was in the hospital and we had to go check her out of the hospital for a dress fitting. "What's wrong with her?" my new fiancé asked. "How can you check someone out to be fitted for a dress?" I had to explain that she was in the hospital to lose weight, and we were indeed able to check her out. We had to take very good care of her, though, because she was so weak from not eating. She kept warning us that she could faint at any moment.

M y mother happened to be close friends with the wife of a man who owned many buildings in New York, including a lovely hotel on Central Park South. Later, this man would behave badly and leave my mother's friend for a woman whose nickname was the Queen of Mean, but that was all in the future. For our honeymoon, my mother's friend gave us their penthouse overlooking Central Park.

On our wedding night, after we'd been to bed, my husband turned on television and watched *East of Eden*. In the morning, over breakfast, he read the sports page. A few years later, I would write a very bad short story about this: The main character, the wife, is incredibly naive, but somehow, in the space of the short story, she comes to a deep understanding and acceptance of her new husband's honeymoon behavior, his lack of attention and conversation, his self-absorption.

Four months later, I would pack up and follow him to Vietnam, where I lived in Saigon for a year, until the war escalated and navy dependents were evacuated.

But in between the madness of our beginning and the drama of our ending over a quarter century later, there were times of tenderness, of being good parents, and of truly loving each other. There were years of building a family with two beautiful and beloved daughters, summers of family vacations with our parents and siblings and extended families. Years of fixing up houses, establishing roots in a community, acquiring large dogs and many cats, growing tomatoes. There was happiness. There were also terrible fights, with threats and yelling and plate smashing, all of which I believed were part of passion and love. We worked out roles for ourselves: I was creative and dramatic, and he was solid and conservative, a man who went off to work every day as a stockbroker, who worked long hours and was steady and firm as a rock. I could act out—he grounded me.

We went sailing in Greece one summer on a cousin's boat, and it was the best month of our lives. I was the one who said, one warm, lovely Greek evening, no doubt fueled by many glasses of retsina, "Oh, let's buy our own boat and sail to Greece with the girls."

And we did! He quit his job. We had a good nest egg. A year later, he bought a forty-two-foot sailboat and was no longer steady and firm as a rock. I was beginning to have grave doubts about this idea as we sailed out of Newport Beach Marina one dark, cold December night. We headed toward San Diego, the first leg of our journey to Greece. Our daughters jumped ship at the first stop in Mexico and returned to Los Angeles to live with our best friends. We sailed onward.

My parents said we were both nuts. I wanted to believe our behavior was more like an opera, with over-the-top passions, crazed desires, adventure, lofty arias of joy and anguish. And maybe it *was* like an opera—but a road-company version. People behaving badly—the music off-key and the voices not up to the task.

By the time we got through the Panama Canal, I knew I couldn't be away from our daughters any longer. I flew home, and for me the boat became a place to visit in the summer.

How and when does a marriage begin to unravel? Was it because of our haste in getting married, the fact that we didn't know each other, was this the fatal crack in the foundation? Or did we grow in different directions? That's the cliché, isn't it? *We grew apart.*

The beginning of the end of our marriage came one August afternoon in Yugoslavia, as we sailed our boat into a harbor near Dubrovnik. A young bikini-clad girl, riding in a speedboat with friends, called out my husband's name as they whooshed past. Apparently, he knew her. We docked and he took a shower and got all spruced up, then left the boat, telling me that he was taking her out for a drink. "Well, fuck this," I said to R., who was one of our best friends and was sailing with us that summer with his daughter and another couple. It was he and his now-ex-wife who had briefly taken care of our daughters eight years before, when we had bought the boat.

We all went to dinner that night, the girl from the speedboat included. I behaved in a very dignified manner, actually quite charming (later, I'd call it my queen of England imitation). I sat at the head of the table, monopolized the conversation, and ignored this teenager my husband seemed so enamored of. Fueled with a rage that acted like a powerful drug, I was all energy yet, also in calm control. My husband whispered to me how rude I was to not include her in the conversation, and how amazing she was, how accomplished!

"You're disgusting," I told him. After dinner, he lingered on the pier, talking with her. The rest of us got on the boat and I started the engine, prepared to sail away without him. Which got his attention. *Nobody* started the engine of this boat but the captain. "Fuck you," I said when he jumped onboard and grabbed the wheel from me. (I was saying "fuck" an awful lot that summer.) And then I lay on our bunk in a fetal position for the next two weeks, until I was due to fly home. I was forty-nine years old. He was fifty-one and looked like a movie star. I had little brown spots on my skin from all the sun. I couldn't write a word and I looked like the oldest living woman in Yugoslavia. Years ago, I didn't even know where this country was, and he was the only person I knew who understood the whole history of Yugoslavia.

The woman he stays out with until 4:30 AM is a young widow, not the teenage whiz kid from Yugoslavia—though she, too, will show up again later. The next morning I sleep late, having been awake all night. When I go into the kitchen, I find a note saying that he's taken the widow (whom I will soon begin to refer to as the Tart) sightseeing.

I felt sorry for this woman when her husband died the year before, in his early forties. We had met them sailing a number of years earlier. She has a loud voice and large breasts. She drinks and smokes a lot and has long blond hair and is ten years younger than I. And though I didn't particularly care for her when we were all sailing, here she is now, a widow. And she's in Los Angeles visiting, and my husband takes her out for dinner, and I can't go along because I'm teaching. "Give her my best," I called out the night before, as I was leaving for my class. And now he's taking her sightseeing all day.

Weeks ago, we had planned a dinner party for tonight. My cousin is in town, our friend R. is coming, and our girls, who no longer live at home, will be here, too. So, while it may be the end of life as I have always known it, I have a dinner party to get ready for. Groceries to buy! Chicken to prepare! I go to Safeway. I try not to scream or weep as I go up and down the aisles, tossing chicken and salad greens, ice cream and cheese, into my cart. I have been the queen of denial, and here I am, unraveling at Safeway in Palos Verdes, California, in front of the cheese counter. I resist grabbing strangers to tell them about the outrage and pain of it all.

But, as they say in those infomercials, wait! There's more!

A few weeks later, the old cliché: the credit card bill discovery. We've been going through an odd détente, he sleeping in the guest room, occasional dinners with our daughters, I visiting my mother in New York for a weekend, both of us being civil. Or, in my case, numb. He has told me the Tart's sister was with them until 4:30 AM, and I'm beginning to think that perhaps we'll get through this after all.

Then one morning, I'm looking over our credit card bill and I find flowers ordered the night he went to dinner with the Tart. And then, a few weeks later, a charge of about a hundred dollars in the city where she lives. Did he order the Tart a present? I look up the number for the shop, call it, and ask what it sells. A bewildered voice replies, "Food. We sell food—we're a restaurant." Then I find his plane tickets, because he always saves his plane ticket stubs in the left-hand drawer of his desk. (Certain things only I knew about this man: the plane ticket saving, his knowledge of the history of Yugoslavia.) He flew to see the Tart the weekend I visited my mother in New York.

I confront him. Though the word "confront" has a healthy ring to it, a positive sound—taking a strong stand; holding one's own ground—I am not positive, not strong and healthy. I shout and cry and bump around the house, throwing things at him. I tell him that I'm going to call the police if he doesn't get out. And then I yell that if he doesn't leave, I'll stab him to death with a kitchen knife.

All of this takes place on a warm May afternoon, with the windows wide open. And somewhere in the midst of the screaming, the plates and miscellaneous objects flying, the threats, my rage and despair blasting out the windows into our quiet suburban neighborhood, I have a moment of clarity. I realize that the shattering of a shared life, the terrible unraveling of love, has indeed made me crazy, but not as crazy as he is.

And so we were divorced. He remarried—not the Tart, not the whiz kid, but someone even younger, the same age as our daughters. I remarried, too. A lot older and no longer dumb in the ways of the world and the heart, I learned that marriage can be calm and steady, and that you can feel deep, passionate love without all the operatic intensity.

I saw him recently at a family wedding. As he walked toward me, I felt the casual kind of affection for him that you feel for a cousin or an old high school buddy. He greeted me with "Well, we're not getting any younger, are we?"

"Speak for yourself," I said, trying not to rise to the bait, but failing. My face felt hot and my head buzzed.

He was hard to talk to. A bit self-absorbed. Had he always been this grumpy and negative? How could he have been the cause of all that drama—the sobbing, the broken plates, the threats of murder? Had I made him up?

"Was he always like this?" I later asked R., my second husband.

He smiled. "Yes," he said.

TALKING THE TALK

Caroline Leavitt

I t's a sultry Madison day and I'm just nineteen, hanging out in a grubby University of Wisconsin dorm lounge with my boyfriend of two months, Will, a twenty-five-year-old grad student in botany. The television is on, but instead of watching, we're facing each other and I'm listening raptly as Will tells me his new theory about plant communication. I admit it: The thing I love most about him isn't his pale blue eyes, his whippet body, or his glossy long hair. No, what I love most is that he never stops talking.

I'm shy, or at least that's what my mother's always told me; it's one of many bits of information from her that always make me feel queasily unsure of myself. She's always told me to go for the bashful boys—"It won't be so taxing on you," she says, "if you find someone like you"—and though she means to be kind, thinking of myself as shy makes me crazy. Quiet is the last thing I want, in myself or in a lover, so when I go on dates, I write down topics of conversation to memorize, I hum during the silences, I do anything I can to fill up the spaces so I won't be left behind because I'm too quiet.

With Will, that never happens. I love his constant deluge of words, the way Will can expound for twenty minutes on apes learning to communicate and then veer into a discussion of why Hemingway really hated Fitzgerald because he was jealous of him. There's no such thing as an uncomfortable silence with him, or really any silence at all. I don't have to torture myself to think of things to say or do, and when I do manage to get a word in edgewise, well, Will is off on another tangent. Just listening to him makes me insanely happy.

Now Will begins to tell me this outrageous story of how he was kicked out of Yale the semester before, for pretending to be a professor in order to scam some expensive textbooks. It's the first time I've heard this story, and it makes me unsettled. "They kicked you out?" I keep repeating, but Will ignores me and keeps talking. "I talked my way out of it," he assures me. "The deal was, I had to leave Yale, I had to apologize to the publisher, but here I am in Madison, and I like this program even better, so it all worked out."

The room smells like plastic and cigarettes, but we're the only ones here, which pleases me because, really, that's how we've lived our lives so far, like we are truly our own private world. I'm worrying about a creative writing class I've signed up for, unsure if I've got the voice or the chops for it, and when I tell Will, he ruffles my hair. "I'll help you," he promises.

Just then, another student comes in, a guy I don't know, a face

I don't even notice because I'm too enamored of Will's. We both nod, but no one says anything. This person I don't know sits down, lights a cigarette, and starts watching the TV. Will and I exchange glances. Damn. Our safe little world of two has just ended.

Will touches my cheek. "Be right back, going to get some soda," he says, and he leaves. Just like that.

I miss him. Without him, I become more aware of things. Like the ticking of the clock in the room. Like the guy sitting there and the deafening silence I have no idea how to fill. I tell myself I have to say something, anything, because it's too uncomfortable to just sit there, so I turn to the guy. "Do you want me to change the channel?" I ask lamely.

"Nah, this is cool." He barely looks at me.

So that's it. He's got as little to say as I have. I sit around, trying to watch, and it begins to bother me that Will isn't back. How long does it take to get a soda?

"See you around," I say finally, and the guy nods and I walk out into the hall and slam up against Will.

His eyes are burning. His mouth is a tight line. "Where'd you go?" I say, but he starts walking away from me and I have to follow him, struggling to keep up. I grab his arm. "What's the matter?" I ask, and he finally turns.

"Were you waiting just until I left? Was that it?"

"What are you talking about?"

"You want to go out with that guy, is that it?"

"Will, no," I say, trying to grab his arm, his sleeve, the back of his shirt. He walks outside the door, into the sweltering Wisconsin heat, with the mosquitoes like kamikazes around us, and I grab his hand. "I love you," I tell him, and I watch him calm down. I've never said the words before to him, but I blurt them out because I know words have power, especially those. He stops short, considering me. "I love you," I tell him again, and something within him seems to uncoil.

"Okay, then," he says, finally. "Okay." He takes my hand and he begins to talk, telling me this story about a kind of plant that traps small animals, about robots trained to do small household tasks, and then we're both laughing, riding on his stream of talk.

I first met Will because I dared to speak. It was my second week at the school and I didn't know anyone, and I felt tense and miserable, so I walked across the campus. When I saw Will, tall and thin, with a shock of long black hair, I don't know why, but I grabbed his arm. "Hello," I said. Will stopped, considering me.

"I don't know anyone," I said.

"Well, now you know me," he said.

At first, it was a dream relationship. Imagine, a boy so besotted he'd stay up watching me sleep! He'd bring me presents, take me out to dinner, and just stare at me as if he couldn't believe his good luck. He held my hand or had his arm around me all the time. We were inseparable, glued at the hip, and when I was sick, he brought me tea and soup and rubbed my feet, he sang to me to get me to sleep, or else he simply talked, telling me story after story until I lulled off. After our second week together, he stopped me at a street vendor and held up a perfect silver ring and slid it onto my finger. "Now we're engaged," he said, and paid the $5.

Of course, my parents weren't pleased. "How could you know

someone well enough to want to marry him in just a few weeks?"
my mother asked, appalled.

"We talk a lot," I said.

My friends were aghast, especially my roommate, who told
me in confidence that Will talked so much, she couldn't concentrate
and had to leave every time he came to our dorm room. It didn't
matter, because by then I was living with Will in his tiny studio and
barely going back to my dorm at all. We had plans: We were going
to live in California, where he'd be a botanist and I'd write. We'd
have three kids and travel all over Europe. We'd never be apart.
Every night, Will told me the story of our lives while I listened, my
head pressed against his chest.

Fast-forward three months. I've started a few short stories in class,
and though it still scares me, I find that feeling Will behind me
makes it easier to go into the class. "If you're nervous, just look at
your ring," he tells me, and I do. I write for hours every night while
Will studies, but when my pages come back, the professor always
says, "Interesting start, but dig deeper, Caroline. Reveal yourself
more to us."

I have no idea what he means.

One day, Will and I are walking down the main street, arms
around each other, laughing. Will is talking nonstop, excited
about something he's just read about the secret life of gnats, and
I'm feeling fueled by his words, when a woman suddenly plants
herself in our path. She's young, my age, and, from what I can
see, desperately unhappy. Her face screws into a grimace and she
shoves Will so hard that he bangs up against me and I fall onto the

sidewalk, scraping my palms. "Hey!" I say, but she doesn't see me, even when I scoop myself back up.

"Oh, look at little baby Will," she sneers. She shoves him again. "This is for Joanie," she says, and then she spits (she spits!) on him and moves on.

Frozen, Will doesn't move. I grab his arm, but he wrenches it from me." What was that about?" I ask. "Who was she?"

He shakes his head. "Doreen. The sister of an old girlfriend," he finally says. "She's crazy. We broke up, but she refused to believe it. Her sister's just pissed, that's all."

He tells me his ex's name is Joanie. She's beautiful, he says, a ballet dancer with hair down to her butt. They lived together for five years, he proposed (this makes me twist my own silver engagement ring on my finger), and then something happened. "What?" I ask, thinking if I know what it is, I can stop it from happening to us.

"I hit her," he says.

That's when I stop walking, when the world suddenly seems to have gone white. I blink at him, as if I've heard wrong. He's never struck me or even broken a dish in anger. "I hit her," he says again.

The whole time he's talking, he doesn't look at me. He tells me how she began to want more, how it impacted their relationship, which began erupting into arguments. "Like what?" I ask, and he gives me a look. "Like a wedding date," he says. And then he tells me that their arguments got more heated, until one day on the street, Will pushed her so violently she fell on the pavement.

"Jesus!" I say, horrified, and then I see that Will's eyes are pooling with tears and something unspools within me. This is the man I love, the man who holds my hand all through dinner, who spoons me at night and whispers stories to me until I fall asleep. "So you didn't actually hit her, you shoved her," I say, and Will nods. "It was an accident," he insists, but he's not looking at me when he says it.

I begin writing more. I write about a woman whose boyfriend hits her, and, for the first time, I don't show that story to Will. I use it, though, to get accepted into an advanced writing class. The first week, we have to read our work aloud. Usually, I hide in the back of all my classes, but this time I raise my hand. "I'll read first," I say, and I do. I read the story about the boyfriend hitting his ex, about his new girlfriend taking it in, getting disturbed, and when I look up, fifteen other writers are looking at me with interest. With respect. "This feels very honest," the professor says, and I feel myself shine, as if I'm glowing from within. "It has something to say, and I think you should try to send it out to the little literary magazines."

"Wow, where did that come from?" another writer in the class asks me. Beside him, another woman smiles at me. "I really felt that like a punch," she tells me. "I wish I had written it." A group of them are curling around me, wanting to talk, wanting to know me, but what I want to do is run and tell Will. I could be published! I have talent! The other writers want to know me!

I excuse myself, and then I race all the way to the library, where he's cataloging trees for a botany book he's doing, and I tell him breathlessly, "I could be published!"

"Where?" Will asks curtly. "Who's going to publish you?"

I start to feel tongue-tied, to lose my train of thought. "They all thought my story was great . . ." I say, and Will waves his hand dismissively. "Aren't you happy for me?" I blurt.

"I'm working, too," he says. I think of all the writers in the class, how they wanted to hear what I had to say. Something like a small fist clenches in my stomach. "You're not going to ruin this moment for me," I blurt, and I storm out, not listening when he calls, "Caroline!"

I run all the way back to my writing class, imagining what I'm going to say to the other writers, having all these conversations in my head. Maybe we can all head to the Rathskeller and talk. But when I get to the class, everyone's already gone. I sink into one of the desks and put my head in my hands. By the time I get up, it's dark outside.

On the way home, I see her. Darleen, Joanie's sister, is walking toward me. She gives me a wary, cautious look. I don't know why I feel compelled, but I walk up to her and I apologize for Will. "He didn't mean to shove her," I say, and she looks at me.

"Why am I not surprised to hear you say this?" she asks. Then she tells me that Will didn't just shove Joanie; he broke her wrist, he sent her to the hospital. He insisted it was an accident and she forgave him, but the day of their wedding, a week later, in a big church in Madison, he simply didn't show up. She looks at me with pity.

"You don't have to listen to me," she says.

By the time I get home, I'm sick. My head is swimming with arguments for why Joanie's sister could be lying, because if she isn't, that means I'm in love with a monster. I open the door and Will is throwing things into a backpack. I thought he'd be angry, but he's excited. "Let's hitch upstate a bit, camp out," he says. "Come on, it'll be fun."

"I need to talk to you," I say. "I want to talk about the story I wrote. I want to talk more about Joanie—"

Will's eyes hood. "Why?"

"Because they're both important to me." I swallow, and then I blurt out that I ran into Joanie's sister. I tell him what she said.

"And you believe her? She hates me. She'd tell any sort of lie to get us to break up."

"How do I know it's a lie?" I can't believe I've said that.

Furious, Will turns from me and stuffs more clothes into the pack, his and mine. "We'll talk when we get there," he says. "It'll be quiet. We'll be able to work things out."

I throw things into the bag, even though I don't feel like going anymore. We walk in silence, for the first time since I've known him. His body is stiff as a straw. His mouth seems ironed shut. We stop at the main drag, where the traffic is heaviest, and Will, still not looking at me, jabs out his thumb.

A blue sedan passes, then a station wagon. An elderly woman ignores us, as does a car filled with girls. The heat is pasting my T-shirt against my back. My hair is damp and I wish I had thought to bring a rubber band to tie it back.

We're at the side of the road, but no one is stopping and Will is getting irritated. I'm annoyed, too, and hot, and I can't stop seeing Joanie in my mind's eye. I can't help hearing what her sister said Will did. "You told the truth," my writing professor said about my story, "you made us see it," but was I telling the truth to myself now? And was Will? Did he even know what the truth was?

"Let me try on my own," I tell him. "When someone stops, you can jump out."

"Without me?" he says, and I nod.

He slinks, sulking, back into the shadows, and I stand up and jab out my thumb. I smile at the cars, and the very act of smiling makes me feel better. Instantly, a sporty little red sedan zips up to me. A guy grins at me, leaning over to open the door, and for a minute I imagine what it would be like to get in the car and close the door, to drive off and leave Will at the curb.

The guy's smile fades as I feel Will coming up behind me. "Oh, no room for two," the driver says, winking at me and disappearing, his tires peeling.

Will's face is terrible. Scowling, he takes a step toward me. "What?" I ask. And then he growls—he really growls. And he says, "You loved that, didn't you? You loved the attention. You loved the way that guy looked at you, like he was devouring you with his eyes."

His voice is getting louder and people are looking. "Will, cut it out," I say.

"I can't trust you for a second," he says. "Who knows what you'll do?"

I've had it. I've had enough. "You know what?" I say. "I'm not going. You go upstate by yourself."

"You slut. You whore." His face tightens.

No one's ever called me that before. No one's ever said anything that cruel or ugly. His mouth is opening, as if he's about to say more, and suddenly I don't want to hear it. "You—" he says, and then I slap him as hard as I can, and he steps back, astonished, one hand to his cheek. He's talking, but I don't listen. I don't hear a word he says, and I keep walking away from him.

I move out that day, back to the dorm and my roommate. He doesn't call and neither do I, but I don't regret it because I keep hearing him calling me a whore, something that makes everything he ever said to me before seem somehow ugly, too. When I see him arm in arm with a new girl on the street, the same way Joanie's sister saw us, he stiffens. His arm falls off the girl's shoulder. I'm surprised by how little it hurts. I take off my ring and hand it to him. "You forgot this," I tell him. His new girlfriend blinks at me, shy as a deer. Neither she nor Will says anything, but they stand there as I walk away from them.

I never really see Will again. But maybe I begin to see myself more clearly. I start feeling that I am a woman of words, that I have important things to say. I'm not lonely because I'm writing so hard, and because I start lingering after class, speaking up, saying what's on my mind. "You're so gregarious," someone tells me, and I laugh, because who would have ever thought to say that about me? I may still not be a woman of as many words as Will, but at least I know that my words, when I speak them, are the right ones for me.

PERESTROIKA IN
PLAIN VIEW

Victoria Zackheim

In 1987, the world watched in fascination as Soviet leader Mikhail Gorbachev introduced *perestroika*, the economic and political reforms designed to bring a new and perhaps liberal restructuring to the USSR. With Gorbachev in control, doors previously closed, locked, and sealed against the West were suddenly opening, and the question so many had dared not ask was finally making its way around the world: Is the Cold War coming to an end?

Whether it was ending or merely easing its grip on United States–Soviet relations, events were taking place that indicated dramatic changes were afoot. One of these changes became evident in June 1989, when two top-ranking members of the Soviet Communist Party Central Committee were joined by the leading political observer and journalist for *Izvestia*, plus several dozen American scholars, Sovietologists from Berkeley and Harvard, and a handful of translators among them, for a historic event: a conference on Stalinism.

The conference alone was significant, to be sure—could Soviets discuss this man and his tyranny without fear of reprisals when they returned home?—but what added an almost celebratory air was the venue. The Soviets and Americans were convening at Esalen, located on the magnificent coast of Big Sur, considered in those years to be the touchy-feely center of the New Age universe. How would party bigwigs Leonid Dobrokhotov and Alexander Tsipco respond to this enclave for the rich and powerful on the California coast, perched in its magnificence above the drama of Big Sur? What would political observer Alexander Bovin write about the Russians and the hot tubs? The Russians and the organic foods? The Russians and . . . us?

I was thrilled to be asked to participate as a visiting writer, but also curious to witness firsthand how such a meeting would play out. That all of this conversing and perhaps even head butting would take place at Big Sur, where I've always hoped my soul will reside upon leaving my body, made it all the more enticing.

I made the drive to Esalen from my home in Palo Alto, on the San Francisco peninsula, with high expectations. The Soviet-American Exchange Program, started by Esalen's founder, Michael Murphy, was an exciting (and, some considered, risky) plan to bring the two superpowers together to promote a partnership of peaceful coexistence. The executive director of the program, Jim Garrison, was a brilliant and innovative scholar with whom I had worked throughout his run for the U.S. Congress. Jim and I had become friends during our political days, and I enjoyed watching him move effortlessly into the international arena, where he founded the Gorbachev Foundation and, nearly a decade later, the State of the World Forum, a nonprofit designed to bring together a network of global leaders dedicated to a sustainable global civilization.

Within an hour of my arrival, it was clear that I was surrounded, not only by a breathtaking vista, but also by an energy field emanating from serious scholars and politicians determined to find a better way to coexist in the world. A world that, at the moment, many believed was edging close to destruction.

A conference with hundreds of participants often demands that sessions be closely monitored and that guest speakers and the audience adhere rigidly to the subject and time constraints. When it is a group of forty, however, the edges are softened and the restraints are loosened, leaving more time to meet and chat, even negotiate. At our first gathering, it was clear that our hosts were guiding us toward a friendly, open, and hopefully enlightening event. Chairs were formed not in neat rows, but clustered for comfort and intimate conversation. There were no podiums to stand behind while speaking, no barricades to separate the "good guys" from the "bad guys," and no suited men—that is, none that I could identify—hovering on the periphery with an invisible KGB or FBI stenciled on their foreheads. Instead, our Soviet guests mingled, their interpreters at a deferential distance, ready if needed.

At least, that was the case for Leonid Dobrokhotov, who communicated in excellent English, and Alexander Tsipco, who seemed to follow the English quite comfortably but responded in Russian. Both men were engaged and engaging, their exchanges lively and provocative. I was struck by how fully they jumped into the thick of things, asking questions and craning to hear the responses, as if anxious to learn about their hosts, the American participants, and life in a country so unlike their own.

In sharp contrast with the two Soviets was journalist Alexander Bovin. Unlike his traveling companions, he made no effort to speak English. In fact, Bovin made a great show of insisting that his interpreter remain at his side. Whenever a statement was made or a question posed, he immediately tipped his head, concentrating on the translation. Whatever his prowess with languages, every English phrase directed his way prompted a contemplative stroke of his droopy mustache and an apologetic shrug. I watched him with growing interest, detecting something that aroused not so much suspicion as curiosity. Before his translator had a chance to repeat the question in Russian, it seemed that Bovin was already prepared with a response. Did he anticipate the question, or did he perhaps understand what was being asked? Whenever the interpreter spoke, Bovin's eyes sparkled mischievously, making me wonder if the banal response his helpmate gave was an accurate translation.

It was July, and the Soviet politicians wore pallid masks reflecting too much time indoors. During the breaks, their hosts urged them outside, reminding them that vitamin D was plentiful in the California sunlight and extolling the benefits of returning to the USSR tanned and rested. I believe it was Tsipco who joked they shouldn't appear too healthy, lest their comrades at home think they had shirked work for play.

The weekend raced by, and I took great pleasure in forging a friendship with my roommate, Natasha Stepanova, one of the translators. As we dressed each morning and prepared for bed late at night, we shared stories about our lives, the plight of women struggling for equality in two very different societies, the challenges of being a working mother, and whether this newfound diplomacy could actually make a difference. It struck me that Natasha was more optimistic than I, which was no easy feat, since I'm the one whose glass is always half full. With my four grandparents having emigrated from Russia, I had always thought of the Soviets as naysayers, hardliners, and anti-Semites. This conference would be a turning point for me, one of those moments when I had to rethink my prejudices and consider what our Soviet guests were discussing: acceptance and forgiveness.

I recall so clearly the ripple that ran through the room when these three men candidly expressed their sentiments regarding Stalin and the havoc he wreaked. When Dobrokhotov spoke the names of Stalin and Hitler in the same sentence, there was an audible intake of breath throughout the room. These were the same men who, only years earlier, would never have dared speak ill of Stalin, and yet here they were, participating in an open discussion about how the former leader—at one time a veritable god among men—had orchestrated one of the bloodiest purges in history. We all knew that while the citizenry no longer praised en masse the joys of Stalinism, there were still many who dared not speak against him. And yet here, on the coast of Big Sur, and thanks to the policies of Gorbachev, three prominent Soviets were doing just that.

How often do we get to share a piece of history? In 1959, during the Democratic National Convention, I was a teenager, a straw-hatted "Kennedy girl" who danced in a snake line through the delegates after John Kennedy won the nomination. As acting escort to Sargent Shriver's mother, I remember how the elderly woman tried not to appear pleased when I introduced her as a relative of the next president of the United States. That convention, and all it embraced, was history. And in many ways, so, too, was this conference on Stalinism.

As the guest invited to document the event, I filled a large binder with notes, which were later tucked away in some storage box. (I haven't seen them for perhaps two decades, but that does not diminish my sense that, in a small way, history truly was being made that weekend, and I was heady with the thrill of it all.)

By the middle of the second day of the conference, jokes were being thrown around, titles of importance were being nearly ignored, and friendships were being struck. No one gave special treatment to the founder of *Mother Jones* magazine, or to the producer of three major film successes who was working on a miniseries on Stalin, or to President Reagan's White House representative. I joined small groups for leisurely walks before and after the sessions; a few scholars slipped away for a soak in the famous Esalen baths cut into hillside rocks, stone monuments to the California version of self-actualization. Other groups met at the Buddha statue and then explored the grounds together, snacking on organic nibbles before returning to the Big House for the next discussion. Despite the camaraderie, some of us were half waiting for the Soviets to drop the bonhomie and shift into the party line.

It never happened. When Tsipco warned against idealism and then expressed a need to return to Christian values, a few eyebrows were raised. When journalist Bovin (through an interpreter, of course) expressed an opposing view, arguing that Christian values were often dangerous and that too many cultures were destroyed in the name of religion, there was a rustling of bodies shifting in chairs. He referred to the years of Stalinism as an era of violence, lies, and intimidation.

By the end of this session, some of us were wide-eyed with surprise, while others could hardly mask their delight. And by the end of the day? It was evident that a threshold had been crossed, and that the conference's agenda had unexpectedly rewritten itself.

On the final day, following the last discussion—when scholars and communists agreed to meet in the future to see where all of this was going—the entire group convened for closing remarks from our hosts. Jim Garrison spoke about the openness of the participants, and how this level of communication heralded great hope for our futures. Michael Murphy expressed his delight at the friendships made and at the future meetings that would most certainly evolve. The Soviets stood before the group and expressed their thanks. Bovin, who remained seated to the side, voluminous belly drooping onto thick legs, added his comments of gratitude through his interpreter.

As we milled about, unwilling to say our final goodbyes, a photographer from *The Sacramento Bee* raised his camera and pointed it at the corpulent journalist. Bovin suddenly grabbed me and pulled me onto his lap. The camera flashed and I, red-faced and laughing, leapt to my feet, never imagining that this would become a nearly full-page photograph in the *Bee*'s coverage of the event. When a copy of the paper was sent to me, there was the journalist, seated Buddha-like, his expression one of utter delight, while I, though laughing, looked embarrassed. This was the time of the women's liberation movement, and I appeared to be anything but liberated!

In my room, as I packed and prepared to leave, Natasha suggested we spend some time together before I headed home. We decided to don our bathing suits and join the others on the cliffs overlooking the surf. This was where the baths sent out clouds of therapeutic steam, where massage tables were set up and tight muscles relieved, and where serious contemplation of nature was possible. There were, however, no contemplators that day. Instead, we found a relaxed and rather raucous group: A few Americans had tossed off their bathing suits in a quest for the perfect tan. The three Soviet guests chose not to follow. Natasha and I exchanged glances and quietly removed our suits. We immediately covered ourselves with large towels and stretched out on the tables.

Bovin was resting on the massage table to my left. The elder statesman of the group, and an enormous man, he wore one of the largest bathing suits I'd ever seen. At that moment, it occurred to me that he looked like a giant walrus. I'm not sure what got into me, but some mischievous impulse caused me to turn to him and say, "Bovin, take off your bathing suit!" Before I could settle back and resume tanning, Alexander Bovin, the journalist, attorney, and scholar who would become the USSR's—and, a few short years later, Russia's—first ambassador to Israel, hoisted himself onto an elbow, turned toward me, and in perfect English responded, "My dear Vicki, it is considered extremely rude for a man to reveal his communist balls in a capitalist society." And with that, he rolled onto his back, closed those sparkling eyes, and smiled.

THE HE OF SHE

Maxinne Rhea Leighton

Looking back, it's hard to comprehend how, with a grandmother who called herself a Bolshevik feminist, I could have gotten myself into this kind of situation. When my grandfather Max, after whom I am named, went to America, he left Peschka alone with three young children in a small town in Poland at the height of the pogroms. My grandmother earned money selling homemade vodka and singing and playing the piano. Peschka realized just how strong she had become on the afternoon that two Bolshevik soldiers on horseback, searching for her still, charged into her house through an open door. As the raging terror-mongers ripped up the floorboards, she walked calmly across the room, picked up her broom, and began sweeping away the dirt the horses had brought in. When they tore back outside, she kept on sweeping, her eldest son, Julius, my father, watching in silent horror.

Grandma told me this story when we sat together in her apartment above the family candy store, after I told her how Carl Rapino had pushed me down in the schoolyard and called me a fat, dirty pig. When I asked her why boys did such things, she said, "Some simply have hateful hearts; others are peacocks that prance because they can't fly. Good for birds, not for people. Learn the difference, little one." I didn't understand what she meant, but she also told me I was beautiful, and that made me feel better.

In the 1960s, when women were talking about liberation, my grandmother found a name that fit what she felt inside. "I am a Bolshevik feminist," she pronounced, "Yah, that's who I am." Because I grew up in a house where English was no one's first language, except mine, I became the interpreter of broken sentences and thoughts. (When my grandmother told me that women should be "adjucated," it became a joke between us that she confused "educated" for "agitated." Same thing with "Bolshevik," which for her was not a political idea, but was about liberation. Until that horses-and-soldiers incident, she had never had the last word with any man.)

Unlike other members of my family, it was my grandmother who was supportive of my plans to attend college, whereas my father wanted me to be his idea of the typical daughter: stay home, marry a religious man, and have lots of children. I thought he was nuts. Peschka said that he still believed he was back in the old country. "It's America and you don't have the body of a peasant, like the other women in this family." The next thing I knew, she was comparing my waist to Katharine Hepburn's, which was fine by me because I was crazy about Hepburn and Spencer Tracy in *Woman of the Year.*

When I landed a job in publishing after college, I thought I'd found a career path that in some small way paid homage to my grandmother, the keeper of the old stories and the innate journalist who commented on the times through the lens of her own perceptions. Marilyn Klinghoffer, the assistant personnel manager in human resources, interviewed me for the job. She had curly black hair with a natural strip of white and was around my mother's age, but was not afraid to wear color. With a buoyant voice and a warm smile, she administered the editing test. This family of magazines was not exactly *Parabola, Rolling Stone,* or *Newsweek,* but it was a foot into the publishing world. "There are no openings in editorial, just in production," said Marilyn. "Once you are in the company, you can move around."

"Start small, grow big," Peschka used to say.

My first day of work, I walked into the entrance on Forty-fourth and Broadway, Times Square, New York City, and rode up the escalator, decked out in the new suit I had bought at Dress Barn. I couldn't afford much, but it was the best Kate Hepburn I could muster: a brown-polyester herringbone look, straight skirt, cinched waist, a little padding in the shoulders. I went straight to personnel for orientation, filled out paperwork, and got my ID and some loving words of advice from Marilyn: "Don't spend your hard-earned money buying new suits," suggesting she thought I was trying too hard to look the role of a successful woman in publishing.

I was introduced to my new boss, Felicia, a woman who towered over me. I loved fashion and clothes and recognized her suit as one I had seen in *Vogue*'s spring collection. She had her own office, with a window, and her door had a very large lock.

Growing up in my home, there was no lock on our bathroom door. "If you need a lock on the door," my mother had declared after I complained, "then you're doing something inside you shouldn't be doing."

Compared with Marilyn in personnel, Felicia wasn't all that openhearted. As I came up against her hearty handshake, I noticed she had one of those mustaches my grandmother was always waxing off. All the women in my family had one; tweezing and waxing began not long after the first tampon. I wondered why she was dressed to the nines but didn't bother to eradicate that shadowy fuzz.

The production traffic coordinator, Heidi, showed me to the desk next to hers. She had a raspy voice, and the hair falling down to her waist was prematurely gray. I always noticed hair because, by the age of eighteen, I had begun to embolden my identity with color that spoke sass, and had already run the gamut from brassy blond to fiery red. Heidi had some strange music going on in her head, which I kind of liked. When that girl was stressed, she'd go around the office cutting phone lines. Most people thought her strange, but I'd grown up on Coney Island, watching the human blockhead on the boardwalk hammer nails up his nose. In that context, Heidi wasn't so odd.

But all of this paled next to "Felicia's Rules"—the foundation of her department.

Rule One: Never call each other by a given name, only by initials. (It was a power/masculine thing, common in business, Felicia explained, but what did I know about business? My father and Peschka owned a candy store, with a soda fountain that I worked on weekends.)

Rule Two: Think like a man, dress like a woman. (I thought again about Kate Hepburn, who, even in pants, was undoubtedly a woman.)

Rule Three: If anyone is after your job, do what any man in a competitive sport would do: Go for the kill. (In the Coney Island Projects, where I played basketball, I was a whirlwind, but it was just a game—no one got hurt. Sure, kids got stabbed or shot on the court, but that was over something personal, like the time some guy stole my friend Odette away from her boyfriend.)

Rule Four: You must join in the monthly department chant. (This was an all-women's huddle, held behind Felicia's locked door, in which, calling on a locker-room mentality, we had to repeat, "I'm a man, I'm a man. I'm a man, man, man." With three monthly tabloids to get to press, the job was fast-paced and stressful, so Felicia thought we needed bonding.)

The magazines we put out were about fixtures and hardware, housing construction, and unique places to hold annual meetings, but I didn't care—I was really excited about this job. Other than Felicia and Marilyn, the place was filled with twenty- and thirty-year-olds, a vertical college campus. As for those rules, they were okay, once I got the hang of them.

After nearly two years on the job, I was hitting my stride. Also, I had developed a wonderful friendship with Marilyn. Not since my grandmother died had I met a woman who matched her moxie and spirit.

It wasn't until much later that I realized I had missed some of the warning signals from Felicia. For example, the dog-shit episode. I was proofing the editorial copy on one of the magazines and noticed that an article about Las Vegas read: "One of the most highly popular places for your annual meeting, the streets are paved with dog shit." I queried Felicia and she said, "Not to worry, it's a joke and someone in editorial will catch it." The magazine came out with "dog shit" intact. I huddled with Heidi, who warned me that nothing good would come of this. I should have seen the foreshadowing on the cubicle wall, but I couldn't. Or perhaps I wouldn't.

Cut to the week before Christmas. It was one of those years when Chanukah and Christmas were within days of each other. After we exchanged stocking stuffers in Felicia's office, I was packing to go home. Felicia handed me a tin of cookies with a beautiful red ribbon and an angel ornament. "I baked these just for you, for Chanukah," she said, "since you are Jewish." This was the first time she had acknowledged knowing anything personal about me. And then she added, "I'll have good news for you on Monday." When I asked her to explain, she packed up her briefcase—its soft, leather-worn look was so classic, and it cooed confidence—and said, "Have a great weekend." I smiled brightly, delighted that she had singled me out with this homemade gift.

A couple of days later, I passed around the cookies at my friend's Boxing Day gathering. Everyone thought they tasted odd and refused to swallow. Yes, they were heavy, but Felicia was a former hippie, so I figured she was into grains, maybe wheat germ. It was shortly before bedtime that I began to double over with a pain so severe that I ended up in the emergency room. "It must have been something you ate" was the best diagnosis I could get. On Monday, I called in for my first sick day.

"What did you eat?" Heidi asked upon my return. After mentioning a whole range of food possibilities, from turkey to truffles, I casually mentioned the homemade goodies.

"She baked cookies for you?" Looking like an unsuspecting victim in a B-grade horror movie, Heidi screeched, "Oh, oh, this is not good. Last girl getting promoted, the same thing happened."

"Promoted?" This was the first I had heard of a promotion, and I wasn't quick to accept her assessment. Before I could respond, Felicia beckoned me into her office. "So, how was your weekend, ML?" she asked, settling into her executive chair.

"Well, actually," I replied, "it started out great, but then I ended up in the emergency room. Must have been something I ate." I tried not to focus on what Heidi had just implied. Besides, how probable was it that someone wanted to kill me?

"Emergency room?" said Felicia, with an octave leap in her voice and a capricious grin. "Last one who ate those cookies spent twenty-four hours running to the bathroom."

Last one of what? I wondered, thinking that some kind of stomach bug had been going around the office.

Felicia locked her fingers together and leaned toward me. "Your friend Marilyn," she whispered, "in human resources, she's been looking out for you." I forced a smile, not sure where this was going. "Word came down that we've purchased a new design magazine," Felicia continued. "They want you to run it."

My heart began to race, and tears came to my eyes. "They want *me?*" I said. "That's unbelievable!"

"It is, isn't it?" she responded. "I can't imagine why they'd want someone with such bad fashion sense." I was taken aback but tried not to show it. Wasn't I on the cutting edge of fashion, the woman who bought well-made knockoffs in the garment district?

But Felicia didn't stop there. "I bet you grew up in a house where the furniture was covered with plastic slipcovers," she told me. How could she know that? I should have prepared myself for what came next, but I was so naive. "Do you actually think that after training you, I'd let you step over me and take the job that I've earned?" Before I could reply, she rushed ahead. "I've slogged away for years with that damn hardware and fixtures, and all those pictures of places where I'm never invited to go!"

I bit the side of my cheek to remain silent; I was feeling very shaky. And then Felicia leaned back and smiled.

"I loaded them with paraffin wax," she stated. When she saw my confusion, her smile became twisted. "The cookies, they were loaded with paraffin."

Before I could speak, she slapped her hand against the desk and hissed, "Shut up, you stupid little cunt."

I'm not sure where I found the courage, because by this point I felt like some idiot in a flesh-colored bodysuit. I told her, "Do not speak to me like that." When she said nothing, I muttered, in a mocking tone, "But now that we're at it, tell me something, Felicia: Who exactly is speaking to me, the woman . . . or the man?"

A little smile played on her mouth. "It's the man. Didn't my rules teach you anything?"

I stormed out of her office, grabbed my purse, and ran to Marilyn in human resources.

"Felicia did *what?*" she shouted, after hearing about the paraffin and Felicia's confession.

"That's right," I said. "She poisoned me. But it wasn't *she*, it was *he*." When I saw Marilyn's bewilderment, I explained that Felicia was driven by the man in her, the *he*. "So what you are saying, Max, is that there's a powerful *he* who drives her ambitions and makes *her* aggressive?"

It sounded so reasonable, so human resources–like, the way Marilyn phrased it. Was I supposed to excuse this woman because of some psychological split?

Marilyn encouraged me to file a complaint, but I knew it would be my word against Felicia's. It wasn't like I'd secured the cookies in some evidence locker. Besides, I kept hearing my father retelling the story of how he thought the Bolsheviks were going to kill his mother, which always ended with "The world is a scary place." And then he'd say, "Don't make waves, keep your head down." Against Marilyn's advice, I turned down the promotion and remained silent.

A week later, Felicia announced that she had been promoted to editor of a new design magazine. Very soon, however, another level of wrath from the multigendered Felicia was unleashed: I was her replacement. She called me into her office. I stepped inside and said, "Please keep the door open. And thank you, I'm not hungry." I felt stronger and ready to take my honor back.

"You people, you really look out for each other, don't you?" she stated.

When anyone starts off a sentence with "You people," I always know what that means. "*You people?*" I repeated innocently.

"Jews," she spat out. "You're all supposed to be so smart, and look out for each other."

I gave her that old Coney Island–Steeplechase Park funny-face grin. It was effective; she actually took a step back. But the pause didn't last for long.

"First they want to give you a job that should be mine," she seethed. "And now they think you're good enough to replace me?"

At this point, it felt as if the floor of Felicia's office were covered with dirt. Unlike Peschka, I did not pick up a broom in defiance. Instead, I reverted to Daddy's little girl, because the world was a dangerous place. I wrote to Marilyn and to the director of human resources, informing them that I would not accept the job, and then I resigned.

I retreated to my tiny studio in Tudor City and for perhaps a month stared out my window, across the river, at the United Nations building. With my cat, Sasha, beside me, I agonized over a lifetime of silencing myself and devoured packages of Oreo cookies, always starting with the filling and then dunking the chocolate into lactose-intolerant-friendly skim milk.

The year 1985 was exciting and productive. My children's book, *An Ellis Island Christmas,* about my grandmother Peschka and her journey from Poland to America through Ellis Island, was conceptualized and later published. I started a new job that I loved, and I began working with a therapist who helped me open a dialogue between my own anima and animus. This led to a further investigation of the he and the she of me, and to a group of women performance artists who went to bars and public spaces dressed as men. We wanted to understand how we would behave differently in society if we were male. I leapt into the experience: I bound my breasts, bought a strap-on penis at a boutique in the West Village, and publicly played out the role of the masculine self. Best of all, I could do this without the voice of my father ringing in my head.

One night, I came home from work and turned on the news. I was shocked to hear Marilyn Klinghoffer's name. We hadn't spoken in years, primarily because when I'd left my job, I had been ashamed at my lack of courage and convinced myself that she didn't want to hear from me. I turned up the volume and heard "tragic death." My first thought was that Felicia had finally knocked off an employee, but this was far more dramatic: an act of international terrorism. To celebrate their thirty-sixth anniversary, Marilyn and Leon had sailed on the Italian cruise ship the *Achille Lauro*. Four heavily armed terrorists had attacked the ship off the coast of Egypt, herding American and British tourists together and then separating out the Jews. With a gun pointed at her head, Marilyn was separated from Leon, who was wheelchair-bound due to several strokes. I remembered meeting him at company events and seeing how hard he was working to reclaim his speech. I wondered if he had succeeded enough to be able to cry out for help.

Leon was shot in the head, but not before he reportedly bit one of the terrorists. His body, still in the wheelchair, was dumped overboard. Until the Italians liberated the ship, Marilyn did not know of her husband's fate. His body washed ashore five days later. Years later, Abu Abbas, the leader of the four attackers, said that Leon's murder was a mistake. Marilyn did not live long enough to hear this: She died of cancer only four months after the attack, but not before verbalizing that what happened that day was far more impactful than her own tragedy.

It was Leon's voiceless act of defiance in the face of fear that spoke the loudest to me. A man who cannot speak shouts in silence during his final moments. A woman who cannot flee takes a stand with a broom. The wife of a murdered man, ignoring her own fate, warns the world that terrorism will be one of the greatest challenges we will have to face. What is it that makes some of us impotent during the time of choice and gives others the impetus to act courageously?

O n September 11, 2001, I am walking down University Place, the demarcation line between the East Village and the West Village. It's 8:38 AM. The sky is inordinately blue and clear. I hear a roaring sound and, like everyone else, look up. A passenger jet is so low that I can actually see the name of the airline. I figure it's going to hit a building, the one right in front of me. *I'm going to die*, I think. *No way can I outrun this.* And my father's reality of the world's being a dangerous place becomes very real.

Fear courses through me with a calm acceptance. The passenger jet begins to rise. I look into the distance and, seconds before the impact, I have what I can describe only as a presentiment, a moment in which I am able to see everything and nothing. Suddenly, this wail comes exploding out of me, a cry of passion like I imagine one of those women from the old country who grieved unabashedly released. It is as if, after all my years of weeping over the death of my grandmother, something is unleashed inside me and set free—ancient ancestral sounds. I think of my father, who escaped certain death only to be consumed by the fear of what didn't happen but could have. In this moment of terror, with explosions and flames nearby, my father's history of fear and silence, my patriarchal lineage, begins to loosen its grip, and I cry out with ascending screams—the voice of Peschka's granddaughter reclaiming what is matriarchal—in the hope that if I am heard, then what is certain to happen will not.

THE LOST COAST

Jenny Rough

My husband, Ron, and I were parked under a palm tree off Pacific Coast Highway, eating frozen yogurt, when a stranger named Dave called Ron's cell. They had a mutual acquaintance who had recommended Ron for a coveted position at Dave's firm in Rockville.

"Where's Rockville?" I asked, with a plastic spoon in my mouth.

"Maryland, near Washington, D.C.," Ron said.

I dropped my spoon. It bounced off my sundress and fell onto my flip-flop. Ten years prior, when I had applied to law schools, I had pondered moving to D.C. For about two seconds. That same year, when I had visited California, I had known I'd found my place in this world. Over three hundred days of sunshine per year. A blue Pacific. Sushi—*good* sushi—on every block. California throws open its warm arms and invites people to follow their dreams—any dream at all.

My dream was to write. My Midwestern upbringing told me that was impractical, so I moved to California and followed different dreams. A law degree. A federal clerkship. A job at a big firm before transitioning in-house to Pepperdine University, where I worked in the general counsel's office in a building up in the hills, overlooking a grove of coral trees and the blue Pacific.

And love. I fell in love among California's blossoming jasmine bushes and purple jacaranda trees. Ron and I shared picnics at the Hollywood Bowl, beers at a trendy neighborhood spot tucked beside the Venice boardwalk, and strolls along the Santa Monica bluffs. We wandered the Third Street Promenade, weaving through its eclectic mix of artists and street performers. In the independent movie theater, he'd order popcorn and I'd order Junior Mints and we'd mix them together, salty and sweet.

The day we married, standing underneath a canopy of pink roses and long green hops, I promised to "bloom where we plant." I chose the odd phrase after seeing it on a needlepoint canvas. Of course, when I said it, I never thought Ron and I would leave Southern California.

Eighteen months later, I could no longer ignore my urge to write. Ron knew writing was my Grand Plan. One night, as we grilled hamburgers, I told him I was ready to take the leap.

"Do you think you're rushing into this? Maybe you should wait a year," Ron said.

We fixed our buns and sat on the balcony couch.

"I've been waiting my whole life," I said.

Ron was worried about money, but I was sure I could earn a decent living as a writer. We chewed in silence and watched the sun set over the Pacific.

"We could start a family," I said.

Ron was ready for kids. I had been hesitating, overwhelmed by the thought of combining a career with a baby. The flexible lifestyle of an artist seemed ideal.

"That would be good," Ron said. And then: "If this is what you really want, we'll make it work."

That first year, my estimated income was a *wee* bit off: hopes of earning $3,000 a month translated into a reality of more like $300. Oops. Ron, who worked at a financial services firm, had been bumping his head against the ceiling of his current job and was antsy for a challenge that involved a direct role in investment decisions. Our mounting bills and decision to ditch birth control pills were putting pressure on him to make more money. So when Dave called a second time, I knew what Ron was thinking: He wanted to take the job in Rockville. Here's what I was thinking: After he'd agreed to my career switch, how could I say no to his?

A month later, I stood on a sidewalk on Rockville Pike, a dirty, traffic-y, retail-jammed route that runs from Maryland into D.C. It was February. I'd dug my wool coat out from storage. The trees were wet and bare, the air damp. I looked up at the brick building looming in front of me. An hour ago, while Ron had toured the ninth floor, I had explored Rockville. No winter farmers' markets—a Safeway. No cute bungalows—bland tract housing. No scent of jasmine lingering among birds of paradise—the smell was more that of . . . dumpsters. And, worst of all, no blue Pacific. When I ate lunch in D.C., my eyes stung. The city had not yet banned smoking in restaurants, and there were ashtrays at every table. Even when we boarded the plane for the trip home, I could still smell the stink of stale cigarettes.

The Midwestern girl in me wanted to be a supportive wife to Ron. The California girl called me to be true to who I was. But who was I, exactly? A writer? Given my pathetic paychecks, I didn't feel I had leverage.

In California, I stuffed my dread, along with my pants, into moving boxes. I walked my dog to the beach one last time. Offered the sun a final salutation in my favorite yoga studio. Said goodbye to my book-club girls, my therapist, my hairstylist, my gynecologist, and my best pal, Kari, all of whom, together, felt like the steady heartbeat that brought just the right rhythm to my life. Then I watched movers load our furniture into a long orange van and drive off.

In the rearview mirror of our car, the ocean washed away first. The mountains flattened. As we drove through Oklahoma, raindrops splattered our car and I followed the windshield wipers as they flung back and forth. Flick: *Give this move a chance, Jenny— it'll open new doors.* Flick: *But living west is an integral part of your core—you're a California girl.*

Upon arriving in Maryland, we checked into the Woodfin Suites, temporary furnished housing that smelled borrowed, like a dorm room. At five, the staff set out bowls of nuts and sour wine. Our plan was to stay there a week, until we found a place to rent. Nothing felt right: Houses were too expensive, apartments too small, duplexes too dumpy, row houses too narrow.

"Isn't the skyline pretty?" Ron said, trying to help me see D.C.'s beauty as we drove around after dinner one night. I glowered at the Washington Monument. Museums and white phallic structures aren't my thing.

"How can this be?" I asked Ron the next morning. We were standing in a tiny apartment in Logan Circle, an up-and-coming neighborhood in northwest D.C. Industrial-size pipes ran along the ceiling. Three of the walls had no windows—a small dungeon. "This place is as expensive as Santa Monica, but without an ocean."

"Hey, a writer lives here." Ron pointed to an ancient typewriter on a desk next to a modern computer and a stack of magazines—*The New Yorker, The Atlantic Monthly*—with the current renter's byline. A sign? Or was the guy splitting town for good reason?

We looked at more places. We liked the interior of a roomier townhouse off Rockville Pike, but it was in a far-flung Maryland suburb called Gaithersburg. The orange van was arriving the next day, and they wanted a delivery address. Ron tried to delay them. With renewed urgency, I attempted another online search, except I couldn't log on to the Internet at the Woodfin. I'd been cramming my true feelings inside for months, and right then they regurgitated. All over Ron.

"I don't want this—I'm leaving!" I snapped my laptop shut and lugged my suitcase out of the closet. I scooped handfuls of shampoo bottles from the bathroom and threw them in my bag. Tore hangers from the closet and tossed my clothes into a heap.

"Where are you going?" Ron asked.

I stormed past him in a frenzy. Out of the corner of my eye, I could see the bewildered expression on his face.

"Back to California," I said.

An hour ago, we had shared a cozy lunch in a tavern and split carrot-ginger soup and I had told Ron I was opening up to the idea of trying out a new city. Now, he was watching me haul possessions out the door and into the car. He walked over to hug me, but I pushed him away and took off.

Five miles from the Woodfin, I pulled into a parking lot to sort out my thoughts. For one beat—one calm moment—the center of my soul fell silent.

Then I lost it.

I screamed and pounded the steering wheel. I beat my fists into the horn with such force that I yelped in pain, and as I watched my fingers balloon, I cried even harder. I clutched my hand and bent over, sobbing, gulping, until I leaned back against the headrest in exhaustion. I had worked so hard to build a life in California. Now it was gone.

Minutes passed.

An hour.

As the sky darkened, I thought of Ron, stuck alone at the hotel. I wanted to go home, but not without him. Backing out of this mess couldn't be too hard, could it?

When I returned to our room, Ron wrapped me in his arms. He kissed my hair. Gentle, not mad.

"Look," he said. His face was intent. "If things don't work out, we can go back."

"You mean it?"

"Of course. California isn't going anywhere."

Ron had said those words before—in Santa Monica, when I had realized the enormity of yanking up deep roots. I clutched onto his promise, "We can go back," with two hands, like a chalice.

We signed a lease for the roomier townhouse in far-flung Gaithersburg; Ron had deferred to my judgment. But right away, I realized my mistake: I was a tree planted in the wrong kind of soil. Unlike in Santa Monica, where I could amble among cafés and organic-food markets, I had nowhere to go (unless you counted Just Tires). In California, the hot spots are abuzz all day. In Maryland, each time I ran out to grab lunch, usually around two o'clock, the restaurant doors were locked. Hungry, I focused on my writing, trying not to be discouraged by the rejections piling up on my desk Two blocks away, a murder. Then a mugging. At night we grilled hamburgers and gazed out our back window at the view: an old, abandoned grocery store. Outside, the clouds brought rain and storms. The winter turned bitter cold.

At gatherings, people would ask, "So, where do you live?" I couldn't stand that question; the answer would lodge in my throat. Ron would step in for me—"Gaithersburg"—and I would chime in over his shoulder, "But we just moved from L.A."

Another irritating question: "So, how do you like the D.C. area?"

I'd answer one way, thinking another. "D.C. is great if you like history and politics." *I hate both.* Or: "D.C. is growing on me." *Like a fungus.*

Each time I scraped together a few dollars from selling freelance articles, I splurged on trips to California. My body would relax the minute the plane crossed the Rockies—I didn't even have to look out the oval window. In L.A., a smile spread across my face as I Rollerbladed along the beach. In my favorite yoga studio, I reached my limbs toward the sky. Kari and I caught up over glasses of champagne. I scheduled haircuts and dentist appointments. I even flew clothes three thousand miles across the country to be tailored because nobody was as good as Elias, the alterations guy off Wilshire Boulevard.

Our parents expressed disappointment in my dislike of Maryland. We belonged close to them, especially if grandkids were on the horizon. Back in Gaithersburg, I would scold myself for not being more cooperative. I gave myself internal lectures. Ron was particularly concerned with the one that went, *Happiness is an internal state. Remember, it's dangerous to think*, I'd be happy if . . .

In the event that we did move back, what would I long for next?

One day, a ray of sunshine: a pregnancy. When I opened my journal to write about the good news, I reread my previous entries and cringed. They were filled with the word "hate." I hated the gray days. I hated Gaithersburg. I hated that California was so far away. *Hate, hate, hate.* I wanted to be more grateful, especially with a baby on the way. I vowed to try harder.

Within weeks, another ray: Ron's old company in California had acquired a firm and wanted him to run the investment department. When the call came, I was boiling pasta on the stove. Wooden spoon in hand, I started jumping around. Ron agreed to fly out and discuss the opportunity in person, and I spun in circles.

"We're going to live in California again," I sang after he hung up. I flung my arms around him.

"Maybe," he laughed.

I hopped back over to the stove. We would raise our baby,

have our careers, and move on with our lives. This Rockville thing was nothing but a blip on the radar.

"I turned down the job," Ron said when he returned.

My heart went limp. "But we haven't discussed it yet."

"Not enough money. And no opportunity to become a principal."

I swallowed hard. Growing up, I'd watched my father walk in the door and announce moves without consulting my mom. In the bubble of our Midwestern neighborhoods, that was how it was done. Wives were the homemakers, men were the breadwinners, and their jobs were favored. In my marriage, I wanted an equal say.

That night in bed, as Ron lay sleeping, I muffled my cries with a pillow because I didn't want the baby to hear my sobs. As soon as I'd learned of the pregnancy, I had been overcome with a fierce, protective love. Yet another part of me felt threatened. Our best chance of moving west would be if I boosted my income. But how would I care for a newborn while tending to a vulnerable writing career?

I lost the baby.

One bloody night, the new life I held inside gushed out between my legs. What had I done? My desire to move back to California suddenly seemed selfish and wrong. In my anguish, had the baby felt unwanted?

The week of the miscarriage, Ron was scheduled to fly out to California to look into a second job opportunity. This time, I'd bought a ticket, too. I was bleeding, tender, and hurting inside and out, but I refused to cancel. I needed California now more than ever.

Ron and I stayed at a hotel in Laguna Beach. While he met with colleagues, I sat in a patio lounge chair, wrapped in a blanket. As I sipped hot water with lemon, the blue Pacific rested my weary soul and the sun dried my tears. But when I stood up to walk, I felt a crippling pain, no doubt related to the miscarriage. I called my old gynecologist. When I explained my abdominal pain, she told me to come to her clinic right away.

I winced as she pressed my right side. "Could be a twisted ovary," she said. She lugged over a sonogram machine.

"So, how do you like the East Coast?" she asked as she searched a screen that flashed images of my reproductive organs.

"It sounds stupid, but . . ."

She tilted her head from the end of the table so I could see her face.

" . . . I miss the sunshine."

"I love it here, too," she said. "I could never live anywhere else."

At that moment, it became clear to me: There are people who *get* geography and people who don't. There are those who thrive in the slower, humid life of the Deep South. Adventure hounds whose souls would perish without the rugged snowy mountains of Alaska. People who live to smell the tall-grass prairies of Oklahoma. I knew, too, there were people who loved the historic architecture of D.C., and that some of those people were stuck in Los Angeles, wondering why they had to live in what they could see only as a superficial city with orange smog.

The doctor assured me I was fine. That was good news. Ron had bad news: The second job wasn't right, either. On the phone, I overheard Ron trying to negotiate more favorable terms—a higher salary, better security. He was only pushing forward for me. What good would it do if he took a position he didn't want? I slipped him a note: *Don't take it.*

"Why?" he mouthed.

"It's not the right job," I whispered.

Another solution would turn up, wouldn't it?

Back in Rockville, we entered the center of winter. I crawled into bed and didn't emerge until spring.

Come March, I had a brand-spankin'-new plan: Ron could telecommute!

Dave's firm had a contingent of clients in Southern California. Certainly, that strengthened the case. But Ron wasn't sure Dave would like the idea. Still, he promised he'd broach the subject at his one-year review, which was two months away.

The review was slated for a Tuesday. The weekend before, I was hanging on by my fingertips. I couldn't wait to move forward with our plan. I was in my car when my cell rang.

"Dave had a massive heart attack," Ron said.

In the middle of the night, his wife had heard him collapse in the bathroom and had performed CPR. He'd been rushed to a local hospital, hooked up to machines and tubes. The company was preparing a formal statement. Ron mentioned something about funeral arrangements.

"Oh my gosh. That's horrible," I babbled. "That's so sad. I

can't believe—" I stopped. Dave's firm was small. Without him, it would close up shop. If Dave died . . . well, if he died, we would be . . . *free*. Even though I was in the car alone, I slid down in the seat, ashamed at my thoughts.

Dave lived. He was expected to make a full recovery, but for the indefinite future, he wouldn't be coming to work. Ron's review, of course, was canceled.

"I can't leave *now*," he said.

Once again, California was pushed away. But I was at the end of my rope. One way or another, we needed a fresh start. I scrolled the Internet, clicking around for a different place to live. Locally.

"What about Alexandria?" I said.

Alexandria was across the Potomac River on the other side of D.C., in Virginia. Its dog-friendly Old Town had brick sidewalks that ambled down to a harbor. King Street, the main thoroughfare, was full of restaurants and cafés that stayed open all afternoon (it even had a year-round farmers' market). Living there would mean a forty-five-minute commute each way for Ron—on a good traffic day—but he was willing to put up with it if *I* promised to give the community a genuine shot. We found a brownstone in Alexandria, signed a lease, and struck the deal.

For two years, I immersed myself in East Coast living. I took sculling lessons along the Potomac. In the evenings, we strolled down to the French-Mediterranean bistro with the garden patio or hung out at the picnic tables at the rustic pizza place. Even my writing career improved when I snagged a gig at a national Sunday magazine.

Our second summer there, it rained all of June, July, and August, and I began pining for L.A. I fell into another rut when

D.C. experienced one of its worst cold snaps in recorded history. My troubles conceiving had been traced to endometriosis, a condition that caused my uterus to shed too much blood. For six months out of the year, my teeth chattered.

"You know how some people have to live in high altitudes because of allergies?" I argued. "I have to live in sunny California because endometriosis makes me cold."

"Nice try," Ron said.

I stayed away from the West Coast. In a weird way, it was easier not to think about California, to pretend it didn't exist. Then our lease ran out. Once again, we were faced with a decision. Two, actually. In addition to the long-term-renewal lease our landlords sent, Dave handed Ron a document obligating Ron to buy Dave's firm if anything were to happen to Dave again and he didn't recover.

We opted to rent month to month, but we couldn't agree on the second contract. Ron wanted to sign, but I was afraid doing so would keep us away from California indefinitely.

"If you vehemently oppose it, I won't sign," Ron said.

"I vehemently oppose it," I said, with zero enthusiasm.

Ron signed.

I'd been away from California for eight months, the longest stretch since we'd moved four years earlier. That November, I flew out for a writers' conference. Once again, all I loved about the west resonated in my soul. As I walked past the colorful bougainvillea on a path leading to the ocean, it became clear: California was here, directly under my feet. It was up to me to claim it.

I had been waiting for Ron to speak. Each day after work, I anticipated his saying something—*anything*—about how he'd finally talked to Dave about telecommuting. But what did he say? Nothing. Absolute silence. And by saying nothing, he said it all.

When I returned from California, I set dinner on the table and took a deep breath. "I think we should become a bicoastal couple."

Going bicoastal was an idea Ron and I had brushed on over the years but mostly avoided. Neither one of us was excited about the logistics of two apartments, airplane flights, and weeks apart. But the more we discussed it, the more doable it seemed. We still hope Dave will be amenable to a West Coast office. Until then, we'll take turns flying coast to coast, building a marriage with two homes. It's not a permanent plan. Once I'm settled, I'll wait for the call from Ron where he says, "I'm ready to move back to California." But I won't hold my breath.

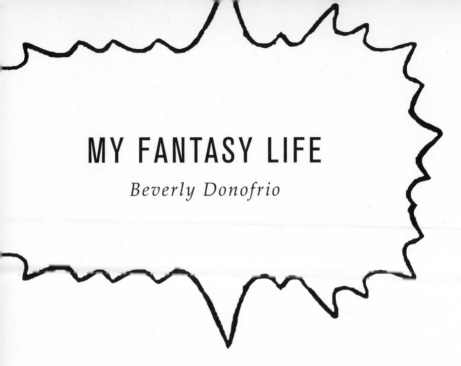

MY FANTASY LIFE

Beverly Donofrio

I was once hired to write an "as told to" book with the wife of a Mafia family boss. The book had been the mafioso's idea; he'd already sold the rights for a TV movie, and he expected to make millions after his wife and I wrote a book in which he starred as the hero—because he believed he was one. His wife loved God and was intensely private. She'd gone to Catholic boarding school and had had no idea that her father was a Mafia boss, or that her future husband was one, too. But when you find your husband's clothes covered in blood in the basement, it becomes hard to keep the old blinders in place. I swear, if it hadn't been for the kids and her husband's iron grip on her every move, she would have escaped to a nunnery.

I arrived to do the interviews, which continued over a three-month period, shortly after the mafioso had thrown a wedding for his only daughter, an extravaganza featuring ballerinas leaping around, carrying torches. He bragged about this wedding but hadn't forked over a penny. Because he didn't have to—he knew that the hotel, the caterer, all those ballerinas, would be too afraid to come after him to collect, and he was right.

I despised him. Every night, back at my efficiency apartment, I'd have to vent on the phone to my friends, who asked, "Aren't you afraid the phone's tapped?"

He didn't have the money. I wasn't buying his bluster and I wasn't afraid of him. I'd grown up under the regime of my own father, an Italian cop—the other side of the Mafia coin—who'd bullied me into dreading the sound of his footsteps, so I'd passive-aggressed him half to death. If I'd had a dollar for every time my mother said, "You're killing your father," I'd never have had to take on this lousy as-told-to-book assignment.

The mafioso stuck around for a while, trying to dictate the story to me, but finally I got him to leave, and three months later, the interviews complete—which included stories of outrageously inventive abuse—he, his wife, and I met at a motel in Northern California. She and I were sitting in her room, when he stormed in, the tube of transcript squeezed in his fist. "What the hell were you thinking?" he said to his wife, slapping his palm with the transcript. "She's a goddamned writer." *Slap.* "You think she's not going to use this shit?" *Slap slap.* "Are you stupid?"

The wife shrank before my eyes, and I roared out of my chair. "Don't you talk to her like that! This was your big idea. You forced her. And where have you been? Shacked up with your girlfriend—"

He took a step toward me and punched the air with his finger. "Just remember one thing. Point your finger at me, and you've got three pointing back at yourself."

"What does that *mean*? What does that *mean*?" I windmilled my arms. "That's Mafia talk."

I used to tell this story often, because I was proud that I wasn't afraid of a mafioso and proud I'd defended his wife. But I never mentioned that I actually did know what he meant by the three fingers pointing back at myself: You accuse, point a finger at, what you are guilty of. I'd basically called him a bully, and in the end I would bully his wife, too. During the editing process, when she asked me to take out a few events she didn't want her grandchildren one day to read, my response was, "Sorry, but you said it; it stays in."

The mafioso believed himself a hero of a noble and misunderstood tradition; he saw himself as a crusader taking the law into his own hands to correct injustices. And he believed that his wife, whom he bullied, ignored, abused, and humiliated, loved and adored him.

I believed I was a wild bohemian mother of a different order, and that my son—on whose seven-year-old head I once broke an egg in front of company, for a laugh—thought I was a good, if unconventional, mother. Until I heard, through the screenwriter doing research for the movie he was writing based on my memoir, that my son was pissed at me and thought he'd had a nightmare for a mother.

The mafioso was delusional. And I was delusional, too.

When I left therapy in my twenties, my psychiatrist, a socialist with a Karl Marx beard to his belly, said, "You have an amazing ability to believe your own fantasies."

He said *what?*

Here's where the other finger pointing back at me comes in. Like the mafioso, I possessed the ability to believe my own fantasies. But I also possessed the ability to believe my boyfriends'. And just about anyone else's.

Call it a willful suspension of disbelief.

Take my first love. Or crush. It was the summer before I turned thirteen, the summer before President Kennedy was shot, the summer before the eighth grade, when I fell for Freddy Driscoll, a tenth-grader. He lived around the block with his two sisters, and I'd heard from the younger that Freddy was diabetic, which meant he couldn't eat sugar, was sometimes convulsed by seizures, and would have to stick a needle into his own skin every single day for the rest of his life. I fell flat-out in love.

I don't think I confessed even to my best friend, Adriana Slovaki, how I pictured Freddy sitting every morning in his white BVDs on the lid of the toilet, bending over like *The Thinker* to jab the needle in his thigh, as a single tear rolled down his cheek. Even though I hated needles and had never once watched one being stuck into my own or anyone else's flesh, I knew that when we were married, I'd kneel before poor, wonderful, imperfect Freddy, cooing comforting words as I eased that needle in, wishing it were I feeling the pain instead of him.

I can't remember the moment I first laid eyes on Freddy, nor can I remember if I heard he was blind at the same time I heard about his diabetes. But, yes, Freddy was blind, and that's why he wore sunglasses.

One afternoon, Freddy's youngest sister, Beth, invited Adriana and me to come over. We carried our orange juice with ice downstairs to her basement recreation room, where we sang to a 45 of the Beatles "I Love Her" and I tried to teach Beth to cha-cha to "Sealed with a Kiss." Beth's older sister, Nancy, came down the stairs and sat on the sofa. "Bev," she said, "I think I should tell you: We just found out Freddy's dying."

I fell to my knees, wailing so loudly that at first I didn't hear the muffled laughter at the window. But then I did hear it, and the running feet. Freddy and his friend Ed had been listening.

I must have looked like a squashed toad, because Beth quickly added, "He's not dying. He told Nancy to say it. He wanted to find out how much you love him, Bev." An explanation I not only accepted but translated into *Freddy loves me.*

Still, a toenail of that squashed toad held on to a pebble of awareness that Freddy had been at best sneaky and at worst cruel. To believe this, however, would have hurt too much, so I ignored it.

Adriana and I hung out every day down the road from Freddy's, under a shady willow, with a whole passel of boys nearer our age. One day toward the end of summer, four or five of us were in a chain shoulder massage when Freddy, who never hung out with us under the tree because he was too old and too cool, pulled up in a Chevy Corvette, stepped out of the passenger door, slammed it, then leaned against it and crossed his ankles. His friend Ed got out, too, flicked his cigarette into the middle of the road, and walked over next to Freddy.

My heart did a conga in my chest. They were both looking at *me.* Freddy stooped until we were eye to eye, lifted his sunglasses, and said, "I can see you."

They all laughed, rolled around on the ground, grabbed their sides, split a gut.

I ran home like hell itself was chasing me, howling so loud that birds jetted out of trees.

I hurt so much, I thought I'd die. But then I didn't.

If my life were a movie, this might have been the inciting incident after which I reappear in my never-to-be-discarded sexy-superhero outfit to hurl Freddy into outer space, his needles catching up and turning him into a pincushion. In real life, it was the inciting incident for many more boyfriends who were not who they said they were. But at least the rest of them believed their own fantasies, too.

There was the large animal veterinarian, a modern-day Albert Schweitzer, who would end world hunger by increasing the production of animals—as protein. I moved with him to a manure-reeking village in Mexico with five thousand people, twenty thousand cows, and two gazillion flies. We kept bull semen in the freezer.

Call me a cheerleader for potential.

There was the alcoholic/painter/photographer/inventor who claimed to have hung out with Warhol at his Factory and who once drove his car repeatedly into the grate of our building because I'd climbed out in the middle of a fight—I gave him all the money I had, $300, to supposedly buy supplies for his "smash paintings." His plan was to throw Coke bottles filled with paint at canvases and make millions. He never produced a single one.

Then there was the ex-commissioner of water for the City of New York, who quit his job at midlife to write a *Watership Down*–like book, only instead of rabbits, his characters were miniature pigs. We drove cross-country together to Los Angeles, and when I introduced him to everyone I knew, I suspected one of the movie people would snatch him up to write a movie, a show, an episode.

I became engaged for the last time on September 11, 2001, to a performance artist, after knowing him for only six weeks.

He'd seduced me by giving me a tape of songs he'd made. On it he imitated a DJ: "This one's dedicated to Beverly Donofrio, the world's most beautiful author." It was "You Are So Beautiful," and I heard it as though my future lover had written every word—for me. In one of his acts, the performance artist wore a jacket with a fake arm; glued to the arm was a violin that was attached at the shoulder. One real hand bowed the violin to "Flight of the Bumblebee," while the hidden hand poked a finger through his fly and wiggled it

I was fifty years old and had a book to write. We were going to buy a big van to carry all our costumes and sets. I would appear in some of his acts. In one, I'd stand erect, wearing a leotard, as he played me like a cello. Meanwhile, he earned $100 a week and he and his son lived with me. One evening, as I was reaching into the oven to remove a sheet of cookies, he wrapped his arms around my belly and hugged me to him. I screamed, "Don't do that! Don't ever do that! My hands were in the fucking oven!" He stood up and looked at me. "How can I show you love," he asked, "if I'm afraid you'll blow up at me?" He slumped into a chair and shook his head. "There's something evilish here," he said. I was inclined to agree.

The night it ended, a few months later, he held a knife over his head and wailed to the heavens, "I can't *take it anymore!*" He was of Spanish descent.

When we broke up a week after that, I didn't shed a single tear. The ball was over. The gig was up. The carriage had turned back to a pumpkin. I was all done, spent, fed up, tired of shading all those houses of cards from the light of day.

I was ready for What Is, and prepared to be depressed.

I shaved my head; people wondered if I had cancer. I didn't

have a disease, I had a determination—to be able to look in the mirror, lift off the dark glasses, and say, "I see you."

That was almost a decade ago. The Mafia-wife book was a flop, and the mafioso died not rich. Freddy Driscoll and my ex–best friend, Adriana Mordarsky, were an item all through high school. The vet cheated on me with a virgin and they moved to Uganda, where he runs a wild-game farm.

After I broke up with the alcoholic/painter/photographer/ inventor, he stalked me for a month and then, a month after that, looked right through me across a bar, not recognizing me. The ex-commissioner of water gave up writing about the pigs and went back to environmental law. The performance artist has become a disc jockey on his own online site. He recently wrote to tell me that he regrets we're not together and that he dreams about me. He sent a picture of himself and a link to a song in which we're still making love in his secret life. I was flattered, but I didn't fall for it.

I've fallen for God. This is where you atheists are going to have to willfully suspend your disbelief. A spiritual life requires that you believe things you cannot see or prove or ever even know.

I'm a natural.

I know that lions do not lie down with lambs. But I believe that one day they will. And I believe in paranormal phenomena that come from God, also known as gifts of the spirit. St. Teresa of Avila, for example—and who even knows how many others—levitated during prayer. Others have manifested the stigmata, had visions, given or received miraculous healings, heard locutions. I myself have had a vision, heard a few locutions, and often smell roses at

Virgin Mary holy sites. And three times, I've smelled something else. It's musk and candles, incense, and flowers—impossible to describe. This fragrance wafts in when I'm in the presence of holiness.

The other day, I met a woman who exuded this fragrance. Fifteen years ago, she quit her job and has been traveling the world ever since, by the grace of God and with not a penny.

When I told my friend David, the crazy psychiatrist, about the woman and the holy smell, he said, "You know that's an illusion. You do know that, don't you?"

To which I joyfully replied, "Well, I know it's not of this world, if that's what you mean."

But you can't count on gifts of the spirit, also called spiritual consolations.

Mostly, faith requires work. I read theologians, I read mystics, I meditate, contemplate, pray, stay silent for days on end, and do yoga. The practices help, but there have been times when I've wondered if my faith is yet another illusion. So one day I cornered my friend Eric—born a Mennonite, bred on the Bible, and one of the most generous men I know. He's also a master carpenter and a fine priest. "Do you ever think there really isn't a God?" I asked him. "That we just believe there is to have hope—that all the pain and suffering will make some kind of sense?"

And he said what I think of as the most crystal-clear, dirt-simple theological statement I've ever heard: "I always think of it like this: Would we have hunger if there wasn't food? I don't think so."

To which I would like to add: Is it possible to believe in God and not be a cheerleader for potential? I don't think so.

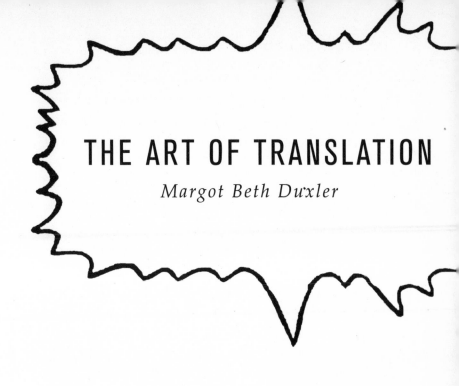

THE ART OF TRANSLATION

Margot Beth Duxler

Imagine a UN translator: vigilant, focused, hearing faster than Mach 2, concentrating to ensure not only that the words are accurate, but, more important, that their meaning is clear. The fate of nations might be at stake, and words alone, when translated verbatim, can have the opacity of lead.

For example, the title of François Truffaut's 1959 film, *Les Quatre Cents Coups*, a coming-of-age story about an adolescent Parisian boy, was translated into English, word for word, as *The Four Hundred Blows*. Though it's a literal and accurate translation, the meaning in English is lost entirely. *The Four Hundred Blows?* Depending on your imagination and point of view, this title could suggest anything from corporal punishment to sexual acts between consenting adults to bad allergies. What the verbatim translation misses is that in French, *faire les quatre cents coups* is an idiomatic expression that means to raise hell, to disdain accepted social behavior—in other words, to be a delinquent who is heading down the road to a life of crime. Any Francophone would immediately grasp this as the anguished cry of distraught parents that their child *fait les quatre cents coups!* To a unilingual English speaker, however, the meaning is as clear as mud.

Of course, to be a proficient translator, superfluency in the languages being translated is essential. But interpreting the meaning that those words convey, reading between the lines, not only hearing what is spoken but also interpreting and comprehending what is meant, are of equal, if not greater, importance.

One famous example of translation gone wrong, probably apocryphal, was the attempt to render the biblical reference "The spirit is willing, but the flesh is weak" from English to Russian and back to English again. According to translation lore, the final result in English was "The vodka is good, but the meat is rotten." Whether fiasco or joke, this resembles a game of Telephone more than it does Jesus's intended meaning as he spoke in the Garden of Gethsemane.

As is often the case, language can create more confusion than clarity, as God, the ultimate jokester, demonstrated so clearly when he put the kibosh on the tower to heaven that the Babylonians were building as a monument to their own greatness, and turned it into the Tower of Babel. Displeased by their arrogance, God punished the population by causing each individual to speak a different language that no one else could understand, effectively ending communication and making construction of the tower—and any other cooperative endeavor—impossible. And thus the Tower of Babel came into being, the icon of verbal misunderstanding and mayhem.

And shouldn't language do just the opposite of confuse and confound? It's meant to distill meaning and clarity out of chaos. Perhaps, as William S. Burroughs said, "language is a virus from outer space." We caught it from our parents, who caught it from theirs, all the way back to the caves of Lascaux and the African plains. We will pass it along to our children, and they to theirs. Some of us are better hosts than others, and the virus aggressively reproduces and mutates. We give our word. We pronounce vows. We swear an oath.

When the princess learned Rumpelstiltskin's real moniker and called him by it, he lost his power and disappeared in a puff of smoke. The naming of the animals was Adam's task, bequeathed as an honor for his stewardship over all creatures, great and small. Adam and Eve were given the Garden to till, not to kill, and a passing glance at the endangered-species list is adequate proof that this particular assignment did not receive a passing grade. This, however, was the fault not of language, but of interpretation. Which is why there are lawyers and there are poets.

My husband, Michael, is one of the poets, absurdly skilled in the art of translating and interpreting the language of emotions. Just as people with synesthesia perceive a single stimulus with numerous sensory systems—for example, seeing specific colors associated with particular letters of the alphabet or with numbers—Michael is gifted with a kind of emotional synesthesia. He perceives and responds to emotion through the multiple filters of intellect, intuition, and humor, which is particularly useful in processing and neutralizing negative feelings and trauma. It works much like antivenom does on a snakebite: You may still have pain or a scar on your ankle where the fangs sank in, but you know you're on the mend.

Twenty years ago, through a synthesis of intellect, intuition, and humor, Michael translated the language of my childhood, when words were weapons, into an unexpected, funny, and ironic declaration of love that still makes me laugh. It cracks other people up, too, but usually not right away. If you were to read a literal transcription—no context, no interpretation—his words would undoubtedly sound like a hostile, rejecting insult. But they weren't. Instead, they spoke a naked and undefended truth.

I'm told that the first word I spoke was "moo." It had nothing to do with bovines or any other domesticated creatures. I was born and raised in Chicago, and the only animals with which I was likely to attempt communication under my mother's watchful eye were the overfed squirrels and pigeons that gathered around the penny-a-handful peanut dispenser outside the corner cigar store, hoping for a treat.

No one in my family had dogs or cats or even goldfish. These first-generation refugee parents wanted nothing more than to distance themselves from their peasant roots, symbolically as well as geographically. They aspired to be sophisticated city folk, until they ascended the socioeconomic ladder of the postwar '50s and fled the cities for the suburbs, and they believed that all animals should be the exclusive domain of farmers.

"Animals will ruin the furniture—they belong outside," my mother was fond of saying. I did not understand how they could ruin anything, seeing as my mother kept every chair and sofa fitted with clear plastic covers, which I referred to as "condoms" as soon as I was old enough to know what condoms were. It would have taken a phalanx of rain-soaked cats and dogs to leave so much as a damp pawprint on anything, including the wall-to-wall turquoise carpet, which also sported plastic runners to keep it spotless in high-traffic areas.

The "moo" I had verbalized was an attempt to participate in my mother's enthusiastic cooing at a rare sight—the full moon visible on the early-morning horizon, the great sky-pearl oblivious to the rush of cars and buses below in the middle of a decidedly urban landscape. I just could not wrap my tongue around the "n" sound yet, so "moo, moo, moo," was the best I could produce from the nest of blankets in my blue perambulator. Family mythology relates that my mother bragged to anyone who would listen that I understood exactly what she meant as she gesticulated wildly toward deep space, crooning, "Moon, moon, moon." She was also unabashedly proud that my first sentence was "Talk book," meaning, "Read me a story." I was born a lover of words.

Until I became fluent enough to express feelings and ideas that differed from theirs, my parents thought my language skills were quite brilliant. As our interests and perceptions of the world diverged, however, my parents began to experience me as some kind of alien whose mother tongue they did not share. Boasting about their precocious language sponge morphed into derision and punishment.

When I was growing up, my mother behaved as though I had hurt her intentionally if I didn't fulfill her expectations of academic achievement, and especially of beauty, which was most of the time.

"Why can't your hair be like your friend Leda's?" she would moan. "Nice and soft and shiny?" Left to its own devices, my hair

was a barbed-wire tumbleweed. Just like hers. Or if, as was often
the case, the zipper on my skirt stuck slightly because I had gained
weight, she would monitor what I ate as if she were a Geiger
counter screening for radiation. Asking for a cookie prompted the
rhetorical "Do you really need that?" And if, by her evaluation, I
was eating too much at dinner, a mumbled "Even a train stops
sometimes" was sufficient to make me push my plate away.
"Remember," she'd say with a tentative smile, "you have to suffer
to be beautiful." If I were beautiful, I might not have minded. But I
was suffering *and* ugly.

Compared with my father's, my mother's reproaches were
relatively mild. He was more direct in his disapproval and was apt to
strike me physically, as well as with words. If it's possible for a face
to become a fist, my father had mastered the metamorphosis. In fact,
the contempt that transformed his visage from human to monstrous
was more threatening than his clenched fist could ever be.

Between my mother's constant criticism and my father's rages,
I learned early that words could be more wounding than sticks and
stones, and saying what I thought or dreamed became consigned
in mirror writing to the pages of my well-hidden diary.

I remember one Passover at my Aunt Harriet and Uncle Bill's
when I was about nine or ten. My cousin and I were sharing a
plate of sugar-coated, multicolored, half-moon fruit gels, which
are a Passover dessert tradition—definitely of the unsophisticated,
nongourmet genre—and a delightful accompaniment to Mogen
David wine. We held the semitranslucent gels up to the light,
pretending they were stained glass, debating the relative merits of
the different colors: red, green, orange, and yellow. "Someday, I'm
going to go to that church in Paris and see the famous stained-glass

windows," I announced, as I popped a cluster of rainbow gels into my mouth. "And I'm going to learn to speak French, too," I said, chewing the sugary goo as I spoke.

My father had overheard from his seat at the head of the table. His face clenched and his lip curled into a sneer. "Where did you get that idea?" he snarled. "From some book? Chicago isn't good enough for you? You have to go to a cathedral in Paris to see what the *goyem* built? Not if you keep eating candy like that! They don't want fat girls in Paris!"

My mouth still full of candy, my eyes stinging with tears, I ran from the table to the safety of the bathroom, where I locked the door and spit the half-chewed sweets into the toilet, trying over and over to throw up. I had no idea how I knew about Notre Dame when I was ten, though "some book" was very likely the culprit. Nor did I understand why wanting to go to France meant betraying my heritage. Twelve years later, I did go to the City of Light, with the *goyem*-built cathedral. And I learned to speak a musical language whose words taste like butter and cinnamon on my tongue to this day, and that I never want to spit out.

It is no surprise that I grew up more than slightly uncomfortable with the XY chromosome carriers of the species. The shadow of my father's ridicule distorted my vision of myself even more than my mother's had, accompanied as it was by unpredictable violence. I always felt in danger of being humiliated and rejected by men. That is, until Michael. From the beginning, he made no secret that he felt our relationship was nothing less than a miracle. He was never short of spontaneous, authentic appreciation of my body, my mind, even the meowing and purring I employed to communicate with all felines and many nonfelines, and he could not understand why I felt so self-conscious and critical of myself.

He was frustrated, too, that his appreciation had so little effect on my self-perceptions. Nothing he said, no reassurance, seemed to help, until the night we were dressing to go to the Viennese Ball, a nostalgic costume event featuring Strauss waltzes and polkas and commencing with an authentic nineteenth century grand promenade to Chopin's Polonaise in A-flat major, op. 40, no. 1.

In its original incarnation, the ball was a yearly fundraising event for the Berkeley Promenade Orchestra, which was one degree removed—or maybe not—from the nerdacious geekiosity of the Renaissance Faire. We had been looking forward to the event for months. We had taken waltz lessons and discovered that the delight of physical synchronicity we shared privately translated with ease onto the dance floor. We were anticipating a fairytale night, nothing less than a trance state induced by the three-quarter heartbeat of the music.

Unfortunately, as I got dressed, the last button on the waist-band of my ball gown pulled a bit more snugly than I remembered from the last time I had tried it on. It was tight, uncomfortable, and suddenly I felt all wrong. I looked all wrong. My eye makeup seemed early KISS, rather than the Audrey Hepburn chic I was hoping for. And I was convinced that my fancy French braid be-longed on the big fat ass of a plough horse, which was pretty much exactly what I saw when I looked in the mirror.

Michael was bemused, clearly not seeing what to me was so obvious.

"You don't get it!" I yelped in frustration.

"No, I don't get it," he confessed. "I don't get it at all. You're beautiful. You're gorgeous. Everybody thinks so."

I groaned. "You're crazy."

He was elegant, Fred Astaire, in his white tie and tails, ready to waltz the night away.

"I'm supposed to look like Grace Kelly," I whined, staring at my reflection in the mirror, knowing that I was seeing myself through my parents' eyes, unable to diffuse their disapproval, which had become my own. No matter how I turned, what the quality or the angle of the light was, all I could perceive was their vision of me: a disappointingly ethnic-looking little girl who was a carbon copy of her self-loathing mother and her authoritarian father. I would never be the golden-haired princess with delicate features they longed for me to be.

Michael stood a few feet behind me, also looking at my image in the mirror. I couldn't read his expression. I sat down on the side of the bed. "I'm just coarse and lumpy and . . . and I'm ugly!" He sat down beside me and looked me straight in the eye. "You're beautiful," he said, "but you're stupid!"

First I flinched, hearing the echo of parental criticism. Then I understood, and I laughed and laughed and laughed until I cried and my mascara ran and my face turned red, and I didn't care. When I could finally speak, I said between bursts of giggles, "Do I look fat in this lipstick?"

"Enormous," he assured me.

Whenever I relate this moment of grace to friends or family, it generally requires an explanation. "How did you know that

Michael was the one?" curious acquaintances have asked.

"When he told me that I was beautiful . . ."

"Ah," they nod knowingly.

" . . . but stupid," I continue.

"He said *what?!*" is the response I hear most often. It's as if they had just seen someone crossing the street wearing an inner tube, flippers, and scuba gear over a tuxedo—it's impossible to know what to make of it. "Beautiful but stupid" has a similar effect, until I explain.

If an alien being were to overhear and translate a conversation between Michael and me, it would be left scratching its pointy blue head, thinking that good means bad, love means hate, *mrrrrow* means "I've missed you," and "butthead" means "beloved husband." We have so many pet names for each other that we refer to each other by our given names only if we are very serious or very angry. It's pretty rare. With us, neologisms are the norm.

As I get older and immediate word retrieval is no longer a given, I am increasingly grateful to have an inventive mind and a sense of humor. I'm likely to forget your name, but I'll remember how you laughed and be able to describe in detail how you waved your hand as you chortled, guffawed, or screeched like a dolphin. I'm also more and more convinced that language *is* a virus from outer space. And I hope no one ever finds a cure.

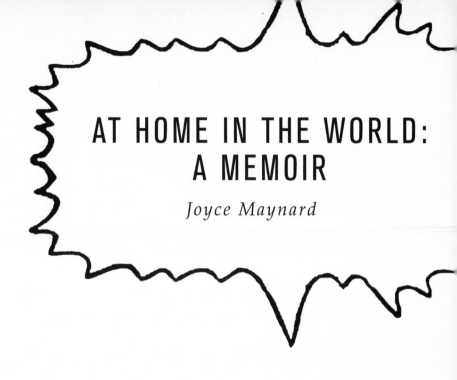

AT HOME IN THE WORLD:
A MEMOIR

Joyce Maynard

A s a freshman at Yale, Joyce Maynard wrote the cover story for
The New York Times Magazine. One of the many laudatory letters
she received came from noted author J. D. Salinger. They began a
correspondence that culminated in nineteen-year-old Maynard's
leaving Yale and moving in with Salinger, a fifty-four-year-old
recluse. In this excerpt from *At Home in the World: A Memoir,*
it is 1972 and Maynard is with Salinger and his children.

I n March, Peggy and Matthew are on a week's vacation from
school, and the four of us travel to Daytona Beach, Florida. Jerry
has chosen Daytona Beach in part, at least, on the recommendation
of Dr. Lacey, who knows of a homeopathic physician there who
favors the high potencies he and Jerry believe in.

Jerry says this Florida doctor can address my sexual problem. I don't question his choice to combine this mission with a family vacation.

It has been a particularly brutal winter in New Hampshire, one storm after another, day after day where the temperature fails to rise above zero. I have longed for the warmth of Florida. But Daytona is a depressing place.

Our hotel sits right on the ocean, and Matthew is happy, as always, because there's a game room in the hotel, and a vibrating bed, and a shoe-shine kit in the bathroom. Peggy is disgruntled. She misses her boyfriend. As Jerry has already explained to me, she and I are sharing a room, while next door to us, Matthew and Jerry are bunking in together. This seems odd to me, knowing that the children have observed the two of us sharing a bedroom since July.

"Let's take a dip," he says. We head to the beach.

Even before we've spread our towels on the sand, we learn a disturbing thing about Daytona. Cars are allowed to drive up and down the beach—fast and loud. Matthew says something, but the sound is drowned out by V-8 engines speeding past, drag racing.

Still, we spend the afternoon on the beach. Jerry warns Peggy to protect herself from the sun, but she's anxious to get a tan. Matthew jumps in the waves. Jerry is trying to read his homeopathic journal. "Come on in the water, Dad," Matthew calls to him. Jerry looks reluctant, but he gets up to join Matthew. I open my book of the *Teachings of Ramana Maharshi,* turning to a random page.

That night, we eat in the hotel dining room. The kids order spaghetti and garlic bread. Jerry and I get a salad, no dressing.

Other patrons of the hotel, surveying our table, would suppose what they are seeing is a single father vacationing with his three children. But my behavior is very different from that of his children. I am careful and anxious.

Our waiter brings Jerry's salad with dressing. The people at the next table have a toddler who is very unhappy, and the wife is complaining because the husband plans to take off and play golf for the afternoon. Peggy mentions a game she's missing because we came here. Worried that all the aggravating details of being away from home will get on Jerry's nerves, I keep quiet.

Not Matthew. He stabs his fork into his meatball and holds it aloft, like an Olympic athlete holding up his medal. "Ta-da!" he says. "Mark Spitz!"

"Quit it, okay, Matt?" Peggy says.

"Guess what, Dad?" Matthew says. "In the lobby, they had all these brochures of neat places you can go see. There's this amusement park with a really great-looking roller coaster."

"I need to get a new bathing suit," Peggy says. "The one I brought makes me look fat."

The next morning, Jerry and I have arranged to see the naturopathic practitioner Dr. Lacey has recommended. Jerry has made the appointment under the name of John Boletus and his friend Joyce. We take a cab to her office, leaving Matthew and Peggy back at the hotel. Jerry has given Matthew change for the game room. Peggy has a bad sunburn and wants to sleep.

Over the phone from New Hampshire, Jerry has told this doctor only that he is a student of homeopathy, interested in consulting with her on a number of matters. She ushers the two of us into her office.

He tells the doctor he lives in New Hampshire and is engaged in various varieties of research. He has an abiding interest in Eastern medicine—acupuncture, acupressure. In the last ten years, the primary focus of his study has been homeopathic medicine. He himself favors the high-potency approach employed by Dr. Lacey, among others. He understands that this tends to be the approach she favors as well.

Sitting here saying nothing, I wait for Jerry to begin describing the particular reason why we are here. But now he and the woman physician are talking about differing schools of thought concerning potencies. The issue of succussing a remedy in water versus taking it in pellet form, under the tongue. He is mentioning the names of particular remedies he has been working with lately. Their names sound like potions from a fairytale: Sanguinaria. Aconitum napellus. Drosera rotundifolia. Gelsemium. Passiflora incarnata . . . Bloodroot. Monkshood. Sundew. Yellow jasmine. Passion flower.

Lately, Jerry has been studying the uses of pulsatilla in the treatment of headache, he tells the doctor. She takes a homeopathic journal off the shelf. "I wonder if you're familiar with this article on the subject," she says. "I myself was tremendously excited when I read the findings here."

"I would have favored the potency of 200x," Jerry says, "having experimented with a similar form of treatment myself on several occasions . . ."

I look out the window. Palm trees. Cement. I think about swimming. I am roused by the sound of my name.

"My friend here, Joyce, is anxious to consult you about a

problem she's experiencing that I have been trying to assist her with," Jerry is saying. For the first time, the doctor turns to me. She studies the single sheet of paper, attached to a clipboard, that I filled out when I arrived. *Female. Nineteen years old. 110 pounds. Five foot six inches. Experiencing difficulty having intercourse. Frequent headaches. Amenorrhea.*

"So," she says. "You suffer from a tightness of the muscles surrounding the vagina? How long has this situation existed?"

"Eight months," I say.

"And the remedies you've considered . . ." She turns to Jerry. He lists several.

"Has she experienced acupuncture before?" she asks Jerry.

"Only acupressure," Jerry says. "I've worked with her pressure points, but strictly for the headaches."

"I want to perform a physical examination," she says. Jerry leaves the room as she instructs me to remove my underpants and shows me where to put my feet up on her table.

Her physical examination of me is very brief. No sign of physiological abnormality, she says, as I'm putting my underpants back on.

"You're very tense," the physician says. "I'd like to try a little acupuncture on you." Then she instructs me to take my dress off and lie on her table in my underwear.

She washes her hands and takes out a little tray of needles. She places one on my abdomen and begins to spin it in place, until it breaks through the skin. There is no pain.

Then she places a group of needles around my nose, and another on my abdomen, and one near each of my ears. I concentrate on the buzzing sound of the fluorescent light and close my eyes.

In my most hopeful moments of anticipation of this doctor visit, I pictured this doctor presenting me with a tiny crumb of some magical remedy I would place under my tongue that would open me like a flower. Jerry and I would return to our hotel, return to New Hampshire, suddenly, gloriously able to make love. By the time we leave her office, I no longer hold out any hope of having been cured. I feel exactly the same as I did before, only horribly humiliated.

Grim-faced, Jerry pays the bill. We hurry out the door. In the cab I cry a little. I have never undergone a pelvic exam before. Jerry puts his arm around me. We say nothing about the experience.

When we get back to the hotel, we meet Matthew out by the pool and then go to the room, where Peggy is just getting up. We put on our bathing suits and take our towels and books down to the beach. Peggy has to lie under a beach umbrella. Matthew sprints toward the water, calling for his dad. Jerry has bought him a kite and he wants Jerry to fly it.

Jerry and I sit on our folding beach chairs alone together for a moment. He stares out at the water, the children, the hungover college students on spring break, the cars racing up and down across the sand. He looks very old. His shoulders are hunched. He rests his forehead in his hand.

"You know," he says, "I can never have any more children. I'm finished with all this."

One of those crazy Daytona Beach drivers has just driven by, making so much noise with his souped-up engine that for a moment I am not sure I heard it right, what Jerry just said to me.

"What did you say?" I ask him.

I see Matthew splashing in the waves, his new orange kite

lying on the white sand. Jerry's bag of bananas and sunflower seeds. The homeopathic journal and the Ramana Maharshi book. The towels, with their hotel insignia. The music from somebody's portable radio—Neil Young singing "Heart of Gold." The sun at high noon. Sand flies on my legs. The smell of suntan lotion.

I see Jerry's face, as familiar to me as my own, and dearer than anything. His long lean body, in old-fashioned swim trunks. His hands raking through his silver hair. My hands reaching for my beach towel and my book and my room key. The sound of my own voice, as if what I am hearing were dialogue from a movie and not my own self speaking.

"I can never have any more children," he says again, staring out at the ocean. "I'm finished with this."

Then he turns to me and speaks, with a coldness I have never known before from him, though we have certainly fought. Here is the chill wind I have always feared.

"You'd better go home now," he says. "You need to clear your things out of my house. If you go now you can have everything gone before the children and I get back. I don't want them upset, having to witness all this."

I get up from the sand. I must be breathing, but it feels as though the air has left my lungs. My vision blurs. I walk back to the hotel.

Back in the room, I peel off my bathing suit and put on my dress. I take my clothes out of the drawers and begin packing. I take my ticket off the bureau where Jerry has left it and dial the number of the airline. "When is the next flight to Boston?" I ask. There's a blizzard going on up north. No planes are expected to fly into Boston until the next day at the earliest. New York is no better.

Sometime late that afternoon, Jerry and the children return to our two adjoining rooms. Jerry has taken Matthew and Peggy shopping. If the children have noticed anything strange about my sudden disappearance, they don't mention it.

"When you've seen one Stradivarius, you've seen them all," Jerry says to Matthew in his Inspector Clouseau accent, putting an arm around his son's shoulder.

"Take your filthy hands off my asp!" Matthew says, also in character.

"I got a flight back tomorrow," I tell Jerry.

"Joyce's father is sick," Jerry tells Matthew and Peggy. Matthew looks momentarily concerned. "But he'll be okay, right?" he says. I say sure.

The four of us go out to dinner. I don't eat. Afterward we go to see *The Heartbreak Kid,* an Elaine May comedy featuring Cybill Shepherd and Charles Grodin as a couple who meet during Grodin's disastrous honeymoon in Florida. I watch the movie more intently than any I've seen all year.

All this time I have been hoping for the moment when Jerry will take me away alone to talk, and we will reenter the familiar space we occupy, when it's just the two of us landsmen. I wait for him to signal me, but he doesn't.

We prepare for bed—I in my room with Peggy, he in his, with Matthew. He says good night, barely looking at me. I say good night back to him.

Lying there in the darkness while she sleeps, all I want is to be able to cry freely. But I know I mustn't wake Peggy. So I go into the bathroom.

The sound of my crying wakes Jerry. He stands in the doorway in his pajamas. "You've got to be more quiet," he whispers. I let my knees give way. He catches me. He sighs deeply.

He sits down on the closed toilet seat. I sit on his lap. His pajama top is wet with my tears.

"I don't think I can live without you anymore," I say. "Don't send me away."

"You know the story, Joyce," he says. "We've been through all this before. Let's not make it harder."

We sit there a long time, saying nothing. Finally, sometime before dawn, I make my way back to bed, although I don't fall asleep. In the morning, before Matthew and Peggy get up, Jerry goes down to the lobby with me. Because he has always paid for everything, I haven't even brought money on this trip. Now he stuffs a couple of fifty dollar bills in my hand. We walk out in front of the hotel, where a row of taxis is lined up. "This girl needs to go to the airport," he says, easing me into the back seat as one would a very frail elderly person. I am looking into his eyes, still hoping he's about to hit his palm against his forehead in that way he has and say, "Christ! What was I thinking of?" and pull me out of the taxi.

"Don't forget to turn the heat down and lock the door after you, once you leave the house," he says. "I'll give you a call." He pats my shoulder and kisses my cheek.

I watch out the window as the taxi pulls away. He looks at his watch and runs his hand through his hair. He turns and walks back into the hotel.

I have no memory of the trip back from Florida.

My friend Jean, to whom I'd given my apartment, tells me that I showed up in New Haven that same day, or the next. She remembers the sight of me on the steps of some dormitory.

I tell her she must be wrong. I have no memory of getting myself to New Haven. Maybe it was later—the next month.

"No," she tells me. "You had a tan. You told me Jerry was still in Florida with his children. You said something about cars on the beach. You weren't making a lot of sense."

I make my way to Hanover. From there I take a taxi over the same stretch of highway Jerry drove with me that first day he picked me up. It's a half-hour ride to Jerry's house.

A lot of snow has fallen since we left, just two days earlier, and Vernon Barrett has not been by yet with his plow. I am bare-legged and wearing sneakers as I make my way up the hill, up the steps, and let myself in the door. The house is so cold I see my breath.

I clean my things out of the closet. I set my records and typewriter by the door, along with the sewing machine I bought, still in its box. I have surprisingly few possessions or clothes. I take with me a couple of books Jerry has wanted me to read—the meditations of Lao Tse, an old novel he picked up for me in a used bookstore called *The Dolly Dialogues,* and a mystery written by Josephine Tey. An introduction to homeopathy. The Xeroxed copy of his dietary regime. I wish I had a photograph of Jerry and me, but for all the months we spent together, there are no pictures of the two of us.

I'm packed and ready to go within an hour. I call my mother.

Just hearing her voice, I begin to cry so hard she can't understand what I'm saying, except the one part that's clear. *Come get me.*

"I'll come right away," she says.

She arrives a few hours later, leaving her car at the foot of Jerry's unplowed driveway. Standing in the cold living room, I see her trudging up the last snowy stretch of road on foot, in a white rabbit fur hat and red suede boots. When she gets to the door, I fall into her arms, though I also know, as we stand there, that I will no longer find the kind of comfort in her arms I once would have.

T he two of us make just a couple of trips in the nearly knee-deep snow to haul my possessions down the driveway. I can't bear to look at the pain on my mother's face.

After everything is loaded in the trunk, I go back in the house alone just one more time before leaving for good, to make sure the heat is turned down again and to turn out the lights. On the window of Jerry's bedroom, where the glass is dusty, I write, with my finger, the name of the child we had talked about: BINT.

I t's over that quickly.

One day, Jerry Salinger is the only man in my universe. I look to him to tell me what to write, what to think, what to wear, to read, to eat. He tells me who I am, who I should be. The next day he's gone.

He had described to me the path toward enlightenment. It had required a kind of discipline and self-denial I did not possess, an ability to let go of ego and lay down desire for worldly pleasures.

I had always stumbled on that path. But I have never questioned the belief that his path is the right one. Not having Jerry to lead me, I feel left behind and lost, not simply alone physically, but spiritually stranded. I've been well acquainted with the sensation of loneliness all my life. Never like this.

SAM

Amy Ferris

He said, "I can't make your mistakes for you."

I was fifteen, fifteen and a half, maybe, almost sixteen, and I was leaving home.

I was all packed and ready.

Trying on my new knapsack—on and off, on and off—resting right there on my back and shoulders, so when I hitchhiked from San Francisco to Medford, Oregon, I looked oh so cool and groovy, and felt oh so cool and groovy, and not so top-heavy. There is nothing worse than wanting desperately to look cool and groovy while hunching over due to excess poundage. There is, I suspect, a lot of bullying and hushed snarky remarks that go along with that particular fashion faux-pas.

I had packed every single peasant blouse and long Indian skirt and tie-dyed T-shirt I could manage to find. I had also tucked, deep in the knapsack, hidden away in a corner, my small bottle of Jean Naté perfume; some makeup: powder blush, mascara, an under-eye concealer in a *very light* shade (I think, but I'm not sure, all were Maybelline); and the pièce de résistance, the one item that would cause me deep, profound shame—the forbidden double-edged Gillette razor.

He drove me to Kennedy Airport, where he would put me on an airplane that would fly me across the country so I could meet up with my friend who would later break my heart into many teeny pieces, some remaining crushed for years and years. He drove me from our home on Long Island, where my mother stood in our door frame, never once stepping out from behind the screen door, her hair in rollers, her lashes coated with mascara, and a cigarette dangling from her lips.

She stood, and for many, many minutes, not a word was spoken.

"Okay. Bye, Ma."

And then: "Shiva. I'm sitting shiva. You coulda just stabbed me—woulda been easier."

Everyone was a stand-up comic. This is the god-honest truth. Every single mother on our block turned out at one time to be Shecky Greene: "You coulda just stabbed me—woulda been easier."

You know what? In hindsight, maybe it *woulda* been easier.

I had dropped out of high school. Jewish girls from middle-class families didn't drop out of high school. They had nervous breakdowns, or went on all-day shopping sprees at Roosevelt

Field, or would cut school and go to the park and make out with various boys, or go to the "one" movie theater and watch a movie over and over and over again, because in those days you could. You could sit in a movie theater, stay all day, and you could also smoke cigarettes. I would be swooning over Omar Sharif in *Funny Girl*. I wanted to be Fanny Brice, married to Nicky Arnstein, and I wanted to speak Yiddish, and I wanted, more than life itself, for a period of about, oh, three months, to stand on the bow of a tugboat with a floral arrangement the size of frickin' Texas and sing "Don't Rain on My Parade." I know, it was a gigantic dream for a very short period of time, and of course the only hitch was that I had no singing voice, none whatsoever. I couldn't have carried a tune if someone had held a gun to my head and demanded that I sing on cue. Singing was definitely out of the question.

Although now that I write and remember this, we did sing show tunes while driving in the car. Any and all car trips consisted of playing a game show, like *The Match Game*, and singing show tunes. On this particular day, driving to the airport, *Fiddler on the Roof* was the show my dad chose to sing, the complete score, from our home on Long Island to the airport in Jamaica, Queens. Singing "If I Were a Rich Man" seemed both somewhat peculiar and deeply moving as I was embarking on a life-changing experience. Of course, the Grateful Dead or Laura Nyro would have been my choice, but my father was much more of a show-tune aficionado. Every single Sunday morning, without fail, he would sit in his favorite recliner in our den, surrounded by shelves filled with books, playing his favorite musicals so loud on our stereo that he would wake our entire family. The sound of show tunes reached the second floor instantaneously.

This was a ritual: recliner, coffee, musicals. And no, no, he was not gay. He was not gay, and he was not closeted. He was a man who loved art and culture and theater and musicals and gambling and poker and his children and most definitely his wife. And I can tell you right now, as he drove me to that airport on that day, while he didn't say it, he knew I was making a mistake and he was not happy with my decision. He was tense and scared and worried and held my left hand with his right hand while he gripped the bottom of the steering wheel with his left.

Making the trip was a decision I blurted out at the dinner table so matter-of-factly, it could have gotten lost in normal dinner conversation: "Hey, can you pass the salt? And a little more steak, less rare, more well done? And hey, by the way, I dropped out of high school, and can I have some more string beans, please? Thank you."

I was at a stage in my fifteen-and-a-half-year life where breathing felt like a chore. I was so miserable and unhappy and I felt so alone in the world. I was running with a bad crowd and stealing dollars, lots and lots of dollars, from my dad's wallet and Mom's purse and drawers—here and there, lots of here and there—and buying hash and marijuana and coke and lying about that. I was acting out all sorts of self-loathing behavior. I will spare you the details, but suffice it to say that there was a time in my life when being bad and feeling bad just blended together into plain old *big bad BAD*.

And so I quit high school and decided to tag along to a commune with my friend who I made out with in the back seat of the car, where we kissed so long and so hard our lips cracked and bled. But I wasn't his girlfriend, and he wasn't my boyfriend.

He said, "I don't like you in that way. I like you plenty, but, you know, not as a girlfriend. I don't love you; I mean, I'm not, you know, in love with you."

But no other girl was willing or wanted to go with him to Medford, Oregon, and so I said yes. Yes, I'll go. I'll quit high school, and I'll stop straightening my hair and stop shaving my legs (which turned out to be the worst crime, the you-are-no-longer-allowed-on-this-commune crime), and I'll never ever go to Ohrbach's again, and yes, yes, I'll hitchhike from San Francisco and spend a night at a small scary dirty creepy motel off the side of the road somewhere between San Francisco and Medford, and yes, we'll have bad, unappealing sex once (or maybe it was twice), and yes, I'll cook macrobiotic foods and sing songs written by Joan Baez and Pete Seeger. And I'll tell everyone that I love *The Three Stooges* when in fact I secretly wish them all ill will, and yes, I will allow myself to be unhappy and confused and keep all my feelings wrapped in a little ball and bury them deep. Just like the Jean Naté perfume, the makeup, and the razor.

"I can't make your mistakes for you," he said as he left me at the gate while my knapsack was making its way to the plane by way of the conveyor belt and the peasant skirt I wore was dragging on the floor and my hair was curly and unruly. He handed me a couple of hundred dollars and said, "Please, our secret," and I smiled and kissed him and hugged him so tight I could feel his heart breaking. "I can't make your mistakes for you," he whispered in my ear, and then he turned and walked away.

And the mistakes piled up one after another, year after year after year.

There was the pregnancy. The one where I behaved like a needy, desperate young woman, using that pregnancy as a weapon to try to get the man to love me, to want me. To want me and the baby.

"Why don't we abort you and keep the baby?" he finally said.

I sat alone in the abortion clinic, until another man, a middle-aged, short, heavy-set, bespectacled man said, "I will help you. Come with me." Half an hour later, I was in a room with about ten other girls who had just had abortions, and I can tell you right now, with complete conviction, that none of us felt good about what had just happened—none of us. And I would go so far as to bet none of us ended up with, or stayed with, the guy we had sex with, the one who got us pregnant. Because none of us in that room, on that day, quite understood or believed at that stage in our lives how vital and necessary it was to love the whole of ourselves, to honor our whole self. I was young and lonely and had absolutely no self-worth whatsoever. Self-esteem was so out of reach for me, I would have fallen down if I had tried to grab hold of it. I was desperately searching and hoping for love. That mistake—*the desperation of wanting to be loved*—later in life became a deep mission: *the desire to become a woman of unlimited self-esteem.* Wouldn't trade that mistake for the world.

Then there was the boyfriend, the horrible, bad boyfriend. The one who, I knew from the get-go, from the moment I met him, was not right for me. He. Was. Not. Right. For. Me. I knew it, and I didn't pay attention to my own instincts. There was a voice that said, *Nah, don't, he's not good for you, this doesn't feel right, don't do this.* I did not pay attention to that voice. Nor did I did pay enough attention to his anger and his mood swings and his need to be right all the time, and to his violent streak and the hole that remained punched in the wall, or the way he humiliated me in public, or the very first time he threatened me, with his big hard hands wrapped around my throat. His hands wrapped so hard, he was choking me. "I could kill you," he said in a hushed, scary voice.

I sat in my car in bumper-to-bumper traffic. A few of my personal belongings were scattered on the back seat, along with a black-and-blue mark stretching from my jawline to my clavicle, as I replayed the entire five years over and over and over and over again, wishing more than anything I had paid attention to that voice, my voice, telling me, *Don't—don't do this.* Why hadn't I listened? What had I not trusted about myself, my own voice? Why did I constantly turn down the volume?

That mistake—not paying attention to my own voice, my own life—later led me to a deep-rooted passion: *the desire for all women to speak up, to speak their truth, to be heard.* Oh, no, I wouldn't trade that mistake for anything.

And then there are the mistakes that bring us shame, the ones that make us weep in the dark, the ones that keep us at arm's length. The ones that we marry. The ones that we try desperately to hide, the ones that have prescription numbers, the ones that are hidden away in cartons. The ones that we forgot. The ones that are thrown up in our faces over and over and over again. The ones that come back to haunt us. The ones that feel so unbearable, we think we'll die. The ones that get us down on our knees. The ones we die with. The ones that make us feel not worthy or deserving. The ones that keep us invisible.

A different airport.
   A different city.
   A different time.

My dad and I were sitting together at the airport in Fort Lauderdale, Florida. Waiting, waiting, waiting at the gate for a plane to arrive from Atlanta, Georgia. We had been sitting for hours. We had arrived at the airport very early, and the plane was four hours late. There were delays and headwinds and storms, and all the god-awful pacing back and forth, back and forth, and checking his watch every five minutes. This was my dad's all-time favorite pastime: worrying. And then, finally, after circling the airport for another hour, the plane landed. Safely. Finally. Finally. And then my father exhaled, this big gigantic huge exhale. The kind of exhale that makes you wonder, *How did he hold that in for so long?* And then, a few minutes later, along with other weary passengers, his carry-on baggage in one hand and his felt hat in the other, my husband—my sexy, funny, quirky, oh-so-very-kind-and-loving husband—got off the plane. And as he walked toward us, I remember thinking, *What if, what if, my father had never said to me, "I can't make your mistakes for you"?*

All those mistakes, all those god-awful, embarrassing, shameful, secretive mistakes that brought me closer to another person, that I swore I would never ever repeat, the ones that seemed to pop up every which where, the ones I couldn't seem to live without, the ones with names like Joe and Richard and Jeremy, who kept me waiting for hours in restaurants and hotel lobbies and late-night bars, the ones who never called back, never showed up—all those mistakes *led me here.*

DR. FEELGOOD IN THE SNAIL GARDEN

Kathi Kamen Goldmark

Five pretty young women—tossing their long hair and applying lip gloss, a little overdressed for the occasion—knocked on the door of a nondescript Hollywood Hills apartment.

Their guys weren't with them. A week into a rock & roll tour in support of their first hit record, the guys could have been anywhere—Corpus Christi, Oklahoma City, or some other exotic locale. This evening was a get-acquainted dinner for the ladies, hosted by the band's manager; let's call him Jerry*. I was the one in leather fringe and too much patchouli oil. This was required by law in the 1970s, because I was the drummer's girlfriend. Audrey, my best new L.A. rock 'n' roll friend, was the bandleader's girl-friend, so she was allowed to dress more like a normal person.

Dinner turned out to be a culinary novelty, an actual yard-long overstuffed deli sandwich, pointed at with pride by Jerry's wife, Joanne, a plump redhead with a grating voice and a talent for annoyance. In those days, I was all organic brown rice and seaweed, but I ate politely—my mama had taught me how to be gracious and mind my manners—and, honestly, I loved those mounds of tasty, salted meat on soft white bread. As down-market as a meal could be, to me it was a rare delicacy to be savored and enjoyed, a guilty pleasure.

Jerry cleared his throat, making sure he had everyone's full attention. His conversational tone shifted into lecture mode as he began by welcoming us to his home, then outlined the unique joys, duties, and challenges of being a rock and roll girlfriend. He felt he needed to point out that there were three basic and essential rules, and if we paid attention and followed them carefully, we'd be just fine.

Rule Number One: There was only one acceptable dry cleaner, and we were urged to take our sweethearts' stage clothes there and there only.

"Two-hour turnaround, and these cats know how to do rhinestones," Jerry insisted. We all nodded. It seemed a little silly, but sure, we could do this. I saw a couple of the other girls begin to take notes. I didn't have a pen (I never have a pen) and decided I'd crib from Audrey later on. More wine was served, along with a pudding-based dessert exactly as elegant (and tasty) as the yard-long deli sandwich.

Rule Number Two: Jerry hit his stride as we were told to send all of our household bills, in handy preaddressed, stamped envelopes, to a business manager's office in Hollywood. That sounded like a pretty wonderful plan to me. (Did it occur to anyone to ask about accounting or recoupables? Nope. We were, in our defense, barely into our twenties.) Plus, we would each get an allowance. The idea was that our men needed us to be able to keep the home fires burning without a lot of personal or professional distractions on our end. They were, after all, doing something *really hard*—touring the world in an indulged up-and-coming rock band, in an era of unprecedented indulgence—and they were *doing it for us*. I glanced at Audrey, who rolled her eyes. One of Audrey's eye rolls could sink a battleship, even then.

Rule Number Three: Like a preacher coming to the core of his sermon, Jerry rolled into the big finish, his voice dropping to an intense whisper as he tried to look solemn and professional. Not so easy for a middle-aged white guy in a 'fro and a Nehru jacket.

"You know, ladies, for weeks, even months, at a time, the guys won't be able to enjoy the comforts of home. And there will be temptations—oh, yes. Other women will want to be with them. . . ." He paused for dramatic effect.

His point, when he finally got there, was that there were groupies on the road, guys in bands had no ability or inclination to resist available sex, and this was going to have to be okay with us. To our credit, I suppose, none of us pointed out that he had just dumped a total load of crap. We were starting our glamorous new rock & roll life, and there were sure to be some adjustments along the way. We owed him the benefit of the doubt, right?

"But don't you even *think* about fooling around on them," he declared. "They need you to stay faithful and true. It's different if someone is screwing around in your own bed, in your own home. They need to know they can count on you."

Why, that rascal, he'd buried the lead!

One of our perks, in addition to hot tips on dry cleaners who could do rhinestones, turned out to be Dr. Frank, a bona fide member of the medical profession, a man with wild, frizzy hair and an even wilder smile. Dr. Frank was *there for us*—whether that meant opening his office at midnight to administer magical VD-be-gone penicillin shots to the guys on their way home from the airport or dispensing the monthly Valium[1] prescriptions that allowed us ladies to get our beauty sleep without calling our boyfriends in the middle of the night, every single night, while they were doing god-knows-what with god-knows-who. And honey, the Valium helped. Those little robin's-egg-blue ten-milligram babies became a form of salvation.

After he got to know us a little better, Dr. Frank added quaaludes[2] to the mix, and for a couple of years all I had to do was show up for my monthly appointment at his seedy little strip-mall office and pick up my prescriptions: sixty Valium and thirty 'ludes that cost about seven bucks, total, to fill at the local drugstore. Only problem was, there was no way I could take all those quaaludes.

I had defied Rule Number One—use the "cats who do rhinestones"—immediately. There was a nice dry cleaner right on our corner, and I liked the owner.

As for Rule Number Two—keep the home fires burning—I took advantage of our free rent- and bill-paying service plus allowance and enrolled in a master's degree program at a university without walls, volunteering at a small private school in return for supervised hours toward an MA in drama education. A win-win, except for the fact that pharmaceuticals were piling up in the drawer of my bedside table. Who had time to do drugs?

Ironies aside (I spent months putting on a play with a dozen twelve-year-olds for one night of applause in a funky auditorium, while my sweetie played every night for screaming thousands), it was a great gig. I loved the kids, and working at a school got me out of my own head. My schedule was flexible enough that I could join my drummer boy on tour now and then. And I was so active and busy that I lost weight without really trying—suddenly a svelte size 6, I needed new clothes for my glamorous rock & roll life. And that's where the quaaludes came in.

Eddie was a musician friend in New York who "knew people." To be more specific, he knew people who *really liked quaaludes*. So whenever we took one of our frequent trips east, I brought my stash and he sold the pills for me, individually, at an approximately 3,000 percent markup (less his 15 percent agent's fee), and handed me wads of cash, which I in turn took to Bloomingdale's and used to buy a fabulous size 6 rock & roll wardrobe. We've all heard of people selling valuables to buy drugs; I sold drugs to buy gorgeous, soft denim bell-bottoms appliquéd with velvet and lace; tiny blouses made of stitched-together silk scarves; vintage hats and gloves; platform shoes with fake goldfish swimming around inside Plexiglas heels. (Shall I mention another source for great outfits? The gorgeous Eurotrash twins with the Sunset Boulevard boutique who gave me deep discounts because they were both screwing my boyfriend? Perhaps that's too much information.)

But enhancing my wardrobe was only one of many really weird things about my life in those days.

One of the others was, increasingly as time went on, Dr. Frank. I don't exactly remember when he started wearing the copper pyramid on his head (he claimed that the pyramid shape channeled mystical energy and powers, and urged me to wear one, too), but it was about the same time that I jumped on his scale with a huge paperweight and a couple of rocks in my shoulder bag. Not only did he not notice the paperweight, he didn't notice the purse. But when he recorded my weight—eight pounds heavier than last month—he clucked his tongue and wrote out a prescription for something called Preludin,[3] a *really* fun appetite suppressant that was especially effective when taken with half a quaalude and a slug of Cuervo. Who needed food? Or sleep? Boyfriend? What boyfriend? Rule Number Three—indulging lover's promiscuity while remaining faithful—happily bit the dust at last.

So life went on, not always jolly or fun, but jolly and fun enough. There were nights when I became obsessed with worry over the whereabouts of my sweetheart, who had developed a penchant for going out for a six-pack and disappearing for a day or two of alcoholic-blackout frolicking. Audrey would come over to talk me down or ride around with me, looking for a drunken drummer under roadside bushes in Laurel Canyon. She never once rolled her eyes at me, though I'm sure she was tempted. In calmer moments, we imagined schemes for getting more attention from the guys, based mostly on episodes of *I Love Lucy*. (We could rent disguises and try out as backup singers! Meet them at the airport in gorilla suits and tutus!)

At home there were jealousies and tantrums: whiskey glasses thrown at walls, wild rides to the beach, hot- and cold-running love. I worked, wrote songs and plays for my kids at the school, and went out to rock & roll shows dressed to the nines. Through the roller-coaster ride, there were anchors: Jerry, trying to control us; Dr. Frank, to take the edge off.

A day finally came when all the excitement of our glamorous life, which lately had pretty much boiled down to watching my boyfriend get drunk and pass out on the sofa (while I made lame excuses about his whereabouts), wasn't so exciting anymore. I made the tough decision to move out, get my own tiny apartment in West Hollywood, and support myself with my brand-new master's degree and teaching credential. There were shakeups in the band, too: personnel adjustments, resentments, settlements, and lawsuits. The drummer left town and I tried not to notice. I'd moved on.

Reality kicked in quickly: Whoa, I had to pay my own rent and show up for work every day? Who'd thought *that* up? But independence made it worth figuring out a way to pay the bills. My gorgeous clothes still fit; all I had to do was starve myself and work out like a maniac. There were dates with a variety of interesting men. And Dr. Frank was always there when I needed him, until one day he wasn't.

I came home from work and turned on the TV news: something about a "doctor to the stars" getting busted for inappropriate prescriptions. When I glanced at the screen and saw a familiar frizzy head topped by a copper pyramid shielding his eyes from the camera, I knew the pharma-party was over.

A new job came along and I moved to San Francisco, where my new boyfriend didn't run off on drunken benders—at least not without me. I also discovered my own rock & roll voice and started a band with a couple of friends. (Was it a coincidence that the robin's-egg-blue Stratocaster I chose to play was the exact same color as my dearly departed little ten-milligram buddies? Over thirty years later, I still find that color deeply soothing.) But I never found a new doctor, at least not one as generous with his prescription pad. Somehow, the time had rolled around to start being a grown-up.

One day, years later, my phone rang. Dr. Frank calling. He'd moved to San Francisco and found my number in the phone book. Only his name was no longer Frank—it was something wispy, like Ariel, which should have been my first clue. Would I like to get together and catch up? he wondered. I'll admit it: Visions of that prescription pad danced in my head as I prepared for our meeting in a ramshackle Victorian in the Richmond district.

I barely recognized the man who opened the door—skinny and grizzled, his hair covered, this time, by what appeared to be a white towel, he offered to show me around the "compound." Dr. Frank had become a member of a religious community following a guru he called Father. He had contacted me not in the gesture of friendship I'd assumed, or to offer the pharmaceutical guilty-pleasure joy I'd secretly hoped for, but because he thought I was a live one. He wanted me to become a follower of Father's, too, and launched into a fever-pitched come-on.

As on the night of that fateful long-ago lecture explicating the proper deportment of rock 'n' roll girlfriends and Rules Number One, Two, and Three, I listened politely. I heard about Dr. Frank's psychic awakening, on through pyramid power and then a series of vision quests followed by a fortuitous meeting in Woolworth's automotive accessories department that led him to Father, who had given his life new meaning. His eyes, though spinning around in opposite directions, lit up whenever he talked about Father. There was room for me, too, in Father's life. I would be welcome.

Finally, he asked me if I had any questions.

"Yeah, I do. How does the community support itself?"

"Ah," said Frank/Ariel. "Look out the window, into the back yard. See those snails in the garden? We have lots and lots of snails. People think of them as pests, but we catch them out of the garden and sell them to French restaurants as escargots. There are always more snails."

I could barely see them in the fading light, but yes, a closer look revealed that there were lots and lots of snails.

I told him I'd give his proposal some thought and made a hasty retreat. Then I ran to my car, trying to remember every detail so I could report this event to Audrey, who by then lived three thousand miles away.

I read my drummer's obituary in the *San Francisco Chronicle* and drove north for over four hours to get to the funeral, held in a small coastal town. The room was filled with friends, girlfriends old and new, his gorgeous adolescent son. But I was the only one there who'd been around for the rock & roll ride that had defined his career and his identity. Of course, they got it all wrong. Someone brought a mix tape of tracks he hadn't even played on, ignoring a soulful lead vocal from the first album and the background parts where he'd hissed on the "s." They talked about a man I didn't recognize: a father, town booster, and philanthropist. And they remembered a flawed, haunted guy facing private demons, too recognizable for comfort. I sat there, knowing no one, listening quietly. When it was time for people to stand up and share, I stayed seated and silent.

I noticed the absence of former bandmates, as well as that of Jerry and Dr. Frank. Had it occurred to anyone to contact them? Was everyone still embroiled in litigation? Was everyone even alive? Who knew?

On the long drive home, I imagined what they all might be doing right then: the other musicians deep into new projects, Jerry laying down his sleazy law to a roomful of new, lovely girls, and bright-eyed Dr. Frank, intent on digging up backyard snails for Father. I pulled over to cry and say my own private goodbyes.

Then I drove home, remembering certain moments of those years of trashy elegance, thinking that sometimes there's a fine line between a pest and a delicacy.

And sometimes there isn't.

Pseudonyms have been used throughout this essay.

1. At the time, Valium was viewed as a "mild" tranquilizer, one that we now know to be mightily addictive.

2. Quaaludes are a powerful muscle relaxant with a slightly aphrodisiac effect and a tendency to reduce a person to a lump of happy, amnesiac pudding.

3. You will find, all over the Internet, deeply nostalgic posts from people who wish they could still get this drug in the United States.

BEATING LOVE TO THE PUNCH

Jane Ganahl

As someone who's spent a healthy chunk of her adult life a) single and b) writing newspaper columns, books, and blogs about relationships, I'm sometimes asked why I still have a sense of humor about the demented dance of dating, and why I have experienced so little heartbreak, despite having weathered two divorces and too many love affairs to count. Simple, I respond: I learned early on to be the one to leave first. Don't wait for the size 14 loafer to drop. Beat him to the punch, and keep your dignity intact.

It's not the most enlightened way of dealing with the opposite sex, but it's worked pretty well for me. And I'm not as cool and heartless as I may sound. Generally speaking, by the time I leave a relationship, its heart has not been beating for some time. I was just never one to hang around and poke sticks at the corpse, checking for signs of life.

I hadn't had sex with my first husband—a Swedish god who oozed charm like a rock star—for months, he never told me he loved me, and in fact he never wanted to talk at all. I cried myself to sleep at night as he stayed out late with his buddies. Yet when I told him I wanted out, he was dismayed.

"But I still love you."

I do recall pausing momentarily, but I could see, big as a freight train, more hurt coming down the track. So I condensed my heartbreak into a ferocious verbal assault and let him have it. When I was done, there was no turning back.

My technique of leaving in this manner was years in the making. My early training, while harsh, was brief. And strangely satisfying.

Spring 1964. The girls' bathroom at Woodside Elementary School. I stood at the mirror and awkwardly slathered on pink lip gloss in preparation for a life-changing event just five minutes away, feeling apprehensive and weird and gloriously alive. I stared at my face, gave my perky flip one more smoothing stroke, and started for the door. It opened before I got there, and in walked Vicki.

Uh-oh.

She closed the door behind her and stared at me. The thoughts flickering across my mind were *Will our sixth-grade queen bee try to punch me? And if so, can I take her down?* She was taller by a few inches, but I was tougher and more athletic. Perhaps I could get her in a headlock? It might be gratifying to watch those fake eyelashes come unglued and float south, like black snowflakes, while her angel face contorted in the crook of my elbow.

It had been a chaotic year. The United States of America was grappling with a presidential assassination, race riots, and war in Southeast Asia. And I was dealing with a question larger, yet far more personal: Did I really want to be a girl?

This question evoked a pluses-and-minuses list in my head.

The minuses of being a girl:

- *that whole menstruation thing (which had yet to smite me)*

- *the breasts that had only begun to bud but already were interfering with my ability to catch a football*

- *the makeup-and-hair thing, which I was really bad at, as evidenced by the uneven glopping of pink across my lips*

Plus, the girlier of my friends actually practiced laughing behind their hands, geisha style, and never disagreed with anything the boys said. Which made no sense to me: Boys were often idiotic, and I did not hesitate to let them know when they were.

The pluses of being a girl:

- *This could be neatly summed up in one word: Steven.*

Steven was captain of every sport played at our school. He was clean-cut and had a dazzling slash of a grin that reminded me of Darrin on the TV show *Bewitched.* He wasn't smart—he was in the slowest of the three sixth-grade classes—and he wasn't nice, but I didn't know it then. And he was Vicki's. At least, he had been yesterday.

Vicki looked at me with an odd expression of neither malice nor sadness, as if she were groping for something to say. My old friend was now the enemy, blocking my exit and keeping me from my date with destiny. With Steven. With my first kiss *ever.*

Sure, Steven and I had locked horns on the field more than once. Several times, actually. When I insisted on playing football with the boys during recess and was picked (always last) to be on his team. And if I missed the catch or kicked the ball backward over my head, he was always the first to groan and say, "Oh, *man,* I told you girls shouldn't play sports!" I would pick myself up and hiss at him like a pissed-off kitty: "Hey! I would never tell you that you couldn't play with dolls, sissy-boy!" His face, when that happened, would turn the most charming shade of scarlet, and you could see the tension snap his patrician jaw shut. When I told my mother of my almost-daily run-ins with him, she barely looked up from the pot of ham and yellow rice she was cooking. "He likes you," she smiled. "He's just flirting."

I almost fainted. Steven, flirting with me? Could it be possible? But he was with Vicki! I'd heard they'd even petted—gone all the way to second base. But he was fickle—he'd been with several girls since kindergarten, when I'd first espied him with his little cardigan sweater and perfect hair, sitting intentionally next to Sarah, the prettiest girl in the class. Maybe he was ready to be done with Vicki and ready for a girl who was, you know, smart? And not a simpering fool?

Suddenly, I was no longer interested in my punting skills, and began working on my femininity with the fervor of a born-again Christian. I stopped wearing pants and started wearing dresses, tugging uncomfortably at the skirt and neck and waist, all of which felt straitjacket-like. I combed my hair twenty times each day, worked on curling it up at the ends like Jackie O., and even took to wearing makeup: a gash of turquoise on each lid, and pink lip gloss. My mother said no mascara until eighth grade, noting that girls who wore mascara or fake eyelashes looked easy. I didn't want to look easy, I just wanted to look pretty. And it seemed to be working. Now when I walked by Steven, he turned to watch me go.

My friend Cathy, who was even more challenged in the femininity department than I, noticed. "He keeps looking at you!" she said, giving me a sharp elbow in the ribs, with no small hint of jealousy. "I bet he's going to break up with Vicki and ask you to go steady!"

I dared not even think about that possibility, for if I did, I'd spend science class writing the name Jane des Georges over and over again, instead of doing drills on the periodic table of the elements. Platinum . . . ring. Copper . . . like my hair. Plutonium . . . because our love is nuclear.

I was at my locker, when the bell rang for school to begin. When I looked up and saw Steven leaning on the locker next to mine, I almost fainted. He was grinning like always, but this time he seemed a bit nervous, twisting his class ring around his finger in circles. *His ring? Oh, God . . .*

"Could you, like, meet me after school by the backstop?" he asked with a suave wink. The backstop, surrounded by oak trees and relatively private, was a notorious make-out spot. I thought my knees might buckle. "Sure," I stammered, with feigned confidence. I tried to wink back but ended up blinking both eyes simultaneously and fiercely. Steven hesitated, then ran off to class.

I couldn't wait to tell Debby and Cathy what had happened, and they, in turn, reported the gossip to me: Steven had broken up with Vicki and was going to ask me to go steady. Where had they heard this? I demanded to know. From Vicki herself, they told me, and she seemed quite distraught.

Oh, man, not only was I going to get my first kiss with the boy of my dreams, I was now the school Jezebel. The next thing you knew, I'd be middle-school dance queen. Steven would bow and hold out his hand for the first dance at the end of the year, and we would be the envy of all the kids as we foxtrotted our way into infamy.

But first, I had to get through this interminable day. I found my sister and told her I was going to walk home a bit later, mumbling something about cheerleading tryouts I had to practice for. Then I enlisted Debby and Cathy to hover nearby, like amateur reporters covering the breaking news event.

With t-minus five to go, I slipped into the bathroom for the nervous prekiss routine. It was then that I ran into Vicki. We stared at each other, and it slowly dawned on me that this might not be a chance encounter. "Hi, Vicki, what's up?" I asked with feigned casualness.

"I just had to tell you . . ." she began, then stopped, looking stymied and almost tearful.

With a rush of remorse, I reached out to touch her arm. "I'm sorry, Vicki! This was not my idea. I guess Steven's just kind of fickle."

Vicki turned away and didn't look at me after that. "No, Jane, you don't get it. What day is today?"

I had to think a moment. "April first?"

She said softly, "Right, April Fools' Day—get it? This is all a big joke he's playing on you. I'm sorry."

I felt like someone had hit me on the head with a baseball bat. "A . . . joke?" I breathed, my voice quaking. Vicki opened the door and walked out, leaving me alone. Despite the fact that she was my erstwhile competitor, I knew she wasn't lying. For a moment I felt a pang, wondering what kind of asshole boyfriend would require his girlfriend to stand by and lie by default. Then I stared at the mirror, took a paper towel, shoved it under some running water, and began to scrub the pink off my lips and the turquoise off my eyes, as if that action would prevent the tears from collecting and spilling out.

I emerged from the bathroom, my bare skin rosy from scrubbing, and ran with determination down the field toward the backstop. Debby and Cathy were standing nearby, as planned, and Steven's friends were also off to one side, acting like they just happened to be there.

Steven was leaning against the backstop, one foot tucked under him and looking like James Dean. I hated him more than I'd ever hated anything or anyone up to that moment, but decided to let him say his rehearsed lines.

"I just wondered . . ." he began.

"What did you wonder, Steven?" I forced a smile.

"I was wondering if you . . . you know . . . would want to . . ." He was twirling that ring again, and I lost it.

"You were wondering if I wanted to be your goat? The butt

of your joke? Because this is just a joke, right?" With each word, I felt my voice rising to a chaotic shrillness that was unfamiliar to me. I could see Debby's and Cathy's smiling faces fall, and they began to move toward us, arms outstretched, as if trying to catch a falling baby.

"*Right?*" I shrieked.

Steven was taken aback but continued to smile icily. "Okay, yeah, it was a joke," he said. "What are you gonna do about it?"

I stood there for a moment in mute fury, then balled my hand into a fist and thrust it into his stomach with all the force I could muster. He let out a howl, grabbed his midsection, and doubled over in pain. Tears coursed down my cheeks. As I pulled back to punch him again, Debby and Cathy took my arm and restrained me. They guided me away, and we began walking back toward the school building. I could hear Steven's friends laughing—at me or at him, I wasn't sure—as Steven got back on his feet.

"Who'd want to go steady with a flat-ass like you?" he yelled after me. "You're just a stupid flat-ass! Stay off the football field! Go play with your dolls!"

Through my tears, I looked at my friends. "Guess I'll have to get some dolls," I sniffed. Then we all laughed. My head whipped around as we kept walking, and I saw Steven's friends consoling him. As soon as he looked my way, I flipped him a triumphant bird.

The story flew around school like a bad flu: Steven had been in the process of pulling a cruel prank on me, but I'd bested him and busted him in the gut. He avoided me after that. And I learned he had done this before to a few other girls, always the ones who spoke their mind and refused to play girlie games. But I was the last. Vicki, like a predecessor to Tammy Wynette, stood by her man: They remained together through high school, at which point I lost track of them. And, despite her poor taste in men, she and I became friends again, not long after she bravely stood up for me and spilled the beans. I don't think I ever thanked her, but I should have.

Since that time, I've kept my eyes wide open in love. And for good reason. Even during periods of relative bliss, those moments would come: He'd stop listening to my work-related dilemma if a pretty woman came on TV; he'd stop laughing uproariously at my funny comments; after a fight, he'd no longer want makeup sex. I knew what it meant: Time to go, time to head to the backstop and nip this pain in the bud.

Have I been too defensive in love? Kept my metaphorical dukes up? Probably. But at least I've been the one to smile through my tears, knowing I beat love to the punch.

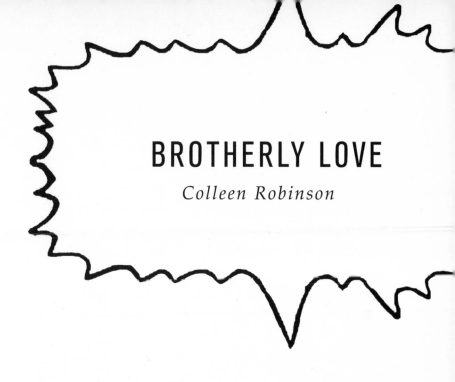

BROTHERLY LOVE

Colleen Robinson

Until I was thirteen, I was a happy girl. The turmoil of the 1960s didn't impact my world, which centered on my large Irish Catholic family. As the fourth of six children, I had plenty of siblings to play with, though in my desperation to grow up quickly, I gravitated toward my older brother and sisters. The eldest, Maureen, I considered glamorous; Mary Beth, a year younger, was the little mom of the family; next in line was Kevin, my confidant. Then there were the youngest, Daniel and David, who didn't get much consideration beyond being "the boys." They were two peas in a pod and spent a lot of time getting into mischief. Daniel, two years younger than I, was the family clown, making us laugh with his one-liners and his funny interpretations of famous comedians.

As a family we were close, but the tragedies that were to dot my teen years brought us even closer: Dad's sudden drowning when I was thirteen; my car accident at seventeen, in which I lost my leg;

David and Daniel's sexual abuse by our friend, the parish priest, during the two years prior to my accident; and then the betrayal by the church, when the dioceses did nothing with Mom's report of the abuses, except move the priest to another state.

It wasn't until I was in my early twenties that I nuzzled my way into Daniel and David's pea pod. It happened when they discovered that I, too, smoked pot, leading us to band together as the closet renegades of the family, the ones defying our Goody Two–shoes upbringing. Everyone in our family was square, but not us three, not anymore. Pot offered us relief from the tragedies heaped upon us, and the ability to become immersed in the joy of the moment.

In 1983, when I was twenty-three, I spent a lot of time hanging out at the house Daniel and David shared—what became known as the "party house." One clear April day, Daniel and I were sitting on the hand-me-down leather couch in the living room, odors of stale cigarettes and beer lingering from a party the weekend before. I knew Daniel was nervous by the way he repeatedly flicked his cigarette. "Colleen," he said, "I want to tell you something, but you can't tell anyone else. Promise?"

"Yeah, sure, Daniel, what is it?"

"Well, I met some really supportive people over the past couple years." He was looking at me, eyebrows raised as if in question. "And I, well . . ." He took a puff and his hand shook. "I'm, well, I'm . . ." He paused again. "Colleen, I'm gay."

In our little universe, this news was huge. I stared, mouth agape, then lit a cigarette. Now my hands were shaking, too. I didn't know a single gay person or what that even meant. "Does Mom know?"

"No," he said, "but David does." As he spoke David's name,

he straightened up a bit, as if supported by the very thought of him. "And so do a bunch of people from school." He looked at me sheepishly, as if embarrassed to have told so many friends before he broke the news to me.

We talked a while more. I was too uncomfortable to ask what I really wanted to know, which was how: How do two men have sex? He would have told me, but I wasn't ready to hear. I remembered going to a bar in London and laughing at the men in drag who were singing onstage; staring in disgust at men kissing each other; writing about the whole "fag" experience to Daniel. My face flushed with embarrassment.

As we spoke, I felt more comfortable with this expanded view of my brother. I also felt concerned, wanting to protect him from the ignorance I had been part of, consumed by, my whole life.

I had been seeing a counselor to help me deal with my feelings about my amputation. Perhaps a counselor could help Daniel deal with the myriad feelings around being gay and his stress around telling the family. It felt like such a small gesture, but offering to pay for counseling seemed like a loving way to show my support. Daniel was reticent when I first offered, but finally decided to give it a try. After his first session, he came out to Mom and Larry, her new husband; they were as shocked as I had been. A veritable lioness, Mom has always been our biggest cheerleader, so it was no surprise when her loving support emerged over the months. When Daniel told the rest of our siblings, I felt he and I were comrades.

After my amputation, I showed the world a strong, confident woman, but inside I was insecure and angry. Daniel understood this duality firsthand. He, too, had been showing the world one view of himself while keeping a huge part of who he was a secret.

As I watched him emerge, his true self intact and his bright blue eyes sparkling like a Kashmir sapphire, I felt I had a best friend in my younger brother.

Daniel's humor kept me laughing; he made himself laugh, too. It was the therapy we needed. We'd look at each other with glee, throw our heads back, and allow the laughter to take over, always a cigarette dangling from our hands. His laugh was a defiant cry to the heavens, saying, *You can't get me down—nothing can*. I felt safe when I heard that laugh; I was being held in someone's heart.

It was around that time that we both read *Out on a Limb*, by Shirley MacLaine, and we were equally intrigued. The New Age movement was blooming and we felt like we were, too. Past lives, channeling, metaphysics, UFOs—it was all mind-blowing. Coming as we were from our deep-rooted Catholic upbringing, the movement provided an alternative understanding for why these things had happened to us. The church's answer was that it was God's punishment; the metaphysical answer was that it was part of our souls' evolutionary growth. We were comforted by the ability to give up the angst of our past.

While I was away at college, Daniel called. The cracking in his voice told me it wasn't good. Before he could explain, I was already gripping the phone.

"I saw the doctor today."

"Daniel" was the only word I could muster. I wanted to reach through the phone and hug him, but I waited for him to speak.

"Colleen, I'm positive."

Sweat formed on my brow and my heart sank to my knees. "Oh, God, no," I whispered. I heard him cry. After a moment, I asked, "What does that really mean?"

He sniffled, and I knew he was wiping his snot on his shirtsleeve. "Sixty percent who are positive get sick, so . . . " He paused and took a deep breath, and so did I. "Maybe I'll be in the forty percent who don't." Ever optimistic, that was Daniel.

"Damn straight you won't," I announced. When his sniffles turned to sobs, I realized the depths of my helplessness and just wanted to take care of him.

"But this means I'll never be able to have a child," he cried, and from him escaped the sadness that comes from a crushed dream. I felt sick to my stomach and light-headed. My instinct was to escape, but this was my brother. No matter how much I wanted to protect him, AIDS could not be treated with counseling or money.

I feared I would lose him. Why did he have to die? I thought of Dad and how hard it was to lose him, and knew that my experience with death and grief had not prepared me for my brother's death. After Dad's death, people always said that God wanted Dad with Him. I wasn't sure whether I believed in God anymore, but I did believe that Dad's soul lived on, and I wondered if perhaps Dad wanted Daniel to join him.

Synchronicity was at play in our lives. Daniel, now living in Seattle, went back to school to study acupuncture, and I needed a place to live, so, six months after his phone call, we rented a house together. Shortly thereafter, he invited Mom, and Larry, and me to the Christmas concert put on by the Seattle Men's Chorus.

Watching the hilarious and poignant show put on by 125 gay men, I realized that Daniel had found a new and loving family.

After he joined the group, I watched his life become increasingly joyful. He was finally with people with whom he could be completely himself. I attended parties with my brother over the following year and marveled at how inclusive, kind, and generous his friends were with me. But it wasn't long before some of them began to show signs of AIDS, and then they started to die.

I felt great reluctance about leaving my brother during this difficult time, but I accepted a new job and moved across the state. We spoke by phone often, with too many of those calls revolving around the many friends, acquaintances, and acupuncture clients who were sick and on the brink of death. There were times when my brother's grief was so profound that he could only weep. Other times, I sensed his numbness and felt helpless. Helpless and terrified. Was every word he was saying to me something I would be saying to a friend in . . . when? Six months? Two years? I found it impossible to be as present with Daniel as I wanted to be. If his friends were dying, then so, too, would he.

I often found myself driving and listening to "Bring Him Home" from *Les Miserables*, planning Daniel's funeral and wondering how I'd survive his death. As Jean Valjean implored God to bring Marius back, I sent my own silent and tear-filled prayer to a God I'd long ago stopped trusting. Who would I go to with my problems? Who would support me the way Daniel did? I was nearly paralyzed at times.

In 1989, I applied to the Peace Corps, but as I delved deeper into the application process, the ramifications of leaving for two years hit me. What if Daniel got sick while I was gone? Our family was supportive, but how could I be happy in the Congo while my brother was here, without me, dying? I removed my name and instead took a job as resident director at an AIDS housing and health care facility, where I came face to face with the reality of AIDS in America. I saw drug-addicted and mentally ill men and women from the fringes of society scraping by and who, without our help, could not manage the medication regime they required to stay alive. I tried to separate them in my head from Daniel—he was educated, had a loving family, and had no heroin addiction or need of shelter—but as I got to know the patients better, I saw that they were more like Daniel than I wanted to admit.

Daniel and I saw each other frequently, often going out to eat together on Capitol Hill, the gay-friendly area of Seattle. Because he was in the Men's Chorus and had a big client base in his acupuncture practice, walking down the street with him was like being with a celebrity.

For all the love he gave others, I knew there was a special place in Daniel's heart for me. He was my biggest cheerleader. If there has ever been a man in my life who has made me feel beautiful, it's Daniel. Walking into a restaurant, seeing me, he always exclaimed in delight, "You look fabulous!" and then gave me one of his signature hugs. With Daniel, I could talk about my insecurities around my leg and men, about my concerns that time was ticking and I wasn't finding a man to love me. "Pigs, all of them!" he'd say in support, a twinkle in his eye. "None of them is good enough for you." And sometimes he stopped what he was doing, looked at me, and said breathlessly, "Coll, you're just so beautiful." And from Daniel I could hear it, I could take it in, because I knew that he saw me, all of me, and that even though he was familiar with my whiny side and my bitchy side, I could still take his breath away.

We spent every Christmas Eve together for years. The chorus had a traditional midnight performance, and I loved watching Daniel sing with such joy. We took turns staying at each other's houses after these performances, sometimes not getting to sleep until it was nearly morning. We always set the alarm so we could have plenty of visiting time, and we always started our day with a strong pot of coffee. Enya's recording of "Silent Night" filled the room as we exchanged stockings and gifts. Inevitably, we would cry. No words, just tears that flowed and then were gone. Although we never admitted it, both of us feared this would be our last Christmas together.

Daniel remained positive—literally and figuratively—for eight years, until he developed an opportunistic infection, CMV, a virus that made him nauseous, feverish, and weak. As I was falling in love with my soon-to-be husband, Daniel was soaking his sheets from night sweats and having an increasingly difficult time doing his job.

After all those years, Daniel officially had AIDS. There was no massive explosion in his body, as I had feared, but a quiet, insidious infection that sapped him of his energy.

Over time, I saw his frustration mount. An uncharacteristic anger began to emerge from this normally cheerful and buoyant man, and I was scared. My sense of ineptness about how to support him through his grief was nothing compared with his frustration and anger. I wanted to be the person he could go to when he needed to vent, so as he yelled, I sat there listening and nodding, even though I was shaking on the inside from the intensity of his fury. At the same time, I felt guilty about my upcoming wedding and joyful future while he was facing the possible end of his. This idea was brought home dramatically when he became too weak to continue working and was forced to go on disability.

I couldn't marry in the Catholic church; that world was dying a slow death in my heart. I would have been happy with a New Age minister, but Mark, my fiancé, wasn't comfortable with that. One day, I discovered via an advertisement on the back of a matchbook that all it took to become a legal minister was filling out a simple form. I looked into it and found that it was a bona fide venture. This was the perfect answer. Daniel was the only person who knew Mark and me as a couple well enough to marry us. His health had stabilized, albeit at a low-functioning level, and we felt confident that he would have enough energy to participate in our wedding. When Mark and I asked him to sign up so he could be our minister, he wept, whispering, "I'd be honored," joy reflected in those twinkling eyes.

On my wedding day, Daniel was vibrant. He conducted the service with a strong voice and a welcoming spirit, and then danced until the evening ended. I felt such joy—elation, really—committing myself to the man I loved. I knew how much Daniel wanted that in his life, too, but his future was so uncertain, and having AIDS made it hard for him to meet new men. That day, my joy was tinged with guilt for all that my brother would never have.

When I became pregnant, Mark and I decided to buy a house that could accommodate Daniel, a place with no stairs and that could adapt to a wheelchair. But as my belly swelled, I became more and more attached to the being inside me. Suddenly, death was too big for me. How could I care for a new baby and a dying brother?

Many family members pitched in to help load our belongings and move us across town to our new house. Not Daniel; he was too weak. The afternoon of our move, while we were eating pizza, Mom, Larry, and Daniel stopped by to see the house. I stood across the sparse living room and watched everyone but Daniel eat and laugh. My brother remained in front of the fireplace, looking gaunt and frail. The sparkle in his eyes had dimmed; I had to turn my head. A new life was growing in my body, while his was wasting away. Would he be around to watch my baby grow up? The mere suggestion of Daniel's absence made me sick to my stomach.

Ten years earlier, Daniel would have died from this.

But he didn't die. He lost nearly two hundred friends, acquaintances, and clients over the years, yet he continued forward, like a soldier surviving war, carrying emotional battle scars from the trenches.

Daniel wears his heart on his sleeve, and I saw his heart swell with love and contract in pain as he tended to, and then lost, one friend after another.

I have been on the periphery of his experience, offering what little support I can, yet surviving the beginning of the AIDS pandemic has always been Daniel's own experience, full of grief and pain. Daniel reminds me of the old saying "We all come into this world alone, and we all leave this world alone." He has taught me that the true joy in life is how we support and love each other in those fleeting days and years between birth and death.

MY REAL FATHER

Rose Castillo Guilbault

My mother always spoke well of my father, the man she had divorced. He wasn't movie-star handsome, she'd begin, *"pero era atractivo y simpatico."*

His nose was slightly crooked, his mouth too large, his face too long. Limpid eyes the color of green Mexican rivers reflected a liquid serenity. But like a ripple across water, they could suddenly change from warm and calm to hard and cruel.

It was his style, she would tell me, the way he moved confidently, the way his clothes draped gracefully on his slender frame, and, yes, his arrogance, that very attitude that made people around him bristle, made him attractive to her. He carried himself as if he were better than everyone and he didn't care that they knew.

He dressed in pin-striped suits and two-toned shoes. A white linen handkerchief, scented with a light citrus cologne, always peeked above his breast pocket. Never mind that he was a traveling salesman, selling trinkets to curio shops in border towns like Juárez, Nogales, Mexicali, Tijuana, stopping along the way in dusty Yaqui Indian villages where the indigenous people still wore huarache sandals and white cotton pants, hoping to make extra sales, *pueblitos* populated with low-slung adobe homes, dirt floors, and mesquite fences like the one where he'd met my mother. He dressed the part in which his ambitions cast him: a successful entrepreneur.

They met when she was twenty; she married him at thirty. Her mother told her she knew nothing about him or his people, that he was much older. She hesitated accepting his marriage proposal for many years. And yet, all the while, he patiently courted her: serenading her, always a gift in hand, and remembering her at every town in his sales territory by sending a postcard or letter.

"His head was full of ideas for starting businesses. He showed ambition" was her explanation for finally marrying him. That, and the fact that she was known as *la quedada*, literally translated as "the one left behind."

I don't remember when she found out he had a former wife and family. "It's in the past," he said, closing the subject.

She chose to believe him.

When I turned five, her best friend took her to see a child in a neighborhood not far from where we lived. He, too, had the familiar river-green eyes and the crooked nose. When she confronted her husband, he answered, "You are my only wife," surprised that his philandering would offend her.

This was the story I heard my mother tell many times as I was growing up in the Salinas Valley, where we had moved after she divorced him and married the man who became my stepfather.

I admit I liked hearing about my father, Tito; he seemed more a character in a movie than a flesh-and-blood man. My mother kept two black-and-white photos of Tito in a white envelope, mixed in with a letter from her beloved mother, a photo of herself as a young woman, and one of a nameless boyfriend her mother had declared unsuitable for marriage because he had been divorced. These were stored at the bottom of her blue travel case, covered with letters from home and important documents, like marriage and birth certificates, my school vaccination certificates, and report cards. Inside also lay a sad-looking, hand-size naked baby doll with a sweet round face and two nubs where her hands had been. I remember not liking this toy and leaving her outside, behind the metal tub in which my mother hand-washed clothes. The elements chipped at the bisque paint and crumbled the doll's extremities.

My mother saved it because "it was a gift from your father; I thought you might want to keep it." Also saved on my behalf: a tiny silver knife charm and a black stone that could "one day be a ring." It was a peculiar assortment of keepsakes, odd bits of unsalable inventory handed to a grateful little girl. I accepted the significance she conferred upon them, believing, as I'm sure was her intent, that I had been special to him.

I remember staring at his photos, searching for a hint of recognition. No matter how hard I looked, no spark ignited my memory.

I'd beg my mother to tell me more. She always complied with a warning: "Don't tell your father we talked about Tito."

"Why?" I'd ask.

"He wouldn't like it," she'd say firmly.

My stepfather was the opposite of my biological father. José Celedonio Garcia left a crowded barrio in one of Mexico City's poorest areas to enlist in the *bracero* program, the agricultural guest-worker program that started in the United States during World War II and lasted until the early '60s. He was an urban young man, used to the hustle and bustle of an already sprawling and overpopulated capital city, where he worked in his stepfather's struggling welding shop.

José longed for adventure. He wanted to visit the United States but had no money to travel. Like so many other immigrants with few options, he took a gamble. He had never been on a farm, nor did he know anything about agriculture, but he was strong and a hard worker, and those seemed to be the main criteria for the job.

His passport photo from 1954, the year he left for the United States, shows a high-cheeked, brown-skinned young man with slicked-back, wavy black hair and gentle brown eyes. The corners of his mouth are turned slightly upward, hinting optimism. He wears a stylish, boxy, shoulder-padded suit, like the kind Ricky Ricardo wore in early episodes of *I Love Lucy*; his shirt is white, knotted at the neck with a skinny, multicolored tie.

What dreams did he have when he pulled the suit off a hanger, rubbed the material between his fingers, and stared at his reflection on a narrow mirror in the crowded, chaotic *colonia* emporium? On what occasion did he imagine himself wearing that suit in the United States?

I can only remember seeing the suit hanging in the back of a closet, the thin, navy blue fabric faded and dulled by layers of fine dust that blew in from the nearby fields.

He was known as Pepe by my mother's family, a nickname for all men named José. To his boss, a Spaniard, he was Garcia, which he pronounced *Gar-thee-a*. His own family choose Cele, short for Celedonio. American acquaintances greeted him as Joe. My mother affectionately called him *Viejo*, Old Man, while the other farm workers respectfully addressed him as Don José. And, as a child, I avoided calling him Papa, mainly because my mother never told me what I was supposed to call him. "Tito is your real father," she had stated. She probably meant biological and was simply trying to make it understandable for a child. My childish logic concluded that if Tito was Papa, then José could not be Papa, too.

This reluctance did not mean I had a lack of affection for my stepfather. I had liked him immediately. We met him at the restaurant my mother's cousin owned, in the Salinas Valley town we visited after she left Tito. José was the only customer who made a special point to talk to me, and not just the adults. He came up with the idea that I should use a juice can to collect tips. When I produced one at his next visit, he ceremoniously reached into his pocket, lifted his hand to show me a shiny nickel, then dropped it in the tin can, where it spun around, making a pleasant clattering sound.

Later, when he proposed to my mother, she asked me if I would like him to be my father. "I won't marry him unless you like him," she declared. Even at age six, I felt it was too serious and weighty a decision to give a child. What did I know, other than that he was nice and gave me nickels? Was that enough for my mother to marry him?

Our life as a family was defined by our move from town, out to the farm where José was employed. He was offered a house, free of rent. "Imagine how much money we can save. We'll be able to buy our own home," he said, convincing my mother, who preferred living in town. We traded our three-room apartment, a short walk from everything we needed—groceries, the post office, friends, and school—to a five-room white clapboard cottage far from town.

Farm work was hard physical labor. Up at dawn every day, José laid miles of irrigation pipes, artfully plowed long, neat rows in the fields, hacked at recalcitrant weeds that sprouted before the crops began to grow, and drove tractors through whirlwinds of dust. When he wasn't in the fields, he was in the barn, fixing tractor engines, soldering tools, or repairing broken irrigation pipes. He built my mother a hutch, a walk-in chicken coop, and a carport for his car. "You are a very talented carpenter," my mother encouraged him.

When our car broke down, he never went to a mechanic. With only a book as a guide, he confidently took apart the engine until he figured out what was wrong. Then he expertly replaced the smallest, oddest-shaped part, down to the nuts and bolts. It was the only time the boss's three sons came over. They surrounded the hood and stood, heads bowed over the engine as if in prayer, to witness this mechanical miracle up close. The engine parts lay on the ground on top of a greasy tarp, strewn like pieces of a jigsaw puzzle.

"Gee whiz, Garcia, how'd you know that goes there?"

"Where you going to put that part?"

The boys bombarded him with questions as they shoved each other out of the way, in their excitement not to miss any part of the engine operation.

Standing near the tarp, away from the car, I felt my chest expand with pride at my stepfather's abilities. It felt good to know he was my dad.

My mother's sisters thought well of him, too. "*Es un buen macho*," they'd cluck approvingly. In Mexico, the term has a kinder connotation than in America. It ennobles men. It means they are good husbands, providers, hard workers, and bear their burdens in silence.

But it was this silence that proved to be a greater burden on my mother and me. My stepfather seemed incapable of communicating his feelings and troubles. Instead, he'd suddenly turn moody, taciturn, descending into a sullen silence. His behavior was confusing to me, and upsetting. Sometimes, like clouds passing through, his bad mood lifted quickly; other times, the storm settled within him, possessing him for days. The silence screamed throughout our small house, my mother and I nervous little mice, tiptoeing from one corner to another, waiting for the storm to pass. When my mother was able to cajole from him a reason for the silence, work-related complaints were generally the cause. The boss, a hard-driven Spaniard who dressed in nothing but khaki clothes (like a fascist, my mother pointed out), was impatient and mercurial. In the California fields, with this man in charge, the historical relationship between conquistador and Indian was re-created. And in the Mexican tradition, practiced from the time of the Aztecs, the worker swallowed whatever humiliations were dealt in situations he felt powerless to change.

My parents had their differences. My mother was entrepreneurial; my stepfather lacked ambition. She imagined buying and selling homes and using his carpentry talents; he feared overextending himself. She envisioned him opening his own car-repair shop; he dismissed it as a fantasy.

And then there was the money issue: He couldn't save any. Any time they gathered a small amount, there were multiple reasons to spend it: a new car, driving to Mexico to see the family, tools, cameras, gadgets.

My mother became troubled, unsure how to navigate the rough shores of their relationship. I was her confidante. "You are the only one I can talk to," she implored, but I felt burdened by what she shared. I wanted them to solve their problems, and for him to come home happy. I wanted her to stop crying.

"I walked away from one bad marriage."

"If it was so bad, why do you always say nice things about him?" I demanded.

"Because he is your father. Every time I look at you, I see him. You even have the same facial expressions and gestures—how is that possible? You've spent all your life with me!" She'd smile tenderly. "I can't hate him. He gave me you."

Over the years, she shared new details about Tito. He was born in Spain, had lived in New York; his father was Basque, his mother French. His parents owned a circus; he had grown up with servants. He had been a partner in one of the first radio stations in Mexico.

As an adolescent, I began to question these fractured bits of information. Was any of this even true?

After seven years on the farm, the boss gave up the lease. There was no question we would move into town. My mother sought seasonal work in the vegetable-packing sheds. With that income, her long-held dream of home ownership was achieved.

While my parents learned to negotiate their issues, I became a full-blown American teenager and introduced new drama into our lives. My emotions were like a dormant volcano: They churned and sputtered inside me, straining to explode. I focused all my hormonal rage at my stepfather.

I resented his continued mood swings as much as I did his wasteful spending, which kept us poor and made my mother cry in frustration. I hated the way he slurped his coffee and exclaimed, "Ahh" after each sip, burped like a bullfrog after each meal, farted in public, and snored so loudly the house seemed to shake every night. And most of all, I hated seeing him come home at night, denim overalls caked with dirt, eyes red-rimmed, hair covered with dust, shoulders slumped from grueling fatigue, and the feeling of overwhelming pity it evoked in me. I was seeing him through American eyes: as an aging field worker who, after so many years, still spoke heavily accented, sometimes unintelligible English, dressed in plaid shirts and checkered pants, and stubbornly held on to, even for a modernized Mexico, old-fashioned Mexican social values. Feeling my blazing eyes on him, he did not understand my hostility. It was now he who did not know what to do.

I went on my first date and he stopped talking to me for weeks. For good measure, he disabled my car to keep me from leaving the house. I'd comfort myself thinking, *After all, he's not my real father.*

I did not want my parents' life. I left for college, even though, at the last minute, José tried to bribe me into staying by offering a brand-new car if I attended the local community college. My mother was touched by his gesture. I was disgusted. He couldn't afford to pay for my college; how could he afford something they didn't even have? By now, my mother, who had wearied of her role as referee, agreed it was best for me to leave.

College allowed me to sprout wings. I followed my career dreams and my heart. I married my college sweetheart, and five years later, we had a daughter.

My parents mellowed as grandparents. They found their true calling in life. At thirty, being a wife, mother, and a broadcast journalist who had overcome my own struggles softened my hard edges. I became tolerant of my immigrant parents' idiosyncrasies, appreciative of their sacrifices, and understanding of their limitations.

I remember this interval in our lives as a season of harmony. After a drought of conversation, my mother and I had much to discuss about child rearing. José was endlessly content and patient playing with his grandchild. Our times together were filled with laughing, watching the antics of my toddler, and relaxed reminiscing about our past.

Then something totally unexpected happened. My cousin invited me to visit with our mothers' youngest sister, who had moved to Tijuana. It had been over ten years since I had seen my Aunt Melinda—much too long, I decided—and I quickly accepted the invitation. After the hugs and exclamations of "It's been too long," we fell easily into our familiar patter, reminiscing and gossiping, as if it had been only a month since we'd last seen each other.

Then, abruptly, as if remembering something she'd been meaning to tell me, my aunt dropped a bombshell. "Your father lives here."

"We see him at his store," her daughter added. "He's always dressed very nicely."

I was stunned. I had come to regard Tito as a book I'd read long ago, a work of fiction. Now here they were, my aunt and cousin, telling me he was a living, breathing human. "Does my mother know?"

"Well, yes," my aunt nodded. "He's been here a long time."

Intuitively, I understood why she would have omitted this fact from our conversations, and I made a spontaneous decision.

My father owned a curio shop in downtown Tijuana, the kind that caters to American tourists. My aunt informed me that he also owned a warehouse that stored his merchandise; he owned other properties as well. How did she know? He'd told her. "Still a braggart," she chuckled. My mother's family had never liked Tito.

"I want to meet him," I told them. "Can you take me to his store?"

I was nervous when we arrived. But with my two cousins, my aunt, and my cousin's husband, I was with my tribe, safe and supported. What would he say when he met me? Would he try to hug me? Would he disavow me? Even though I had watched all those movies about adult children finding their long-lost fathers, I wasn't clear about what I hoped the outcome for me would be.

My aunt took over once we were inside the store. "We want to see Tito."

"He's not here today," a young man replied politely, though he looked at our little group warily; it was obvious that we weren't customers.

"Where is he?" my four-foot-eleven aunt demanded.

"He's at home."

"His daughter is here to see him. Give us his phone number."

Clearly, I was not a daughter the clerk had met, and who knew if he even had a daughter with whatever number wife he had now? The young clerk stared at me, wide-eyed with curiosity; I felt myself blush. What was I doing here? Had I really thought this through?

Back in my aunt's home, I took a deep breath and dialed the number written on the back of the store's business card. All eyes were on me. My thoughts were blank, my emotions calm. A man answered. "May I speak to Tito del Castillo?" I stammered.

"Speaking. Who is this?" He had a strong, assured voice.

"I'm Rosela, Maria Luisa's daughter." I just couldn't say "your daughter."

He was obviously taken aback. "*Pero muchacha,* what are you thinking?" he started, then stopped. I could hear him organizing his words. "Well, it's unexpected, you know."

I giggled. Oh, God, how could I? I mentally shook myself, reminding myself of my mission. "I want to meet you. I'm here today with my aunt. Can I meet you at your store?"

"No, that's impossible today; I'm with my family. Can you come another day?"

"I'm just here today; then I return to the States."

"That's too bad. Some other time." He paused. "Well, goodbye."

The dial tone hummed like an angry bee. The phone was stuck to my ear, my hand incapable of setting it back in its cradle. I was shocked by the brevity of the conversation and by the wily way he had disposed of me, as one would a telemarketer: politely and quickly.

"He didn't want to see me," I laughed, making light of it to my mother when I returned home.

My mother's calm eyes darkened and then seemed to emit sparks like fireworks in Cinco de Mayo celebrations. Her mouth pursed and her nostrils flared as she spat out her response. "The *desgraciado* didn't want to see you? *Ese pinche cabron,* that fucking asshole, hasn't changed after all these years!" The barrage of expletives and the intensity with which she delivered them made me regret I had told her. My mother never swore.

"Mama, I don't care. He means nothing to me. It was more of a journalistic interest to learn about that side of my genes."

"*I* care," she told me. "He insulted you by not seeing you. He insulted me! Don't ever try to see him again!" She was angrier than I had ever seen her. Was it possible that after thirty years she had finally realized how much she hated him? That she no longer had to pretend for my sake?

I did try to see him again. I called several times. A woman always answered, and each time she told me patiently, in a bored voice, that he was no longer there and I was not to call anymore.

My husband, who had lost his own father at age three to a plane crash, thought I should pursue him, that I should show up in front of his house and ask him everything and anything I needed to know. Had his parents really owned a circus? What had they died of? Had he been born in Spain or Mexico? Had he loved my mother when they married? So many questions.

They remained unanswered. Two years later, my beloved mother died, and with her, my interest in Tito.

I was angry at her death. Why her? She was the one I was close to. Why not my stepfather? Nevertheless, my husband and I invited him to live with us. I was afraid he would perish living by himself. He didn't say yes or no, but he stayed for thirteen years. It was not always smooth, but he was always helpful. Another grandchild was born, my second daughter. He relished his role as grandfather.

As my daughters grow, I observe that he acts the same way with them as he did with me, yet they have none of my hang-ups. They are not embarrassed by their old-world *abuelo*. They ignore his teasing that so irritated me. They are oblivious to the coffee slurping. His bedroom is their hangout.

His moody personality still makes an appearance, but it does not control me. I press him into conversations that used to make him uncomfortable. What kept him from buying and fixing houses? What was it like being a *bracero*? What made him so angry when I was young? He does not hesitate in answering any and all questions. He opens wide the doors to his interior life, no longer ashamed or too prideful to show his vulnerability. He is a simple and uncomplicated man who strove to do the best he could with what he had, and never pretended to be someone he wasn't.

He spends the last years of his life helping his friend Margarita with her restaurant in San Francisco's Mission district. He helps her open it every morning and serves a free breakfast to a group of elderly neighborhood women who can't afford to pay. He stays in the restaurant throughout the day, chatting with the regulars, doling out advice to young men and women who seek him, and offering words of wisdom. He is the sage of Margarita's Restaurant. Always punctual, he returns home to pick up his younger granddaughter from after-school care. Every day he takes her to the neighborhood grocery store for a snack, where, she tells me, they call her "a very important customer" and give her extra treats. He remembers to buy a snack to bring to his elder granddaughter, now a teenager but still a little girl to him. He is seventy-nine years old and has achieved a pleasant rhythm in his life.

Margarita tells me that they enjoyed an outing, going to all the places that have significance to him: the houses he lived in in the Salinas Valley, the house in which my first daughter was born, the park where my parents wheeled her to play.

"Recojiendo sus pasos." Margarita shakes her head sadly, referring to the Mexican expression "retracing your footsteps," a superstition that states you visit old haunts as a way to say goodbye to this world before leaving for the next.

And, as if it were a prophecy, he passes away a week later.

It is my duty to go through his things, deciding what papers to keep, what clothes are to be donated, and what items will be given to family or kept for the granddaughters. I find his wallet in the nightstand. It is filled with the usual items—driver's license, credit cards, photos of the granddaughters, and a few dollars. Tucked into a side pocket is a piece of paper folded into a small square. Unfolding reveals a yellowed, brittle newspaper article. It is a story that was written years ago about my receiving an award. At the top of the article he has written the date and, in his elegant script, the words *My daughter, Rosela.*

TINA

Karen Quinn

I have no memory of the very first time my father looked at me the way fathers do, with eyes that said *I love you*, but I do remember the last. It was three days before he died. Mom had called the night before. "You'd better come now. It's almost time."

I packed in a rush, leaving my husband and two small children, flying from New York to Denver, never believing for a second that the end would come. For six months, he had been fighting pancreatic cancer. Intellectually, I knew that it was terminal. Still, it never occurred to me that he would actually die.

Only a month earlier, he had awakened in the middle of the night to go to the bathroom and had collapsed on the floor, hitting his head. Blood gushed from the wound. Mom called an ambulance and he was rushed to Rose Hospital. The next day was Valentine's Day. From his bed, he called my brother, Michael, to his side. He managed only a whisper. "Do me a favor. Go over to

International Villa and buy your mother something really special from me. I don't want her to think I forgot." He adored my mother. They were married almost fifty years, with a four-year divorce break in the middle. Issues over money, communication, and trust had breached their relationship, but the years apart made them realize how much they loved each other. Their remarriage was the happiest time in both their lives.

It was a crazy day in the hospital after Dad's fall, with blood transfusions and tests. Dad checked back with Michael. "Have you gone shopping yet? Don't forget. I promise I'll pay you back." Michael found it endearing that Dad kept assuring him that he'd be repaid. He finally slipped out and bought a beautiful crystal perfume bottle, which my father proudly gave to Mom that night. (Michael told me that the one thing he wanted from my mother after she passes on is that perfume bottle. Dad never did pay him back.)

Now, with the end near, I arrived in Denver. The light was low in my parents' bedroom when I spotted him, a slight lump in the rented hospital bed, his head resembling a skull on the pillow. His lips were pursed as if he'd eaten something sour; his eyes opened and closed and then rolled back in their sockets so that only the whites were visible. My father, Sonny Nedler, was nowhere to be found in those eyes. Michael stood behind me. "He's in a coma. He doesn't know who we are." I didn't know this was what a coma looked like.

The lump in my throat swelled and hardened all at once. I sat by my father's side and took his hand, kissing it. "Daddy, I'm here. It's Karen. I'm right next to you. I love you so much." His head twisted, his face contorted. I prayed he wasn't in pain. Then, all at once, he opened his eyes and focused on mine. He was back, no question. He beheld me with the same eyes that used to twinkle when he laughed, the eyes that would pierce my heart when he caught me doing something wrong, the eyes that regarded me with so much love just before he gave me away at my wedding.

Our gazes locked. He gasped slightly and started to smile. This encounter took one second, maybe less, but he saw me. He knew I was there. I knew he knew I was there. Then he slipped back into his morphine-induced state. It was an eye blink, a moment I never articulated to anyone, but the image imprinted itself on my mind forever. When I think of my father dying, this is what I remember: that second our eyes locked and he told me with those eyes that he loved me for that very last time.

The next night, we cradled him as he took his last breath. Only then did his face relax and he looked like our father again. But of course, he wasn't there.

I've always been a firm believer (well, hoper) in reincarnation. When the rabbi came to talk to us about the funeral, I asked him what Jews thought about whether the spirit lives on after death. I wanted him to affirm my desire that Dad would somehow live on, to tell me something that would ease my grief. He explained that our brand of Judaism didn't believe in that, although Madonna's did. Gently, he touched my shoulder and said, "But don't you worry, your father will live in your heart forever." I remember feeling terribly disappointed that he could do no better than a Chinese fortune cookie.

Despite what the rabbi said, some highly suspicious incidents led us to believe that Dad's spirit was with us after he passed. The night Dad died, my grandmother's potted flowers flew off her kitchen counter and over a coffee table, making a huge mess all over the floor. When Mom walked into the kitchen the next morning, lightbulbs exploded around her. On the day we buried him, as I was putting on my mascara, the bulbs around the bathroom mirror began blinking, as if to say, *Don't bother, you'll just end up with raccoon eyes.* He was right. I did.

In the months after Dad's funeral, I oscillated between life as usual and bouts of terrible sadness. There was a job to attend to, a husband to care for, two young children who needed me. Tears came easily, especially at the end of the day as I lay in bed. About six months after he died, I had a vivid dream about him. We were trudging up a mountain, carrying backpacks filled with rocks. Exhausted, we finally reached the top, our muscles burning with pain. The backpacks came off and my father took my hand in his. Suddenly, we were flying. Weightless and free, I tightened my grip as we soared above the landscape, light as air. In my sleep, my father's hand felt as real as the pillow beneath my head. It felt so solid that I thought I must have grabbed my husband's hand. As I regained consciousness, I was certain the experience had been real, that my father had been there and had taken me in flight as if to say, *Look, no pain. See, I'm free!*

After that dream, I was dogged by a sense of unknowing that I couldn't shake. Was it really Dad who had visited me, or was I that desperate to believe he was okay? What had become of him? Had the beautiful soul that had been Sonny Nedler disappeared forever when he took his last breath? I wished I could talk to him for just one hour to find out what he had been up to, spirit-wise. What was heaven like? Did he look in on me often? Had he heard I was writing a book? Would anyone besides Mom ever read it? Did he know that Don (his youngest son, my brother) had been diagnosed with cancer? Was he putting in a good word with God to make Don better? Why couldn't someone invent a telephone that connected us with our loved ones on the other side? Apple? AT&T? Anyone? Anyone?

My friend Lois told me about a psychic from England. Like Cole in *The Sixth Sense*, she saw dead people. She spoke to them, too. "The woman's phenomenal," Lois promised. "And for only $200. She's coming to my office next month to read for me. Do you want an appointment?" Naturally, I said yes. I would have paid ten times that if I could have known for certain that I would speak to my father on the other side.

It was a rainy day in November when Marie and I met in Lois's conference room. I had been expecting someone along the lines of Stevie Nicks—flowing robes, wild curly hair, and a witchy persona. Instead, she was the opposite—speaking in a clipped English accent, wearing a crisp gray suit and white orthopedic shoes. As we sat at the conference table beneath the fluorescent lights, she asked me to concentrate on the person I most wanted to hear from. Closing my eyes, I conjured my father, very much alive, smiling and laughing, his eyes sparkling. I twisted the ring on my left finger, the one I'd remade using the diamond he always wore.

"There is a male presence in the room," Marie said. "He's older, has gray curly hair. He wants you to know that he was met by relatives on the other side, his father and a matronly woman."

Yes, yes, I thought, my heart racing. He must mean Poppy Jay. And Grandma has to be the matronly woman he's talking about, although she had lost weight before she died. But maybe she gained it back in heaven.

"He's telling me that he's been spending time with a good friend who passed after he did," Marie added. "Do you know who I mean?"

I nodded, thinking he must be with his old pal from Chicago who had died six months after he did. I was happy to think that they had found each other.

"He wants you to send his love to a person who was very important in his life. The name begins with an M. Michael?" she suggested.

"Okay," I said. She had to mean my brother Michael. I wondered why he didn't mention Don, my other brother.

"He's apologizing to your mother for something he did twenty years ago," Marie said.

I wasn't sure what he meant. An affair? Underwear left on the floor? The skeptic in me thought a psychic apologizing on behalf of her spirit was making a pretty safe bet.

The reading went on for another twenty minutes. The part of me that wanted to believe interpreted about half of what the male presence said in ways that made perfect sense. The other half was a puzzle, as though the psychic were pulling names and bits of information from an ethereal blender.

"Who is Hazel?" Marie said. "There is a woman named Hazel that he wants to acknowledge."

"I have no idea," I said. Surely he couldn't mean Hazel the maid, from that TV show in the '60s. I used to love watching her on Sunday nights. The dad, Mr. B, the wife, Missy, the boy, Sport, and that dog, Smiley: the quintessential American family, except they could afford a sassy maid. Why would Dad bring her up?

"He's spending lots of time with a gentleman named Bennett. Do you know who that is?"

I shook my head, confused. Could she mean Bennett Cerf, the president of Random House, who used to be on *What's My*

Line? Dad had read me Dr. Seuss books; Random House published them. As a kid, I always watched *What's My Line?* Kitty Carlyle was my favorite panelist, what with those fancy blindfolds she had. Could that be the connection? It seemed awfully tenuous. I was stretching.

"Listen," I began. "The male presence in the room, it could be my father. Or maybe it isn't. I don't know. A lot of what he's saying is right on. But a lot of it makes no sense. Can you ask him to say something that will let me know in no uncertain terms that he's here?"

Marie nodded and psychically asked the spirit-who-could-be-my-father to prove it to me. Her eyes widened and she became physically agitated. Gasping, she cried out, "Who is taking his watch?"

"Huh?"

"Someone is trying to take his watch from him, and he's not ready to give it up. But he can't speak for himself. He can only speak with his eyes. He's telling this person not to take his watch. Who is trying to take it from him?"

The reading was unraveling by the second. How could I have believed this woman? I wondered. There was no way to stretch anything in my life to fit that crazy story about the watch. "I have no idea what you're talking about," I said. But still, I hoped. "Ask him to say something else."

Marie sighed. Once again, she appeared to engage the spirit psychically. "Ah, he said that I should just say 'Tina.'"

My heart plunged to the industrial carpeting at my feet. *"He said what?"*

"He wants me to say 'Tina' to you. Does that mean anything?"

My God! It made perfect sense. Tina was my father's dog, a white Lhasa apso, the sweetest dog you could ever know. He had adored Tina and treated her like his favored child. When Marie said Tina's name, shivers went down my spine. (They *really* did, or I wouldn't say it because it's such a cliché.) There was not another thing my father could have said that would have been more telling. At that moment, I knew his spirit was in the room.

As soon as I got to my office, I called my mother and Michael. They worked together in the family business, a jewelry store in Denver. I couldn't wait to tell them what had happened—Dad had spoken to me from the other side. His spirit was with us and he was doing well. We could all stop worrying about him.

"He said 'Tina,'" I cried. "Only Dad would know to say 'Tina.'"

My family was impressed. I went on to relate the rest of the reading to them. When I recounted the story about the watch, my brother gasped. "*He said what?*" So I repeated it.

"Oh my God," Michael said. "I never told this to anyone, but on the afternoon Dad died, I looked over at him and noticed that he was wearing his gold watch. I thought I'd better take it off him because he was in a coma and, well, he didn't need it. Plus, his wrists were so frail, remember? I thought the watch might be hurting him. But when I went over and started to unclasp the band, he opened his eyes and gave me a look that made it clear he didn't want it off. So I stopped. It happened so fast. It was a moment, less than a second. But it's the strongest memory I have of the day he died."

I was floored. I'd had my less-than-a-second last moment with Dad, and so had Michael. Neither of us had ever talked about it, and I understood why. It was nothing and everything at the same time. It was a flash of connection that had unspeakable meaning to each of us because it was the very last communication we'd ever had with our father. If the psychic were to be believed, that connection was equally meaningful to Dad. He had spoken his last words with his eyes: *It isn't time. Don't take my watch!*

After seeing the psychic, I made a kind of peace with my father's death. I don't visit his grave, because the one thing I *am* certain of is this: He's not there. Knowing Dad, he would prefer to swing by my apartment on Miami Beach. He visits Mom and Michael in the mountains of Colorado. He checks in on Don in Dallas. Then he goes back to whatever he's doing in heaven. When Mom's boyfriend, Marvin, passed last month, I'm sure Dad was there to greet him, to thank him for taking such good care of her for so long. Last week, we got word that Shirley, the wife of his best friend, had died. Dad was there to ease her journey.

Do I really believe this? I want to. I choose to. Am I sure? No. Maybe death is one big sleep without dreams. I hope not. It's hard to hold on to the belief that my father's spirit lives on, that he's meeting and greeting new arrivals to heaven while checking in on us from time to time. That takes enormous faith. But for me, it's even harder to accept that a random psychic in the days before Google would make two wild guesses about my father that would be so right on—his dog's name and a story that had never been told about a moment in time when two people argued with their eyes over the taking of a watch and all that it stood for.

HE SAID WHAT?: GREATEST HITS

Pam Houston

1. I'm usually attracted to women with thinner wrists.

2. I'd like to give you a big kiss right now, but I've got a mouth full of chew.

3. You're my girlfriend; I'm the one who gets to say what looks good on you.

4. I've just been sitting here looking over my life insurance policy, and it seems that there's no way I'm going to benefit from the money I'm putting in here every month. So if you want the thirty grand after I'm dead, I think it's only fair that you start making the payments.

5. My wee-wee touched your buns.

6. Well, bitch, then I want my pizza back.

7. Any chance you would consider a threesome?

8. Don't tell your mother.

9. I love you, but you are just too smart.

10. I need to perform an exorcism on you at the W Hotel in Chicago.

11. I am so deeply afraid that I am nothing but weak and worthless. So I take the people who want to get close to me and try to break them, so they become as weak and as worthless as me.

12. You know, you would get a lot further in life if you just learned how to fake it a little.

13. If you leave me, I will kill you.

14. Well, in that case, we'd better get back to Colorado before they change the abortion laws.

15. If you leave me, I will kill myself.

16. Would you be okay if I needed to wander in the desert for a year or two on a vision quest?

17. When D. H. Lawrence did it, you thought it was sexy.

18. I love you so much, it would be okay with me if you never said another word.

19. You are so beautiful on the inside.

20. You are so beautiful when I'm inside you.

21. You are either with us or against us in the fight against terror.

22. Frankly, I just don't think you are spiritually advanced enough for me.

23. Women in third-world countries are used to being treated so badly, they actually think I'm treating them well.

24. I want to say this in a way that makes you think I am a normal person.

25. All those Wednesday nights when I told your mother I was at the poker game, I was really across the tracks at the cathouse. It was so dark in there, you were lucky to find your pants when you were finished. It was so dark in there, you could only see the whites of their eyes.

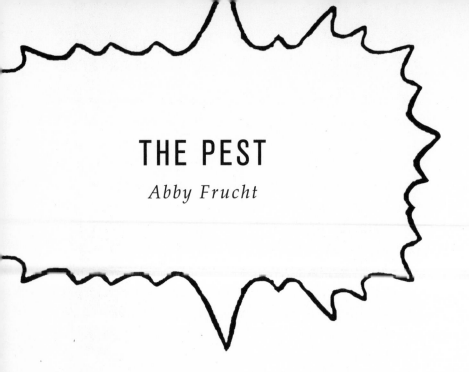

THE PEST

Abby Frucht

It begins with a pestilence of flies.

Every May in Oshkosh, from underneath the mercurial eye of Lake Winnebago, there emerge a zillion flies, each smaller than your favorite dangly earring. Reeking of the sturgeon in whose feeding grounds they've hatched, the flies are so numerous that at the height of the two-week season, houses turn black, cars skid on winged corpses that blanket the roads, and if you step outside for long enough to fetch the day's mail, you become the unenviable star of your own horror movie. When hatching season ends and you shovel the carcasses off your backyard patio, you need two Hefty bags to cart them away. Then you power-wash the house, blasting off goop like a sticky black felt that oozes green sludge.

Of the few good things that might be said of these animals, they never bite and they lower the property value enough that people like my husband and I could afford a house on the water, an optimistic investment representing a doomed effort to rescue our marriage.

On the other hand, it's the flies who introduce me to Rick, who looks like George Clooney. I'm shopping for a power-hose attachment in Rick's family's Home Construction Emporium, when an X-shaped man, his blue jeans vivid with compressed, wholesome energy, steps up to show me how to screw the parts together. As if startled to find, amid the aisles of hardware, the only other flesh and blood for acres around, he offers in earnest, "You slide this male component into this female component," then pauses, flustered, assessing my Darwin-esque get-up, cutoffs with tights, survival of the desperate-est.

I don't know whom I'd imagined I was dressing for that day—not my husband, certainly. Even were my divorce not already a foregone conclusion, it would've become one soon after, I on my back on the desk in Rick's office amid blueprints for drafting structurally sound houses, an irony contrived as if to cast blame on him for my crumpling domicile.

I move into a scrappy upper on Irving Street, blocks from the lake and a slog in snowy Wisconsin winters, the driveway as vast as the Siberian railroad. To clear it on school days, I use the same dented snow shovel I'd used on flies. Rick owns a plow, but since he no longer needs to fight for my affections, he only speeds past to dig out his sister, betting I won't catch sight of him from over the snowdrifts. Like every proper Wisconsin male, he owns a tow hookup, too, but when my car won't start on the coldest day in January, he scoffs, "A published author keeps less than a quarter tank of gas in minus-twenty-degree temps?!" Plus, he hates my unpatriotic Saab, which used to be my parents'. They've shipped it to me so I'll have something safe to drive, like when I drive to Rick's new house, whose principal appeal seems to be how far away it is from Irving Street.

When, after months of pretending not to be ditching me, Rick finally instructs me to leave him alone, I have to travel fifteen miles to bang on his door. On occasion he relents and lets me in, grimacing just enough that I can see the unusually long canine teeth, like vampire fangs, of which he is giddily, savagely proud, often opening wide to display the gleaming points. "I saw you out Rollerblading today. You look like a dork in that helmet thing," he might comment, as fondly as he is able, while leading me to bed. Then he'll turn on some Eagles and sing to me during lovemaking, the whispered lyrics like stones dropped into the well of my gullibility.

My younger son in kindergarten, I have no clue how immature I am, so pathetically fretful, skinny, and wan that a close friend asks, on our way to buy groceries one afternoon, "Abby, do you think maybe you're anorexic?"

My answer is no, I am only in love.

When my sisters and I were children, we built a ladder out of twigs for training our pet newt to climb. For days we'd scoop him up, perch him precariously on the bottom rung, and give a gentle set of nudges, coaxing one bubble toe up at a time. Exercising our rights to the fantasy world of childhood, we believed our newt was climbing to please us, just as, exercising my right to the irrationality of adulthood, I believe that if Rick sings "After the Thrill Is Gone" into a certain opening leading into my body, it means the thrill is back again. It isn't, though.

I run into him escorting a prettier girl around Hollywood Video. She's creamier than I, not so trashily dressed, her legs not as bony, her feet newly shod. She doesn't glance twice in my crest-fallen direction. Nevertheless, later that week, my doorbell buzzes at midnight, Rick's self-appointed hour for showing up unannounced. Wearing only a scarf that I've knotted sarong-style, I nearly tumble downstairs in my hurry to greet him. Will he stay the night this time? And will he tell me, like last time, "You're still the best"?

Though I feel sorry for Rick when he says such things, especially since at this year's Construction Emporium Employee Awards party, Rick's favorite employee confided in me that the other employees hated Rick, thinking him an even bigger pisshead than his brothers, and though I take this as my calling to protect Rick from himself (in my sarong-style nightie, which is really a pashmina my parents bought me, I'm determined to bring out the best in him, *the dark and the light*, the *better let somebody love you before it's too late* in him), I still gird myself against him when I open the door, which snags the carpet, baring a splinter of raw pine board. But Rick isn't there. On the porch stands a fat man I've never seen before, his breathing adenoidal, his eyeglasses murky with fingerprints, his faded, flecked jacket zipped improperly. Beyond him the sidewalks stretch empty and dark, but for a street lamp marking where I fell on my ass on Valentine's Day.

"Hello, Abby," breathes the enormous stranger. "I was just passing by. I recognized your address from the telephone book."

"Hello, Greg," I make myself say to this most unwelcome, in-the-flesh version of the mentally disabled person who's been phoning me monthly to ask my advice about a sequel he's writing for *Lost in Space*, the television drama that hasn't seen airtime since

1968. I've always been kind in putting Greg off, too kind, I now see, the door open between us on twisted hinges, the Lors snoring behind me in their downstairs apartment—nine Hmong family members of four generations, in three remarkable soundproofed rooms. My own boys are at their dad's tonight, so at least if Greg forces his way inside, they won't fall prey to his fourth-grade mind with its hundred-year girth.

"Go home, Greg," I plead, my prior pleadings to Rick to call me, visit me, love me, want me, marry me becoming instantly, absurdly insignificant by comparison. It's not Rick I need; it's staying alive in one piece I need.

The front door has no lock. On jelly legs, I push it as shut as it goes and try to walk back upstairs without showing my bottom. Then I bolt the upstairs lock behind me and don't peek out the window to watch Greg go.

The same friend who asked me if I might be anorexic asks if it's possible Rick's confusion over me has to do with money. Aside from the hopeful spin of "confusion," I'm not sure what she means, his money or mine. And if it's mine she's talking about, is it the fact I have lots more money than she has, or a lot less than Rick? Money's such a dicey subject between her and me, I even wonder if she means to chip away at a more central issue, like how much money *do* I have, anyway? And how about my parents, with their gifts of used cars and birthday checks, the unspoken promise of an inheritance, that IRA they're safekeeping with the exclusive New York broker introduced to them by the family eye doctor? Not wanting to disturb the broker with ignorant questions, since he's a private sort of broker, a secretive wizard, they hardly ever even call him. "We're afraid he'll boot us out,"

Dad exclaims in his elfin way, while Mom stammers, blushing, as embarrassed by money as she is by sex.

But if it's money Rick's hung up about, which irks him more: my momentary poverty or my frugally banked retirement savings? My penny pinching or my chronic debt-free-ness? On my birthday, he enthuses over his "homemade" gift to me, a Prince CD he mixed himself.

"A college teacher still uses a tape player?!" he asks, after I've unwrapped the clumsy package. Then he replays the scene in the movie we're watching, *The Crow*, where lead actor Brandon Lee gets shot by mistake with a loaded weapon. He's watched this same scene six times. "That's the shot!" Rick shouts, over and over. "That's it! Right here! He really dies right here! I can't get over this. I can't stop watching it. It blows me away. What does that say about me?" he asks, pressing rewind again.

"It's not money Rick's hung up about," I answer my friend, her tarot cards spread on the table between us. "It's his mom. She died in childbirth. With him."

For their motherlessness, Rick grew up feeling he was blamed by his brothers; and for making him a widower, he felt he was blamed by his father. The most guilt-ridden day of all is his birthday, which is also, come to think of it, the date we first hooked up on his desk at the Emporium. Because of his tragic history, this need to watch Brandon Lee die over and over still impresses me, even now, as being poignant, dramatic, mythical. Like Rick's canine teeth, those two vampire fangs, Lee's death marks him as if by thirst, by sorrow.

A cat purrs beside me in my friend's living room. The tarot cards turn up four Broken Hearts in four separate readings. It's 1996, but the years, like life, go on. I write my books, raise my boys, teach my classes, join the YMCA, and start dating again. I don't regret my divorce. The only thing I regret is not asking my ex for alimony.

A s I'm walking out the door to meet this new man I'm dating, who likes to take me out sailing—the boat tied midlake to a friend's matching boat so we can dance on the linked decks in twilight, wineglasses in hand—my telephone rings.

We'll marry, Rick begs "I've made so many mistakes. We'll quit our jobs, or I will if you don't want to," and his money will be my money and he'll help me do my taxes and I'll be on his health plan and so will my kids, and he'll do anything for me and he'll be-say-fix-buy anything I want, and we'll live off his early retirement in Europe for the rest of our lives.

I have no wish to tour Europe for the rest of my life, nor quit my job, nor leave the little bungalow I bought for the boys and myself with no advice or help from anyone, not even my parents, who, since Dad retired, have been living off his IRA. It's still in the custody of that secretive broker, about whom Dad sometimes asks, of no one in particular, tilting his querulous head to speak, as if the air itself might answer, "And how's Bernie doing for us these days?" Rick admits I chose an adorable house, despite the noisy location ("The lady with the Saab buys a house on Main Street?!"), but my friend with the tarot cards paled when she saw it: It's the spitting image of the place she grew up in. Plus, it has bats.

"The boys are on their dad's insurance. And do I park them at prissy Italian boarding schools or leave them behind?" I ask. As for Rick's being anything, much less everything, for me, I snort at the concept, though I do love Leonard Cohen's "I'm Your Man."

Then will I at least join him for an evening in Milwaukee to see how I feel? We'll eat, get a room, catch up on old times.

"We don't have old times," I tell him.

For a moment I consider a walk to the grocery store for an onion and a dollar tub of chicken livers. I do this only on nights when the boys are having dinner at their dad's. You dredge the livers in flour, pepper them, fry them up. Then, wrapped in freshly laundered sweats with a good book to read, you're a giant red blood cell, a self-sufficiency machine.

Watching the porter wheel our overnight bags across the fancy Milwaukee hotel lobby, I pull a tip from my wallet, as if to earn some stake in this ill-advised experiment. Our parents took me and my sisters to Portugal when we were girls, girls in embroidered Swiss dresses with attached velvet vests. The guidebook promised "a small train running between hotel and beach," but it was clear right away that, rather than shuttling the guests to and fro, the commercial locomotive on its industrial tracks cut a noisy swath between the sooty hotel and a distant view of ocean. As a girl, I winced at Mom's disappointment, but now I'm vexed like she was, suspecting a trick, even if the trick is a mistranslation instead of a lie.

When Rick turns to face me inside the hotel room, he looks uncommonly meek, or maybe I just now notice his meekness, the x-shape of him suddenly revealed to me as being lowercase. I feel squeamish to find him shrunken in this fashion. I'm reminded of my dad, now smaller than I am and losing his grip—his pants too big, his desk haunted by sheaves of neglected papers—and whose memory, fading, will in time disappear, leaving nothing behind but kernels of sweetness. Unlike Dad, Rick, shrinking, will leave nothing behind, not even courtliness, since what I once mistook for courtliness was really his skill at hiding how nervous he was. I have loved him in error, the way I sometimes love a story I'm writing that can't be revised, a story that has failed me or that I have failed.

A mother might stick by Rick unconditionally, but with so much else ahead of me, there is nothing worth my clinging to in this lackluster hotel room but the challenge between us, some fifteen inches of space across which we position ourselves like thumb wrestlers. Even once we're in bed, I am not dismayed in coming to this tardy realization, only wary, seeing in his face the same thoughts he sees in mine. "Well, we needed to see how we felt," he remarks too lightly, our bodies itchy beneath the uncomfortable comforter. I flash back to a night on the sailboat with that man I'm sort of dating. Our dates are puritanical so far, although I do take some trouble to gaze up his shorts when he climbs the mast.

"*We* needed to see how *we* felt?" I ask Rick. I had thought that we needed to see how *I* felt. I had thought Rick's marriage proposal was why we were here.

"When does Lindsay get back?" it occurs to me to ask. Lindsay is one of his other not-quite-ex-girlfriends, out of town for a while. She's back, he admits. She suffers from terrible depression. "She's not doing too good." If a decade of emails still needs to go by before I realize how sloppy Rick's diction is, and if, in my mind, his emails read even more poorly than they do in reality, I still find them adorable: *Just wanted to say because i was thinking about you, and how i miss you that i use to love our talks when i would stop over and chat. L Rick.*

"She's at my house," he tells me. "I'm all she has. She has nowheres else to go except church. That's something that bugs me, I admit. Your atheism."

"No doubt," I quip. "Like what bugs me is your lapsed Catholicism. Or is it your lapsed Lutheranism? Sorry. I forget."

On the drive home that night, we stop at a sports bar teeming with belligerent fans. I insist on buying my seafood platter, in order to pay too much for it.

Just before bed on December 11, 2008, I turn on the kitchen laptop to learn that "Prominent Wall Street Investor Bernard Madoff has been arrested for allegedly running a $50 billion 'Ponzi scheme' in what may rank among the biggest fraud cases ever."

"I'm finished," Madoff is quoted as saying, and that his books are "all lies."

What this news boils down to is that Dad's IRA, his entire life savings of $1 million, was transformed overnight to exactly $4.62. They'll get none of it back but a theft-loss deduction from the IRS. My sisters and I hold power of attorney. Frail, penniless, and demented, our parents call their walkers "little cars," but they'll have no place to park them if we can't find a way to retrieve some money.

Since I don't generally email Rick—since, rather, it is he who can't let go of the self-negating prospect of us, he who emails every four or five months to "catch up on old times" and to remind me that for seven years running I've forgotten his birthday—instead of emailing to tell him of my family's changed fortune, I watch my fingers play mutely at the keyboard, like striking flat notes on an air piano. There's a girl who shows up at the cul-de-sac near this house I've been sharing for eight years now with my new and (let's hope) final boyfriend, Chuck. She's five. The cutest thing is how she falls. She'll be standing among kids, parents, dogs, bicycles, when all at once she'll tip over like a potted plant. Someone will tilt her back up, brush her off, and leave her to tip back over again. Like her, we fall, are stood up again, brush ourselves off again.

Hi prettu lady! Just wanted to ask how r you and the boys and chuck. Lindsay's doing terrible with her depression, the doctors cant help. her they just keep doing the same tests at, least i still have my land to go too, her depression is getting harder on my but i don't let on I just stay at the land. I still think of you all the time and hop were still friends. Maybe wecan have lunch. i want you to know i still read every night. Rit now I'm realling Cell. I don't know if I told you my brother had a heart attach. It's was pretty bad to deal with but he's going to be. Okay. Let me know if you want to have lunch next week I'd still do anything fo r youu. how r the folks., my dad hardly even works on his cars any more What are you and chuck up to it never ceses to amaze me your boys are all grown upHow about i take you to lunch next week to, catch up on old times?

The friend who asked if Rick's confusion had to do with money is unusually discreet when it comes to asking how things are with Chuck, probably since Chuck's and my style of being mostly perfectly happy together invites little explanation. "That's bad, hon," he said when I told him my parents' money was gone. Then he gave me a hug and continued unpacking his hunting gear.

Since this rambling house we share is on the lake just south of where I lived with my ex, we shop-vac the flies off the deck in May, vacuum them off the kitchen ceiling, then turn off all the lights and sit in the dark so they'll invade us no further. Maybe the classes I took in biology prepped me for regarding these million insects—their legs like bent wires, their ignoble postures—as lessons in the avoidance of cynicism. Just because they exist to screw, reproduce, muck up all available surfaces, and die doesn't mean we do.

"Did you say yes to lunch with Rick because you want to know if he still cares about you, or to reassure yourself you no longer care so much about him?" my friend does not ask. The thing about this friend is she keeps her own secrets, at least I think she does, only she's so secretive, I'm not sure. I wonder if the reason she asks so many questions is that she suspects I keep secrets, too. She hopes to investigate them not so much in order to learn what they are, but to show herself to be the more vigilant secret-keeper.

I said yes to lunch because I want to watch him squirm. I said yes to lunch because I want him to feel guilty about being too much of a cheapskate to offer help for my parents after saying he'd do anything for me all these years, even though I wouldn't take it.

I square my shoulders while making my way to the table, half-coaching myself to turn down an envelope stuffed with cash. But he looks deflated, like George Clooney pinched in the wrong places.

"You're still beautiful," he says, and then he tells me Lindsay's worse and that she won't get out of bed and that they had sex once last year and how unhappy he is.

"You do look unhappy," I observe, conscious of our waitress hovering nearby. I *don't* keep secrets, and anyway the waitress probably hears these kinds of conversations all the time. I was once a waitress, too. Once, a married guy slipped me a note to pass to his mistress at lunch that day.

"Why are you still with Lindsay, then? You only live once."

"Maybe," he says.

I'd forgotten he likes to imagine we all get second chances. It always throws me for a loop, mainly because he means it. "I wonder if you're part of why Lindsay's depressed," I say as gently as I can.

Funny that Madoff hasn't come up, and that we're not, it seems, going to talk about my parents or their terrible loss, their frightening change in circumstance, their unpredictable future. When you sit down with someone maybe twice in a decade, the talk had better steer straight to the heart of things, and not even my dread for my parents' well-being belongs in the heart of this thing with Rick, which beats too feebly to include it. Wordlessly, I place my parents in some other, more frequently visited chamber, a place that has nothing to do with him, but that my sisters and I must occupy for years to come.

So I will have the chance neither to turn down Rick's help nor to rebuke him for not having offered it, nor to feel dirty for accepting it, nor to chastise myself for forcing a mixture of things not meant to blend. I chew on this new set of facts a moment, adjusting the lettuce on my grilled fish sandwich. "I mean, maybe Lindsay would get stronger if you'd just break up with her already and let her live her own life and quit blaming her for all your own regrets," I say. "Have you ever thought of that?"

He doesn't shrug off this question. He doesn't even blink. "I think of it all the time," he says. "It's just," he adds, and now he does shrug a little, "I guess I must love her."

We agree that he must. I finish my sandwich. I order more wine. He's paying.

FATHER KNOWS BEST
. . . NOT!

BJ Gallagher

"**S**he looks just like her daddy," people often said when I was a girl. I was tall, blond, and blue-eyed, with an Irish face. People's comments about my resemblance to Dad made me feel so warm and happy inside—Dad was my hero. I was eager to please him and worked hard to win his approval. I longed to be Daddy's Little Girl. I wanted him to dote on me as his little princess, but he didn't. Don't get me wrong, he did love me—just not in the way I longed for. The thing I wanted most in life was for Daddy's face to light up when he saw me, but it never did.

In college, I recall reading the work of biologist Konrad Lorenz about imprinting in ducks. When ducklings are very young, there is a critical phase in their development when they imprint on their caretaker, bonding to and following the adult. When the adult caretaker is Mama Duck, that's great. But if their caretaker happens to be human, the young ducklings imprint on the human, following him around as if he were Mom. And if the caretaker tries to rebuff and reject the ducklings, imprinting becomes even stronger as the ducklings work harder to follow. That's what happened between my father and me. The harder I tried to please him, the more elusive his approval became. Every time I got close to meeting his expectations, he raised the bar.

My dad doesn't really like children—he didn't even like his own very much. He thought children were just miniature adults. When they didn't behave like adults, he was harsh and punishing. He didn't spank, and hit only rarely, preferring to use his words instead. I discovered that old saw about "sticks and stones will break my bones but words can never hurt me" is baloney. Words hurt—and Dad's words hurt a lot.

"My stooped daughter," he teased about my posture. By age twelve, I had already reached my adult height of five-foot-eight. All the cute boys were shorter, so I slouched to appear smaller. I longed to be one of the petite cheerleader types, but I wasn't. I was tall, gangly, all arms and legs. So I slouched. My father gave me a hard time about it for years. His teasing just made me feel worse. A girl who doesn't feel good about herself doesn't stand up straight. Instead, she shrinks to avoid scrutiny and criticism. Dad thought he was being funny with his play on words—he pronounced it "stoop-ed," as in "stupid." But it wasn't funny—it was hurtful.

"You're too big a girl to dress like that," he said when I wore a miniskirt at age fifteen. "Go change your clothes." It was the '60s, and I had made the miniskirt myself. I enjoyed sewing some of my own clothes and had just finished making the cutest short dress, accessorizing it with long strands of beads and rings on my fingers.

When I came into the family room, getting ready to go out with my friends, Dad looked up at me from his horizontal position on the sofa, his glance instantly disapproving. He said, "You're too big a girl to dress like that," but what I heard was, "You're a fat cow—go cover up." I was devastated. I weighed about 120 pounds, but his words made me feel like a monstrous Amazon. I hated my body.

"Can't you do anything right?" he barked at me as we walked up the courthouse steps. I was sixteen and had gotten in an accident in my boyfriend's car. We had to go to court because I'd been charged with making an illegal left-hand turn and causing the accident. As Dad climbed the courthouse steps with me, I caught my toe on a step and stumbled a bit. His angry words cut into me like bullets from a firing squad. "Can't you do anything right?" he snarled. I didn't need a judge to tell me I was guilty—my father had already done the job of judge, jury, and executioner.

Over the years, I died a thousand deaths as a result of my father's words. They left emotional scars far worse than any physical scars whipping would have caused. He was vicious with his vocabulary, going right for the jugular. I often wished he would just hit me, like my mother did. The bruises she left with her slaps and blows always healed, but the psychic wounds my father inflicted left deep scars that still hurt decades later.

"You're not very good at relationships," he told me when I got involved with one of my professors in graduate school. "Maybe you should stick with what you're good at: work." I suppose he meant well—I gave him credit for good intentions that time—but his words wounded nonetheless. Somehow that deep, masculine voice of authority always sounded like a sentence pronounced by a judge: The verdict is rendered; there is no higher court of appeal,

Dad's verbal gavel would *bang!* down with finality. My fate was decided, once and for all.

Decades have passed since Dad said those painful things to me. His judgments seared my consciousness like a branding iron. Sometimes the scars from his words seem faded and distant; other times they ache with an old familiarity. Will I ever be able to rid myself of his harsh pronouncements?

Self-help guru Dr. Wayne Dyer and spiritual guru Ram Dass had a conversation many years ago in which Ram Dass revealed that he still carries baggage from the challenging relationship he had with his father (who teasingly referred to his son as Rum Dum). Dyer replied that he carried no such baggage and asserted that it's possible to be free of old parental wounds through emotional healing and personal-growth work.

Which of these two gurus is right? My hunch is that because Dyer spent much of his childhood in an orphanage, it makes sense that he might feel free of any parental baggage—positive or negative. Ram Dass, on the other hand, grew up in a prominent Jewish family, the youngest son of a successful lawyer father. Their relationship was loving, but testy.

I think Ram Dass is right: We never fully recover from childhood. We can never completely escape the wounding at the hands of our primary caretakers, no matter how hard we try to reprogram our psyches.

For a little girl, this paternal wounding reverberates through all her relationships with men for years to come. Her father is the first and most important man in her life. For better or worse, his influence colors how his daughter relates to all other males: brothers, boyfriends, lovers, husbands, male friends, bosses, male coworkers, neighbors, and others. More important than training her how to relate to males is how he trains her to see herself as a female. If he cherishes her and treats her with love, tenderness, compassion, and sweetness, she will grow into a woman who feels comfortable in her feminine identity. If, however, he expects her to perform to earn his love, she is likely to grow up to be insecure and uncertain about her femininity.

My father's love was conditional. He loved me as long as I "behaved," and withdrew his love when he disapproved of something I did. We even discussed it once, when I was about forty. I said that I thought real love was unconditional, no strings attached. Further, I asserted that if love is dependent on certain behaviors, then it isn't love at all, but something else. Dad disagreed. He said that of course love is conditional—to think otherwise is sentimental nonsense.

I can't speak for other people, but for me, being loved on a conditional basis left me with a fundamental sense of insecurity. Withdrawal of love as punishment meant that the emotional rug could be pulled out from under me at any moment, without notice or warning. Being loved in such a way made me hypervigilant— always alert to any signal that I was on thin ice. I watched Dad's every move, every facial expression, every shift in body language.

It was like living with a volcano, never knowing when it might erupt in rage and condemnation. Volcanoes are dangerous. Even when they seem peaceful and quiet, you never know what's going on below the surface; you never know when you will have to flee for your life. Perhaps on some deep, archetypal, psychic level, I felt like the young virgin in danger of being sacrificed to the angry volcano god. Home did not feel like a safe place.

Was my father a monster? No. He was simply a flawed human being, damaged by his own childhood experiences. His emotional repertoire is limited; his capacity for tenderness and empathy is small; his ability to forgive is miniscule.

About twenty years ago, I asked my father why he didn't love me. I had had a few drinks at his house one evening, and my stepmother was off in a different room. The conversation with Dad turned to the past. My courage bolstered by wine, I put my burning question before him. "Why didn't you love me, Dad?" I began to cry as I talked. "I worked so hard to win your love and approval, but I was never successful. So tell me, what was missing? What could I have done that I didn't do?"

Dad looked up from his drink with tears welling in his eyes. "I don't know," he said. "Maybe I couldn't love you because nobody ever loved me."

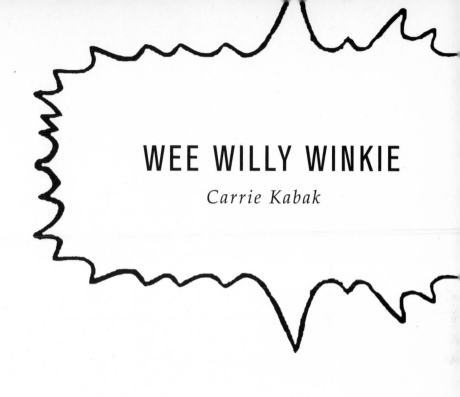

WEE WILLY WINKIE

Carrie Kabak

> *My brother Billy had a three-foot willy*
> *And he showed it to the girl next door.*
> *But she thought it was a snake,*
> *So she hit it with a rake,*
> *And now it's only two-foot-four.*
> —Our Lady of Sorrows playground

By the time I entered college, I wasn't sure I ever wanted to meet a willy. But encounter one I did, and I blame Rowland Jones for making it such a traumatic experience.

> *And what he said made me realize I was still as innocent*
> *as the nine year old who had just taken her first confession.*

Clara has taken her first confession, too, and we're comparing notes.

The visiting priest has a voice like honey, we conclude. He's immaculate, he's spick-and-span, and he's the spitting image of Kookie from *77 Sunset Strip*, so no wonder half the girls in our class are in love with him.

And then the church door creaks open and Kitty Dooley stands before us in the corridor, and we can't wait to hear what *she* has to say about Father Durkan.

"Well?" says Clara.

Kitty puts her hands on her hips. "He did nothing but play with himself," she says. "He started at 'Bless me, Father' and was still at it when he gave absolution."

"We don't believe you!" says Clara. "Do we, Carrie?"

I shake my head. "You're disgusting, Kitty Dooley," I say.

"Priests don't do things like that!" says Clara, wagging her finger. "They are *vessels of Christ.*"

Kitty stomps her foot. "Yer a pair of *amadáns*," she says, "because I'm telling the truth!"

Our Lady of Sorrows church and school sit bang in the middle of England, but the community is, without doubt, very Irish. Most of us live in the suburbs, but Kitty comes from the Dingles, which is riddled with streams and dirt paths. And she lives in a caravan, and she owns a pony, and she eats hedgehogs for supper.

"You're a born liar, Kitty Dooley," I say.

And with that, Clara takes my arm, and we march toward the classrooms, with our ponytails swinging and our pleated skirts swaying.

"Hoi," Kitty shouts after us. "About your Father Kookie—his John Thomas is no bigger than an earthworm!"

"You're so full of gobshite," yells Clara.

A week goes by and Saturday arrives, and the Parish Ladies hold a jumble sale in Our Lady of Sorrows' church hall. But I don't get to go, because Mum says half the stuff could be crawling with lice, for all we know. So Clara calls in the evening to fill me in. The Travelers from the Dingles were there, she says, and so was Sissy Duggan with her squad. Then there was Eddie Boyle with his parents and uncles and aunts and cousins. All our teachers were there, she says, along with their husbands and kids and sisters and brothers and, Oh God, she says, Listen to this, Carrie—Jesus, it's terrible news altogether. "Father Durkan is leaving next week," she says.

On Monday at school, Mrs. MacKeon tells Clara and me to fill every inkwell in the class. So we fetch the galvanized jug, which we fill with blue powder and one quart of water. And we start at the far corner, where Eddie Boyle sits, so we can ask him about Father Durkan. "He's moving to a parish in Donegal," whispers Eddie. But three desks up, we're told he's quitting the priesthood, and halfway along, there's a strong rumor he's getting married. And we hear all manner of tittle-tattling tales before we get to Kitty Dooley.

"I bet yer fella got himself *defrocked*," she says, poking out her tongue.

"La-la-la," says Clara. "We can't hear you."

And Mrs. MacKeon claps her hands to ask for *indoor* voices, *please.*

And in the afternoon we have to write a poem along the lines of *Slowly, silently, now the moon walks the night in her silver shoon,* so I get a chance to check the dictionary. I search for the word "defrock" because I have no idea what it means. "Stripped of priestly privileges," I read. "Punished for wrongdoing." And it makes me wonder if Kitty Dooley isn't full of gobshite after all.

And that troubling notion lives with me for days on end.

Then Father Maloney steps in to prepare us for Holy Communion. And he's an old priest, and a bald priest, with a head like a lump of lard. And the vision I have is disturbing. The image is hazy, but clear enough to see that Father Maloney has a willy the size of an earthworm.

And Jesus, he just won't leave it alone.

And the years pass by, and lessons become grueling and arduous, and Father Maloney retires from church duties but continues to teach Religious Studies. He batters us with catechisms and threatens us with hell, and promises a cloud-filled heaven if we are good. And we learn that children are gifts from God. And he tells us that the Angel Gabriel said, "Behold, Mary, thou shalt conceive in thy womb, and shalt bring forth a son." And we are fascinated, Clara and I, at the wonder of it all, and the more we hear, the clearer it becomes, and we are filled with utter joy. For when Clara marries Elvis Presley, and when I marry Corky the Circus Boy, the power of the Most High will overshadow us, like it did with Mary, and we will miraculously *be with child.*

It all makes perfect sense. Our theory is immaculate, as clean as Ajax bleach, and has *nothing* to do with bosoms or bums or bare ladies, as Eddie Boyle would have us believe. "Little Miss Muffet sat on a tuffet," he says, "her knickers all tattered and torn. It wasn't the spider that sat down beside her—it was Little Boy Blue with his horn."

And he nudges us. "Do you get it?" he smirks.

No, we don't.

*What Rowland Jones said made me realize I was still as
naive as the ten year old who listened to her parents at
the kitchen table.*

My parents have a Morris Oxford, and it's gray, has red leather
seats, and is the epitome of luxury, according to Mum. As
we drive back from Sunday Mass, she tells me, "Sit up, Carrie.
Stop yawning." Did I say my prayers at Communion? Did I sing
the hymns? And she holds her missal in gloved hands and keeps
her rosary beads dangling so the neighbors know we've been to
church. Going to Mass makes a statement. It is the pious thing to
do. We are to appear devout and virtuous, and above all others on
Kingswood Lane.

Once we're through the door, we remove our finery for more
comfortable clothes and the breakfast ritual begins. Mum nicks
rinds to stop the bacon from curling, and she stabs sausages so they
won't burst, and she fries eggs until the yolks are set like bullets.
And while this is going on, it's my job to set three places on the
Formica table, and I must always sit in the middle.

And when we finish breakfast, Mum tells me to *cover the butter,
please, Carrie.* And as soon as I put the lid on the dish, my parents
light their cigarettes and the conversation begins. They discuss
their jobs as they puff through the first cigarette. They rehash the
latest family feud through a second. And then Dad suggests a third
as Mum moves on to members of the parish. Anne Foggarty is no
redhead, she says. Did Tom see all her roots? Sure, she's as gray as
a coot. And did he notice that Sissy Duggan was big with child *yet
again?*

"Why does God keep giving her babies," I ask, "when she has twelve already?"

"The donations come from Sissy's husband," says Mum. "It has nothing to do with God."

And when I tell her I don't understand, she says, "Never mind." And Dad says he ought to mow the lawn, because, *gosh,* judging by the look of those clouds, it's about to rain cats and dogs.

"Let's ask Eddie Boyle if he knows anything about *donations,*" says Clara on Monday.

Of course he does. Donations come in the form of seeds, he says. And he tells us where they come from, and wasn't he trying to tell us that all along?

"Oh, dear God," I say.

"Jesus," says Clara. "How big are the seeds?"

They're as small as a grain of rice, says Eddie. And he closes one eye before pinching his finger and thumb together, so we get the picture.

Then he tells us to guess where they're planted.

We have to think about this, but we soon have a logical answer. The seed goes inside the woman's belly button, of course. Two seeds for twins, we say, and three for triplets.

"Yer such a pair of *eejits,*" says Eddie.

> *What Rowland Jones said made me realize I had a lot
> to learn.*

And our final term at Our Lady of Sorrows arrives, and we all clap our hands because now we're looking good. We're gonna sing a song that won't take long 'coz we're gonna do the twist, and it goes like this. Yeah, round and round and up and down we go again. It's time for sashes, veils, and confirmation, but then . . . our mothers discover the Communion dresses they held back are too small. So there's a flurry of borrowing or buying, or all-night stitching of taffeta and silk, or satin with lace. And the bishop anoints our class with the Holy Chrism, and we are thus sealed by the spirit before the cramming and coaching begins. For we must soon undergo a three-paper ordeal called the Eleven Plus— an exam that will govern our admission to a prestigious grammar school. If we're lucky, that is.

The day St. Ursula's Convent deems me worthy is the same day my parents put 315 Kingswood Lane up for sale. And before the season of mists and mellow fruitfulness, a contract is signed, and I never get to see Clara or Kitty Dooley or Eddie Boyle ever again.

We move to a town surrounded by orchards and hop fields and slow rivers. A town where the houses, pubs, and shops are joined at the hip, but where the Catholic church stands small and alone. And the nearest nonpaying school is Brayminster High, where the girls' names are more like Beryl Tudge than Molly Delaney. And the uniform consists of a white shirt and a red tie, but all else is navy, right down to the knee-high socks, and a strange hat, which closely resembles a quiche Lorraine. Then there are outdoor shoes and indoor shoes, which pinch my toes and make my heels bleed.

And I hobble off to geography to learn how oxbow lakes are formed. I study a war poem in English, mess with magnets and iron filings in physics, and struggle with Venn diagrams in math. And by the time I have learned how to *bully off* in field hockey, I have made a new friend, whose name is Sally Morgan.

Sally has a curtain of hair and wears tortoiseshell glasses. She uses words like "splendid" and "spiffing," and the fact that I'm Catholic fascinates her because, well, actually, she's an atheist.

Her whole family is, to be perfectly honest, Carrie.

And she shoots me a million questions as we bounce home on the number 9 bus. And I answer the best I can. And I stumble over transubstantiation, but I have no trouble at all when it comes to purgatory, heaven, or hell.

"Purgatory is like a waiting room," I say. "And heaven is all around."

And the bus grumbles through Goose Alley, and it crosses Bowdley Bridge, and we get off when it stops at the Green Cock Inn. And as we wander along Briar Lane, I tell Sally that hell is nothing but a blistering, razor-edged abyss. A pit of searing heat and ceaseless clamor. And she laughs so hard she nearly pees her navy knickers by the time we reach her gate.

And I see she lives in a low cottage on the hem of a field.

How many flowers dance in the breeze in her English country garden? I ask. Sally can name a few, she says, and those she misses, she begs my pardon for. Meadowsweet and lily stalks, geraniums and hollyhocks, foxgloves, roses, and little blue forget-me-nots. And we wave goodbye, glad the first day is over but still looking forward to halcyon high school days and years of endless summers.

And autumn tumbles into winter, and we know spring is here when the magnolia blooms on the grounds of Brayminster High. And frogspawn jellies the ponds, and birds build nests in the cedar tree. And the biology teacher declares that since we've covered formation and fission and fragmentation, we really should move on. To other forms of procreation, she says, and namely that of Human Beings.

And so, after lunch, we file into an atmosphere of Bunsen burner fumes and formaldehyde and we are told to "take the benches at the front of the lab, please, girls."

The lights are dimmed and the windows are shuttered. "And we have lift-off," hisses Sally when we are presented with the first slide.

What we see on the screen are the Male Pelvic Organs. But there is no torso and there are no legs—just hoops and loops and a suspended series of canals and ducts. And Miss Cranshaw stabs each complication with a ruler, and I'm baffled by the Latin terminology, and none of it is quite like I imagined.

Then the next slide appears, detailing the female counterpart, and I see a clearing in the forest I didn't even know existed. And it finally dawns on me that seeds are definitely *not* planted in the belly button. And what's more, those seeds look nothing like grains of rice. No. Their heads are shaped like acorns, and their tails are as long as bullwhips.

And they can thrust their way through anything.

What Rowland Jones said made me realize I knew very little about men.

Now that we're fourteen, three pairs of stockings appear on the uniform list, to be obtained from Daisy's Notions at the end of Shamble Street. The stockings are thick and navy and ribbed, and Sally gets a fancy garter belt for her birthday. But Mum buys me a panty girdle that has a secret set of double panels to control and flatten in every which way. It's similar to the foundation garment she wore in the 1950s, she says, when life was more virtuous than it is now.

Lately, Mum's eyes tend to comb my body up and over. And then too slowly down. And she has a strange look on her face when she's doing it.

"Your father's coming upstairs," she says, throwing me a shirt. "Quick—cover yourself up. He shouldn't see you like this."

"Like what?" I ask.

And she points at my chest, and she moves her finger in circles.

And she keeps telling me Dad is too busy to help me with homework—because he's building a set of shelves, that's why. God knows she's been waiting long enough for him to start. No, he can't pick me up from Sally's, because he promised to install an outlet or fix a leaking tap or tighten up a door hinge.

"Take a torch," she tells me. "Just keep close to the hedges on your way home."

Mum's love for me is erratic. Her approval is sporadic. Smiles follow sneers. Gentleness follows gibes. Spontaneous hugs follow spite. And I allow her to bend me and shape me any way she wants me. For as long she loves me now and then, it's all right.

What Rowland Jones said made me realize this statement was true:

Male self-control, though possible, cannot be relied on. Our class saunters into the common room to see this scrawled on the blackboard. We are serving our very last term at Brayminster High, and we're seniors now. Nevertheless, the deputy headmistress has to beg for a little maturity, girls, when the room is filled with a series of spontaneous snorts.

We're introduced to a Special Visitor from the local family-planning clinic—a Mrs. Hilda Kalbfleisch, who has a florid complexion, a hairy chin, and a nose like an aubergine. But please just call her Hilda, my dears, because she won't bite. And she smiles hugely, to show my, what big teeth she has.

For the next hour, Hilda chatters on about coils and barriers and pills that are designed to protect us from the unreliable, the uncontrollable fiend and his foe. We are told to imagine Hilda's thumb is a man's peter as she shoves it up a rubber tube. We are shown a diaphragm that's as big as her hand, and a copper device that's as small as a matchstick, and I'm having a devil of a job working out scales and dimensions and ratios, but what does it matter anyway?

I whisper in Sally's ear to tell her, "Catholics aren't allowed to use contraceptives."

"What are you going to do, then?" she asks.

"When?"

She rolls her eyes. "At college, you twit."

I am astounded and appalled. "I'll make that decision when I'm married, thank you very much."

"You're so quaint," says Sally, squeezing my arm.

What Rowland Jones said made me realize I might need therapy.

A t home, the situation with Mum gets worse. I mustn't talk to the altar boy after Mass, or the paperboy after school. Who gave me that nail polish? That Sally friend of mine? What about the lipstick? Who gave me that note? Hand it over and let her see.

Mum tries to pry open my fingers, and through clenched teeth she's saying, "You will show me that note because I am your mother."

But I snatch my hand away and I run, scaling the stairs two at a time, and Mum is in hot pursuit. And soon she has me backed into the corner of the bathroom, between the basin and the toilet bowl. And tears burn hot on my cheeks.

"*Where is it?*" she spits.

She tunnels her fingers up my sleeves. Then she lifts my sweater and her hands travel to my breasts, and I want to yell and tell her to get off me, but I can't. It's like a nightmare when you want to scream but no sound will come out. And she fumbles and ferrets and scrapes with her nails until she finally finds the note in the left cup of my bra.

I love you, it says in felt pen, and three times over, even though I haven't even seen the altar boy outside of church.

Mum strikes her chest like she's reading the confiteor, and proceeds to accuse me of all manner of things associated with disobedience. Her daughter has sinned in thoughts, *thump*, and in words, *thump*, and in what she has done, *thump*.

When I haven't done a single thing.

The next day at school, Sally holds me as I cry into her blazer. And I vow never to go to Mass again, which is my first declaration of independence. I shall toss the girdles, I tell her, and I shall wear nylon tights, and yes, we *will* bunk the last day of school.

Sally is taking a year off and she needs a job, and where else should she go but to London? Her dad will give her the dosh, she says. And we'll buy tickets to Euston station, and I can borrow some clothes.

And when we get there, the rainfall is as fine as gauze. And Piccadilly Circus is a spin, and a flash, and a flicker of neon lights advertising Cinzano, Gordon's gin, and Max Factor makeup. And smells are hot dogs with onions and exhaust fumes and damp coats. And people are an ever-shifting kaleidoscope of color and movement and weird shapes. And among the myriad restaurants, shops, and theaters sits Regent Palace, where Sally has an interview for the position of hotel maid.

And we dodge through a commotion of blaring horns and wheezing brakes, and I have never felt so exhilarated in my whole life.

And soon, I'll be moving to Cardiff City.

And I'll run on the sands of Southerndown Beach.

And I'll be as free as a seagull.

What Rowland Jones said made me think he was a proper gentleman.

The boy I dated before I met Rowland Jones hailed from the art department and looked a lot like Jesus. And he wore open-toed sandals and seemed gentle, gracious, meek, and mild. But he didn't hang around for long, because I wouldn't let him inside my pants, as he put it. "What do you want?" he asked, shrugging his bony shoulders. "A fucking wedding ring?"

But these days, my beau is Rowland Jones, who wears shirts and cuff links and a jacket in heathery tweed. And his hair is neatly shorn. And his chin is closely shaven. And he drives the streets of Cardiff in a silver Hillman Imp.

"Rowland is decent and upright and full of respect," I tell Muriel, who is big and bossy and quite beautiful. She's my new best friend and we live in Bassett One, which is a block of student lodgings built in concrete, metal, and glass.

"If he's such a gentleman," says Muriel, "why isn't he giving us a lift?"

"His lectures don't finish till eight thirty," I say.

Rowland is a mechanical engineer, I tell her, but she's a bit tired of hearing that. And the sun shines out of his bum, she says. Then she tells me to see to the kettle and get the margarine out of the fridge, along with the jar of Marmite.

We've become very close, Muriel and I, and there are no secrets between us, and so I decide to take the plunge and tell her a bit of news.

"I promised Rowland I'd sleep with him tonight," I say.

Which causes Muriel to drop a loaf of Wonder Bread onto the vinyl-tiled floor. But I'm not surprised at her reaction. I did say I'd rather burn in a blistering, razor-edged abyss than lose my virginity. I said I'd rather sizzle in a pit of searing heat and endure the ceaseless clamor of hell. But Rowland swore on his life that there'd be no pressure on me to perform. He crossed his heart and hoped to die.

"He just wants to hold me close," I explain. "Nothing more than that."

No prodding. No probing.

Muriel picks the fluff from two slices of bread before giving me the eye.

"He'll want to use it," she says.

"Use what?"

"His *coes bach*," she says.

"He said he wouldn't push me to do *anything*," I say. "He said sleeping together would make us feel very close."

"*Twpsyn*," says Muriel, smacking me on the head.

Muriel refused to believe a single word of what Rowland Jones said.

And an hour later, we're standing in a queue outside the Top Rank in matching polyester hot pants, and then we surge through double doors to hand over a fistful of coins for two tickets to witness a sensation, a spectacle, a glam-rock *happening*. And the dancehall is fogged with curling smoke, and when it clears, a stage with a backdrop of shattering glass explodes into view. And Slade leaps to the boards in high-stacked boots. And they wear top hats and tails over tanks that are a clashing jolt of stripes and polka dots. And after a growl of guitars and a punch of drums, Noddy and Dave straddle the microphones to scream, "*Cum on, do we feel the noize?*"

And the floor bounces like a trampoline as feet hammer and elbows jerk and heads roll to the stomping beat. And through strobe lights, I see the flickering image of Muriel lighting a cigarette in slow motion. I see her hair spread and fall, and her necklace twirl and float. And I sweep my hand up, and then down, watching my fingers multiply. And Rowland is an apparition wearing a jacket in heathery tweed, and his shirt is ultrawhite, and I see the glint of a cuff link as he grabs hold of my wrist.

And he apologizes for being late, but the street was packed with cars, he says, and there was nowhere to park his Hillman Imp.

But I guess he found a place in the end.

Oh, yes, he did. And he smiles with a twist to his mouth and a wink to his eye.

What Rowland Jones said made me realize I shouldn't have trusted the bastard.

"What did you really expect?" he said. "I'm a man!"

I stand on the landing of Basset One and I holler for Muriel, and she cries, "What's the matter, *cariad?*" and I do an about turn, and she follows me to my room and we sit on my bed.

"He said I was *frigid,*" I tell her. "Because I wouldn't do it."

"I warned you," says Muriel.

His face boiled like a poached beetroot when I said *no, no, no.* I mean, what would Muriel have done? There were no kisses. No words. I hadn't even changed into my nightie, Muriel. He just opened his fly and presented me with it.

Like it was a prize marrow.

"I was pretty shocked by the size of it, to be honest, Muriel."

It was the first time I'd seen an adult version, Muriel, and I had no idea of its capabilities. It was rampant and unbridled, and it remained in that state as it led him to the door, where he'd hung up his shirt, minus its cuff links, along with his jacket in heathery tweed.

And Muriel slings her arm around my shoulders, and I wait for sadness and sympathy and soothing noises, because, hell, I'm still in a shiver from the shock of it all.

But instead Muriel throws back her head, and the rumble of her laugh sounds like it's rolling up from her bare little toes. And she doesn't stop honking and howling and hooting until I leap to my feet to pummel and pound her with pillows.

And she lies helpless for a while, before drying her tears with my bedsheets. Before her face softens into seriousness. "Pull me up," she says.

And her voice is slow and steady and sincere. "This is what I think," she says.

One day, she says, we'll see the willy as a Beautiful Thing.

"*Jesus Christ*, Muriel," I say. "And when will that happen?"

"When we fall in love," she breathes.

And her eyes twinkle with a thousand million stars.

Purgatory might be a pit stop to heaven, but it teetered on the brink of hell just once too often in the years that followed. But I learned a vast amount about men as I waited for love, and the majority had minds and emotions and feelings, so it wasn't *all* about willies.

They had other qualities that proved to be just as beautiful.

ABOUT THE CONTRIBUTORS

BARBARA ABERCROMBIE has published three novels and numerous children's books, including the prize-winning *Charlie Anderson.* Her latest books are *Writing Out the Storm* (St. Martin's Press), *Courage and Craft: Writing Your Life into Story* (New World Library), and *Cherished: 21 Writers on Animals They've Loved & Lost* (New World Library). Her essays and articles have appeared in many publications, including the *Los Angeles Times*, the *Baltimore Sun*, and *The Christian Science Monitor.* She teaches creative writing at UCLA Extension, writes a weekly blog at www.writingtime.net, and lives in Santa Monica, California, and Twin Bridges, Montana, with her husband.

BEVERLY DONOFRIO'S first memoir, *Riding in Cars with Boys*, has been translated into fifteen languages and became a popular motion picture. Donofrio's second memoir, *Looking for Mary: (Or, The Blessed Mother and Me)*, began as a documentary on NPR and was chosen as a Discover Book at Barnes & Noble. Her first children's books, *Mary and the Mouse, the Mouse and Mary*, and *Thank You, Lucky Stars*, came out in 2007, and a sequel to the *Mouse* book is due out in 2011. Her radio essays have won awards, and she can sometimes be heard as a commentator on NPR's *All Things Considered*. Her personal essays have appeared in many anthologies, as well as in national newspapers and magazines. Donofrio is currently traveling the country, happily at work on her third memoir, whose working title is *Astonished*. Her website is www.beverlydonofrio.com.

MARGOT BETH DUXLER is a licensed clinical psychologist in private practice in San Francisco. She is the author of the psychobiography *Seduction: A Portrait of Anaïs Nin* (Edgework Books). Her fiction has appeared in a number of literary journals and includes the short stories, "All the Time in the World," "Before It Happened," "Bright Colors," "Constellations," "Mairie's Wedding," and "Music." With W. A. Smith, she served as coeditor of fiction for the *Five Fingers Review*; with Edouard Muller, she worked as cotranslator for the first edition of Gault/Millau's *The Best of Paris*. She is a professional fiddler and has performed and recorded with Golden Bough and the Celtic Wonder Band. She is currently working on a novel and a collection of short stories.

AMY FERRIS is an author, screenwriter, editor, feminist, wife, daughter, sister, and friend. Her memoir, *Marrying George Clooney: Confessions from a Midlife Crisis*, is being produced as an Off-

Broadway play (fall 2010). She lives in Pennsylvania with her husband, Ken, and their two cats, Bella and Lotus. Amy can be reached at www.marryinggeorgeclooney.com/blog. This one's for Hollye Fisher.

ABBY FRUCHT has published five novels and a collection of stories, *Fruit of the Month*. She has been the recipient of the Iowa Short Fiction Prize, a New Voices Award, two National Endowment for the Arts fellowships, and the Kay W. Levin Short Nonfiction Award for her essay "Blue Shirt," which was reprinted in Dzanc Books' *Best of the Web*. Her essay "Holes" was included in the Seal anthology *For Keeps*. A mentor and advisor for fifteen years at Vermont College of Fine Arts, she lives in Wisconsin and can be visited at www.abbyfrucht.net.

BJ GALLAGHER is an inspirational author and speaker. Her international bestseller, *A Peacock in the Land of Penguins* (Berrett-Koehler), has sold over 320,000 copies in twenty-three languages. Her most recent books are *Why Don't I Do the Things I Know Are Good for Me?* (Berkley Books) and *It's Never Too Late to Be What You Might Have Been* (Viva Editions). BJ is a regular *Huffington Post* contributor. She has been featured on the CBS Evening News, the *Today* Show, Fox News, PBS, CNN, and more, and is oft quoted online and in print publications, including *O, the Oprah magazine; Redbook; The New York Times; The Wall Street Journal;* and more. She can be reached at www.womenneed2know.com.

JANE GANAHL has been a journalist, editor, author, consultant, and community organizer in San Francisco for twenty-five years.

She is the author of the novelized memoir *Naked on the Page: the Misadventures of My Unmarried Midlife* (Viking), which is in development for a TV series. She is also the editor of the anthology *Single Woman of a Certain Age* (New World Library paperback) and has contributed essays to several anthologies. Ganahl wrote the column "Single Minded" for the *San Francisco Chronicle.* She contributes regularly to *The Huffington Post.* Her work has appeared online on Salon.com and RollingStone.com and in such print magazines as *Harper's Bazaar.* Ganahl is cofounder and artistic director of Litquake, San Francisco's annual literary festival, which in 2008 drew more than 450 writers and more than ten thousand attendees.

BENITA (BONNIE) GARVIN is an award-winning film and television writer and producer. Her original film, *The Killing Yard,* starring Alan Alda, premiered at the Toronto Film Festival and was nominated for a host of awards. Bonnie was nominated for an Edgar and won a special media award from the American Bar Association for the film. In addition to her many projects in the United States, Bonnie also has credits in European film and television. She is part of the adjunct faculty of the nation's most prestigious film school, the University of Southern California, where she teaches screenwriting. Bonnie teaches screenwriting privately as well, and hosts weekend writing workshops around the country. She can be reached at www.fromideatoscript.com.

SHERRY GLASER-LOVE is the author and star of *Family Secrets,* off-Broadway's longest-running one-woman show, for which she received the New York Theatre World Award for Best Debut, the L.A.

Outer Critics Circle Award, South Florida's Carbonell Award for Best Actress, L.A.'s Ovation Award, and a nomination for a Drama Desk Award. Her autobiography, *Family Secrets: One Woman's Look at a Relatively Painful Subject*, was published by Simon & Schuster. Her personal essay "Sheba" appeared in the anthology *The Other Woman* and is a featured piece in the play based on that book. She is also featured in the anthology *Warrior Mothers*, published by Rising Star Press. Her newest stage works are *Oh My Goddess!* and *The Adventures of Super Activist Mother.* Sherry's weekly commentary, *The Voice of the People*, is heard on community radio station KZYX. She is also a founding member of the peace activist group Breasts Not Bombs, which won a lawsuit against the California Highway Patrol, thus insuring a woman's right to demonstrate topless in California. Sherry lives in Northern California with her wife, Sheba Love, and their daughters.

KATHI KAMEN GOLDMARK is the author of the novel *And My Shoes Keep Walking Back to You*, coauthor of *The Great Rock & Roll Joke Book* and *Mid-life Confidential: the Rock Bottom Remainders Tour America with Three Chords and an Attitude*, and has contributed essays to several anthologies. With her husband, Sam Barry, she coauthors the "Author Enablers" column and blog for BookPage .com. Kathi is the founder of the all-author rock band the Rock Bottom Remainders (Stephen King, Amy Tan, etc.) and "Don't Quit Your Day Job" Records, author liaison for several high-profile literary events, and producer of the radio show *West Coast Live*. A 2007 San Francisco Library Laureate and winner of the 2008 Women's National Book Association Award, she likes to think she is ready for anything. Kathi can be reached at www.kathiandsam.net.

ROSE CASTILLO GUILBAULT is the author of *Farmworker's Daughter*, which the *San Francisco Chronicle* named one of the best books of 2005. As editorial/public affairs director at KGO-TV (ABC), she wrote, produced, and presented on-air editorials and commentaries. Prior to that, she was a producer/director at KPIX-TV (CBS). Guilbault has been a syndicated columnist for the Pacific News Service and a columnist writing "Hispanic, USA" for the *San Francisco Chronicle*, and has had essays published in more than one hundred books. A national keynote speaker at colleges and universities, she is currently the vice president of corporate affairs and publishing for the California Automobile Association and publisher of its *VIA* magazine, the twenty-first-largest consumer magazine in the United States, with a circulation of 2.78 million. Guilbault earned undergraduate and graduate degrees in broadcast journalism and writing, as well as an MBA.

PAM HOUSTON is the author of two collections of linked short stories, *Cowboys Are My Weakness*, winner of the 1993 Western States Book Award, and *Waltzing the Cat*, which received a WILLA Award for contemporary fiction, and the novel *Sight Hound*. Her stories have appeared in the anthologies *Best American Short Stories; Prize Stories: The O. Henry Awards; The Pushcart Prize: Best of the Small Presses; Best American Short Stories of the Century;* and *The Other Woman*. She is the director of Creative Writing at U.C. Davis, and she lives there and in Southwestern Colorado. Her forthcoming book is *Contents May Have Shifted*. She can be reached at www.pamhouston.net.

CARRIE KABAK is the author of *Cover the Butter*, a 2005 Book Sense bestseller. She is a professional copywriter and has received commendation as a publishing-related graphic designer and illustrator by *Writer's Digest* and by the daVinci Eye, and was named Illustrator of the Month by the Society of Children's Book Writers and Illustrators. She contributed to the Seal anthology *For Keeps*, and her novels *Tarts and Sinners* and *Deviled Egg* are in progress. Mother of five grown children, Kabak lives with her husband and a collection of dependent animals in Kansas City, Missouri, and is a partner in a specialty-food business. Carrie can be reached at www.carriekabak.com, www.carriekabak.com/graphics, or www.menuboardinc.com.

CAROLINE LEAVITT is the award-winning author of nine novels, most recently *Pictures of You* (Algonquin Books), and is a book critic for *People* magazine and *The Boston Globe.* Her work has appeared in *New York* magazine, *Psychology Today, Salon, Cookie, MORE,* and *Parenting,* and in the anthologies *The Other Woman, Feed Me! Mr. Wrong,* and more. An award-winning senior instructor at UCLA, she lives in Hoboken, New Jersey, with her husband, the writer Jeff Tamarkin, and their son, Max. Caroline can be reached at www.carolineleavitt.com and http://carolineleavittville.blogspot.com.

MAXINNE RHEA LEIGHTON is author of *An Ellis Island Christmas,* recipient of the Marion Vannett Ridgway Award. Her personal essay "The Man with the Big Hands" appeared in the anthology *The Other Woman* and is a featured piece in the play based on that book. She wrote and performed *Design for Love* for MTV's Comedy Central and was part of the Gathering, a women writers' collective at the Whole Theatre in New Jersey. Her first novel, *The Honey Dew Queen of Mermaid Avenue,* is an urban legend of another sort. A graduate of SUNY Binghamton, she holds a master of arts from NYU. Maxinne Leighton is a PhD student in Antioch University's Leadership and Change program. She can be reached at www.maxinneleighton.net.

JOYCE MAYNARD is the author of seven novels, including *To Die For* and *Labor Day*, currently under development as a film. Her best-selling memoir, *At Home in the World*, has been translated into eleven languages. Maynard's most recent novel is *The Good Daughters*. Mother of three grown children and two young daughters, she makes her home in Mill Valley, California. Find her at www.joycemaynard.com.

CHRISTINE O'HAGAN is the author of the novel *Benediction at the Savoia*, and the memoir *The Book of Kehls*, both of which received starred Kirkus Reviews; Kirkus Reviews also selected *The Book of Kehls* as a Best Book of 2005. Her essays have appeared in the anthologies *Between Friends, The Day My Father Died, Lives Through Literature, Exploring Literature, The Face in the Mirror*, and *For Keeps*, in *The Facts on File Companion to the American Novel*, and in *The New York Times* and *Newsday*. The recipient of a Jerry Lewis writing award, O'Hagan was also selected as a Top Irish American of 1993 by *Irish America Magazine*. She and her husband live on Long Island, where she is finishing her second memoir, *The Bees' Knees*. Her website is www.christinekehlohagan.com.

MARY POLS is the author of the memoir *Accidentally on Purpose: The True Tale of a Happy Single Mother*. Her book was adapted into a sitcom with the same name by CBS, which ran during the 2009–

2010 television season. For two decades, Mary was a newspaper reporter and movie critic based in California. She has written for *The New York Times, Self,* Glamour.com, *Red Magazine,* Slate.com, and the *Times* of London. Currently she reviews movies and books for *TIME* and writes a regular pop culture column for MSN Movies. A former Knight Fellow at Stanford, Mary and her son now live in her native state, Maine.

KAREN QUINN did not begin writing until her midforties, after she was laid off from a corporate job, started a Manhattan consultancy helping families get their children into the city's best schools, and then sold the business and decided to write about it. Her first novel was the bestseller *The Ivy Chronicles.* Her other books include *Wife in the Fast Lane, Holly Would Dream, The Sister Diaries,* and *Testing for Kindergarten;* film rights were optioned for *The Ivy Chronicles* and *Holly Would Dream.* Karen recently developed a game called IQ Fun Park to help parents get their children reading for kindergarten testing. She blogs regularly at www.testingforkindergarten.com, www.TestingMom.com, and less regularly at www.karenquinn.net.

DIANNE RINEHART has worked in Moscow, Ottawa, Toronto, and Vancouver as an editor, reporter, and columnist for some of the largest newspapers and magazines in Canada and the United States. She is currently editor of the *Toronto Star*'s flagship weekend *Insight* sections. But her most important achievement to date is co-launching an organization, Give Girls a Chance (www.givegirlsachance.org), to educate girls around the world. Educate a girl. Change the world. Dianne can be reached at www.diannerinehart.com.

COLLEEN ROBINSON is a writer of creative nonfiction and memoir. She has an essay in the anthology *The Spirit of a Woman* and is now working on a memoir about being a disabled mother. Robinson lives in Bellingham, Washington, with her husband and two children. You can read about her musings on disability at http://mymilewalk.blogspot.com.

JENNY ROUGH is a lawyer who switched jobs to launch a career as a freelance writer. She has written articles and essays for *The Washington Post*, the *Los Angeles Times*, *MORE*, *Yoga Journal*, *USA Weekend*, and *Writer's Digest*, among other publications. Her work has also appeared as commentaries on public radio. In addition to writing Roughly Speaking, her blog about nurturing the creative spirit, she blogs for Mothering.com. She is currently working on a memoir about healing from infertility. Jenny can be reached at www.jennyrough.com.

CLEA SIMON is the author of three nonfiction books, most recently *The Feline Mystique: On the Mysterious Connection Between Women and Cats* (St. Martin's Press) and eight mysteries, most recently the Pru Marlowe pet noir *Dogs Don't Lie* (Poisoned Pen Press) and the Dulcie Schwartz mystery *Grey Zone* (Severn House). She has contributed personal essays to such anthologies as *Cat Women: Female Writers on Their Feline Friends* (Seal Press) and *For Keeps: Women Tell the Truth About Their Bodies, Growing Older, and Acceptance* (Seal Press) and written on a wide variety of topics for *The New York Times*, *The Boston Globe*, *Ms.*, *American Prospect*, the *San Francisco Chronicle*, and *Cat Fancy*. Clea can be reached at www.cleasimon.com.

STARHAWK is the author or coauthor of eleven books, including *The Spiral Dance: A Rebirth of the Ancient Religion of the Great Goddess*, long considered the essential text for the neo-pagan movement and in continuous print for thirty years, and the now-classic ecotopian novel *The Fifth Sacred Thing*. Her newest book is *The Last Wild Witch*, a picture book for children. At Book Expo America, *Webs of Power* won a 2003 Nautilus Award from the trade association NAPRA. She cofounded Reclaiming, an activist branch of modern pagan religion, with archives maintained at the Graduate Theological Union library. She is known as a powerful force in modern earth-based spirituality and as a global-justice activist and organizer. Starhawk is a panelist for the *Newsweek/Washington Post* website on religion, On Faith, and contributes to Beliefnet and ZNet. She is deeply committed to bringing the techniques and creative power of spirituality to political activism. Starhawk holds a BA in fine arts from UCLA and an MA in psychology from Antioch West University. She can be reached at www.starhawk.org.

ABOUT THE EDITOR

VICTORIA ZACKHEIM is the author of *The Bone Weaver* and the editor of three other anthologies, *The Other Woman: 21 Wives, Lovers, and Others Talk Openly About Sex, Deception, Love, and Betrayal; For Keeps: Women Tell the Truth About Their Bodies, Growing Older, and Acceptance;* and *The Face in the Mirror: Writers Reflect on Their Dreams of Youth and the Reality of Age.* She is the story developer and writer of the documentary film *Tracing Thalidomide: The Frances Kelsey Story,* and the writer of other films for On the Road Productions. She teaches Personal Essay in the UCLA Extension Writers' Program and writes and records commentaries and book reviews for *The Mimi Geerges Show* on XM satellite radio. Victoria is a 2010 San Francisco Library Laureate and can be reached at www .victoriazackheim.com.

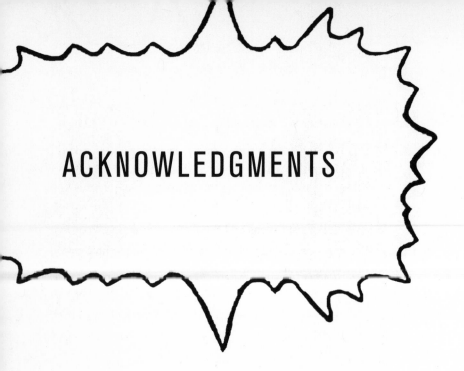

ACKNOWLEDGMENTS

There is no anthology without writers eager to take the plunge, whether the water is Mediterranean calm or North Sea rough. Over the past year, I've had the pleasure and the honor of working with exceptional women, so I must thank them first: Barbara Abercrombie, Beverly Donofrio, Margot Duxler, Amy Ferris, Abby Frucht, BJ Gallagher, Jane Ganahl, Bonnie Garvin, Sherry Glaser-Love, Kathi Kamen Goldmark, Rose Castillo Guilbault, Pam Houston, Carrie Kabak, Caroline Leavitt, Maxinne Rhea Leighton, Joyce Maynard, Christine O'Hagan, Mary Pols, Karen Quinn, Dianne Rinehart, Colleen Robinson, Jenny Rough, Clea Simon, and Starhawk.

When they accepted the invitation to write about that defining moment when *he* said something that changed their lives, I had no idea what they would write. Something funny, poignant, even shocking? The answer is: Yes! It's such a thrill to give such gifted authors as these a topic . . . and then discover what they've written. So authors, thank you, and thank you again.

To my family, as always, my loving thanks for your patience and for sharing my joy. I lament only that my mother did not live to read this book.

My thanks to Krista Lyons and Brooke Warner at Seal Press for believing in this book, and to Andie East for working so hard to introduce it to readers.

As always, endless gratitude to Jill Marsal of the Marsal Lyon Literary Agency. I can't imagine a wiser and more supportive and ethical partner in this crazy world of books.

SELECTED TITLES FROM SEAL PRESS

For more than thirty years, Seal Press has published
groundbreaking books. By women. For women.

No Excuses: 9 Ways Women Can Change How We Think About Power, by
Gloria Feldt. $24.95, 978-1-58005-328-0. From the boardroom to the bedroom,
public office to personal relationships, feminist icon Gloria Feldt offers women
the tools they need to walk through the doors of opportunity and achieve parity
with men.

Click: Young Women on the Moments That Made Them Feminists, edited
by Courtney E. Martin and J. Courtney Sullivan. $16.95, 978 1 58005 285
6. Notable writers and celebrities entertain and illuminate with true stories
recalling the distinct moments when they knew they were feminists.

Dear John, I Love Jane: Women Write About Leaving Men for Women, edited
by Candance Walsh and Laura André. $16.95, 978-1-58005-339-6. A timely
collection of stories that are sometimes funny and sometimes painful—but
always achingly honest—accounts of leaving a man for a woman, and the
consequences of making such a choice.

Naked at Our Age: Talking Out Loud About Senior Sex, by Joan Price.
$16.95, 978-1-58005-338-9. Full of information from doctors, social workers,
psychologists, and sex experts, this is an indispensable guide to handling and
understanding the issues seniors face when it comes to relationships and sex.

*He's a Stud, She's a Slut, and 49 Other Double Standards Every Woman
Should Know,* by Jessica Valenti. $13.95, 978-1-58005-245-0. With sass, humor,
and aplomb, *Full Frontal Feminism* author Jessica Valenti takes on the obnoxious
double standards women encounter every day.

Ask Me About My Divorce: Women Open Up About Moving On, edited by
Candace Walsh. $15.95, 978-1-58005-276-4. A spicy, bracing, riveting anthology
that proclaims: I got divorced, and it rocked my world!

Find Seal Press Online
www.SealPress.com
www.Facebook.com/SealPress
Twitter: @SealPress